Acclaim for *Hand of God*

'Burns is really out of order. Those who have spoken about me in the *Hand of God* are going to get into real trouble. I don't want people to speak in a book that does not say good things about me. If these are my friends, I prefer to have enemies.' Diego Maradona

'It's a corker. The rollercoaster of Maradona's extraordinary life is here in all its painful glory. Burns has written a compassionate, informative, and, in these days of spiralling wages and fallen idols, instructive biography, aided by a magnificent lead character. Stunning.' *Total Sport*

'Like the Gallagher brothers, Maradona's life has had its fair share of sex, drugs, and rock'n'roll. Only more so. For with Diego you can add poverty, corruption, conspiracy, adultery and sainthood . . . What Burns does so superbly is explain why Maradona is like he is and why he is loved, without being an apology for the man . . . Burns gains access to an inner circle of players, trainers and doctors who have previously been tight-lipped. Love or hate the man, his is one of football's greatest stories and so this is the best football book in ages.' *Goal*

'Jimmy Burns' elegantly written and painstakingly researched account of one of the all-time great players steers the reader through all the twists and turns of Maradona's career.' *When Saturday Comes*

'Diego Maradona stopped being the world's finest soccer player and started being a tragic, tormented figure because he was deluded, manipulated and exploited.' *Inside Sport*, Australia

'More than just a biography. Burns has managed to write a portrait and to embed it into a comprehensive description of sports and society over the last three decades. Simply good stuff and interesting reading.' Andreas Herren, FIFA

'The life and crimes of Diego Maradona are chronicled in a revealing biography. This well-researched book shows his life has been a violent mix of sporting brilliance and personal disgrace. The Hand of God weighed down by feet of clay.' Mike Walters, *Daily Mirror*

'This is a praiseworthy attempt to unravel this brilliantly talented but weak-willed man, who lives to fulfil his football dream but could not resist the temptation to abuse his body with drugs. A compelling cocktail of celebration and cheating.' *Daily Mail*

'This is an absorbing account of an often unappealing subject.' Paul Wilson, *Observer*

'A drug-taking prima donna is the subject of this excellent and well-researched book. Shame about the subject. *Hand of God* would have been more accurately titled 'Hands of the Devil' or 'Hand of the Cheat' . . . This first biography of a sporting idol who turned out to have feet of clay will be difficult to surpass.' Greg Struthers, *Sunday Times*

'Burns tells the story of Maradona with much skill and verve. He expertly untangles the various networks of manipulation . . . Our memories of the book will be less to do with Maradona's personality than with those who have so brutally exploited its clear weaknesses. The seamy backstairs politics of international soccer have never been more tellingly exposed. One day, perhaps, Maradona will read this incisive study and learn what happened to his 'magical' career.' Ian Hamilton, *Financial Times*

'Burns is the perfect man to put the Maradona saga into context. He is not just a knowledgeable football fan. He is also an expert on Argentina and a skilled investigative journalist. As a result his book combines a compelling personal story with intelligent analysis of the role played by football in general – and Mr Maradona in particular – in Argentinian politics and society . . . Those who have an interest in the sociology of football, in modern Argentina and in the 'story behind the headlines' will admire Burns' disturbing book which easily transcends the normal confines of sports journalism.' *The Economist*

'Jimmy Burns, is incapable of writing boringly. He has done as good and as honest a book as could be written about the poor boy from the wrong end of Buenos Aires, who went high and has fallen far . . . *Hand of God* is illuminating and atmospheric as it cuts through the web of myth, mystery and full-blooded hypocrisy that surrounds one of the world's most adored and detested sportsmen.' Hugh O'Shaughnessy, *Irish Times*

'This book is exhaustively researched and splendidly written. It includes a fascinating chapter 'Harry Goes to Buenos Aires' which tells of the events surrounding the amazing attempts of Sheffield United manager Harry Haslam to bring Maradona, then virtually unknown, to England in 1978. I can vouch for the accuracy of this particular chapter.' Tony Pritchett, *Sheffield Star*

'Jimmy Burns has written a jaw-on-the floor-fascinating book. Informed by a deep understanding of Argentine and English and a love of football, Burns is ideally placed to tackle the complex development of Maradona from shanty-town prodigy to five-drug cocktailed footballer of USA '94. Burns exposes the sycophants around Maradona and is not shy to point out his pomposity . . . His style is straightforward story-telling; the result could prove to be a modern footballing classic.' John Naughton, *FHM*

'Burns' forensic skills are to the fore in this deft, perceptive study of politics, corruption, exploitation and the occasional dash of genuine sporting genius.' *Time Out*

'Jimmy Burns casts a cold eye on the rearing of a money-making machine . . . This is a solid and penetrative piece of reporting on the resurrection of a footballing God who simply will not die . . . Burns's style is unemotive but the *Hand of God* is an affecting tale.' Hugh MacDonald, *Glasgow Herald*

'Maradona's life, diligently chronicled in this perceptive and fair-minded book, is one of grotesque farce, a billious sequence of operatic catastrophes. Gazza's career compared with this looks like Emmerdale sat next to the Borgias . . . this is not, however, mere sensationalist sleaze. Burns knows Argentina well and his charting of the shanty boy's trajectory towards moral and pharmaceutical meltdown is detailed in this scrupulously perceptive and fair-minded book.' Pete Davies, *Independent*

'An excellent biography. In the detail you would expect from an award-winning investigative financial writer, Burns traces the tendrils of ownership which controlled Maradona's career from the start.' James Lawton, *Daily Express*

'A piece of mastercraftsmanship.' *Hen Span, Het Parool*, Holland

'Shows that Maradona has got a lot of soul . . . the greatest footballer in the world.' Noel Gallagher, OASIS

'Reads like a passionate novel of investigation . . . much more than just a biography, it's about a world of corruption, intrigue, and exploitation.' *AS*, Spain

'A great achievement by one of Europe's most daring journalists.' *El Pais*, Spain

'Few people emerge innocent in this book.' *La Nacion*, Buenos Aires.

'The story of a poor kid whose dreams became true and then turn into his worst nightmare.' *Regina 12*, Buenos Aires

JIMMY BURNS is a prize-winning author and journalist. Among his books are *The Land that Lost its Heroes* (winner of the Somerset Maugham award for non-fiction), *Barça: A People's Passion*, *Papa Spy*, *La Roja*, *Francis: Pope of Good Promise* and *Cristiano & Leo*.

http://www.jimmy-burns.com
Twitter: @jimmy_burns

MARADONA

The Hand of God

JIMMY BURNS

BLOOMSBURY PUBLISHING
LONDON · OXFORD · NEW YORK · NEW DELHI · SYDNEY

BLOOMSBURY PUBLISHING
Bloomsbury Publishing Plc
50 Bedford Square, London, WC1B 3DP, UK
29 Earlsfort Terrace, Dublin 2, Ireland

BLOOMSBURY, BLOOMSBURY PUBLISHING and the Diana logo
are trademarks of Bloomsbury Publishing Plc

First published in Great Britain 1996
This revised and updated paperback edition published 2021

Picture sources: 1.1, 1.2, 1.3 (top) © Giacomino; 1.3 (bottom) © Shutterstock; 1.4
© Giacomino; 1.5 (top) © Yannis Behrakis/Reuters; 1.5 (bottom) © Prosport; 1.6
© A. P. News; 1.7 (top) © Reuters; 1.7 (bottom left) © Prosport; 1.7 (bottom right)
© Sipa/Shutterstock; 1.8 (top) © Reuters/Alamy Stock Photo; 1.8 (bottom) © Juan
Mabromata/AFP via Getty Images; 2.1 (top) © Shaun Botterill – FIFA/FIFA via
Getty Images; 2.1 (bottom) © Jeff Mitchell – FIFA/FIFA via Getty Images; 2.2 (top)
© Karim Jaafar/AFP/Getty Images; 2.2 (bottom) © Marco Cantile/LightRocket via
Getty Images; 2.3 (top) © Pedro Ugarte/AFP via Getty Images; 2.3 (bottom) © Paolo
Bruno/Getty Images; 2.4 (top) © Filippo Monteforte/AFP via Getty Images; 2.4
(bottom) © Debajyoti Chakraborty/NurPhoto via Getty Images; 2.5 (top) © Michael
Regan – FIFA/FIFA via Getty Images; 2.5 (bottom) © Robbie Jay Barratt – AMA/
Getty Images); 2.6 (top) © Xinhua/Shutterstock; 2.6 (bottom) © Chris Brunskill/
Fantasista/Getty Images; 2.7 © Jam Media/Getty Images; 2.8 (top) © Presidency of
Argentina/EPA-EFE/Shutterstock; 2.8 (bottom) © Jam Media/Getty Images.

A catalogue record for this book is available from the British Library

ISBN: PB: 978-1-5266-3941-7; EBOOK: 978-1-4088-2772-7

2 4 6 8 10 9 7 5 3 1

Typeset by Hewer Text UK Ltd
Printed and bound in Great Britain by CPI Group (UK) Ltd, Croydon CR0 4YY

To find out more about our authors and books visit
www.bloomsbury.com and sign up for our newsletters

'God makes me play well. That is why I always make the sign of the cross when I walk out on to the pitch. I feel I would be betraying him if I didn't.'

Diego Maradona

'Pele had nearly everything. Maradona has everything. He works harder, does more and is more skilful. Trouble is that he'll be remembered for another reason. He bends the rules to suit himself.'

Sir Alf Ramsey (1986)

'My main doubt is whether he has the sufficient greatness as a person to justify being honoured by a worldwide audience.'

Pele on Maradona

'Fame was your phone ringing a few times more each week to request interviews you did not wish to give and didn't, fame was people with kindly intentions interrupting your thoughts on the street, fame was the inhibition which kept you from taking a piss in a strange alley for fear of cops and headlines on a front page, fame kept you from making a fool of yourself on the dance floor. Fame was the inability to get boozed anonymously in a strange bar, which meant it was the inability to nurse an obsessive melancholy through a night of revelations.'

Norman Mailer, *The Prisoner of Sex*

CONTENTS

INTRODUCTION

Anyone doubting that Diego Maradona was rather more than just a football player had only to glance at some of the newspaper headlines marking his death on 25 November 2020. From the French *Equipe*'s '*Le Dieu est Mort*' ('God is Dead') to *Olé* in Argentina with 'Immortality: 1960–Infinity', we were being reminded of not just a genius of the game, but an icon and a legend. One of the placards held up amidst the mass of largely poor 'shirtless' Argentines declared: 'It doesn't matter what you did with your life, but what you did with ours'.

Memories came back to me of a day in the early 1990s when I caught a train out from the centre of Buenos Aires to a poor neighbourhood in search of Maradona's beginnings for a biography I had been commissioned to write, drawing on my Spanish childhood love of football and my time working as a foreign correspondent in Buenos Aires in the 1980s. I discovered that whatever I had already seen and read about Maradona's life on and off the pitch, nothing had quite prepared me for what I was to uncover.

My journey of exploration took me to where the streets were unpaved and smelt of open sewers and rotting garbage, and where the hut made of scrap metal, loose bricks and cardboard where Maradona had spent his childhood was preserved like a shrine with flowers and rosaries.

When I heard the news of his death, an image flashed into my mind. It was that of Maradona, scarcely past toddler stage, kicking a football in his ramshackle home. Even at an early age, the kid kicked with force and determination whenever his left foot tired of dancing with the ball.

In later years it was the image of the God-given talent, the magician, that prevailed in many media accounts of Maradona, particularly in Argentina. And yet Maradona himself never forgot the social humiliation of being born in the shanty town. This coloured his world view and boosted his hunger to prove himself in a world where the odds were firmly stacked against people of his background – he was of mixed poor Italian immigrant and indigenous descent. It also secured for him a huge popular following, not least among the world's poor, for whom football was an escape and a connection to other worlds.

The World Cup in 1986 in Mexico is an enduring emblem. In Argentina's quarter-final match against England, he scored that infamous first goal against the old enemy of Argentine history and mythology with his hand, but the referee and linesman allowed it. Only his fellow countrymen excused the mischief. His second goal, which to this day I never tire of watching, was sublime, as Maradona, picking up the ball inside his half, dribbled his way through the English field and defence with perfect balance and rhythm. Poetry in motion.

Those two goals encapsulated the flawed genius that Maradona was destined to be. The first showed Maradona the urchin child who had grown up to be a star, still so unsure of his true self as to feel the need to cheat. The second was Maradona the hugely gifted player of exceptional skill. Lesser players might have had no option but to use their hands. Maradona's tragedy lay in believing he had to do the same, and to justify it afterwards, when his God-given talent should have made it unnecessary.

As for his fellow Argentines, they saw both goals against the English as emanating from someone who spoke to them, and was the best export they had ever had, with a style and vision that was above and beyond the norm, globally recognised as the best player in history. The perception fuelled Maradona's own claim of divine intervention.

In Mexico, where Argentina went on to win the World Cup, Maradona became the incarnation of his nation, redeeming it after the humiliation four years earlier in the Falklands War. He also became a kind of sacrificial lamb who would go on to give his flesh, enduring the inner demons that from then on began to take hold of him, even though he always seemed to pull back from the ultimate fall. He very publicly fought against his drug addiction and alcoholism, and the torments and destruction they brought about in his personal and public life. The last ten years of his life described in this book are a final closure to my seemingly endless biographical encounter with Maradona. These last years seemed to show an ongoing downward spiral and a waste of talent, a squandered God-given gift through drug abuse and family breakdown, apart from a few redemptive moments.

There is much mythology and hyperbole surrounding the life of Diego Maradona, which perhaps has much to do with the Argentine psyche, for ever seeking a redeemer to lift it from its political and economic failure – but which also suggests a different legacy that speaks beyond national boundaries in a time of dislocation and uncertainty, healing and hope.

Maradona is a tragic genius – but also, very human. He was born into poverty, and struggled against the odds. He became, in his time, the best player in the world by a long way and gave many fans great joy. He caused hurt and love. He was rebellious and raged against the powerful and the uncaring, and spoke to the have-nots and the afflicted.

This is the story of a natural-born football talent who grew up to believe he was God and suffered as a result. The first thirty-six years of Diego Maradona's life (1960–96) mirror an age in which football has been transformed from a popular leisure activity into *the* world sport; in which footballers, their fans and club officials are subjected to media and commercial pressure undreamt of thirty years ago. While claiming to be born into and to play for the people, Maradona in fact became a key component in a giant money-spinning machine fuelled by inflated transfer deals, TV rights, sponsorship and merchandising.

I count myself lucky that there are few pastimes I enjoy more than playing football on a Spanish beach in summer, or joining in a very English kick-about at weekends. I love sharing in the collective excitement of the terraces, be it the Nou Camp, Wembley or La Bombonera with my family and friends. I am half Spanish and half English, with a touch of Italian by birth, so I can say, quite happily, that I support Newcastle and Barcelona on a good day, Milan and Boca Juniors on another. I believe in the instinctive universality of football.

I was born in Spain and brought up straddling cultures in Europe and South America, so it was inevitable that Maradona should form a key part of my seduction. One cannot even begin to understand Maradona without watching him play. His seemingly endless bag of tricks, the sheer charisma of his personality, the way he connects with his fans and infuriates his enemies. But Maradona's actions on the football pitch have probably been commented on by sports journalists more than those of most other contemporary sportsmen, and there is a limit to the use to which the English language can be put in describing key moves.

Thus while I have selected certain matches as an illustrative reminder of Maradona's talent for the game, this book is not primarily about a gifted player chasing goals. My main concern has been to investigate Maradona as a unique social, political and religious phenomenon. In so doing I have tried to go beyond the Maradona of the football screens, and to shed some light on the myths and vested interests that have surrounded him throughout his career, from the superstitions and political intrigues of his native Argentina to the complicities of doctors and football authorities in the World Cup. Along the way is a relatively short life packed with incident and personal crisis.

Preparing this book involved not just a great deal of travel and research, at some risk, but the co-operation of numerous people who helped me to penetrate the secretive, propagandist and self-deluded world which Diego Maradona has allowed to be built around him. I am more thankful to Diego Maradona than I would ever have thought possible when I first caught a glimpse of him in 1982, playing badly against the Russians while his country and mine went to war over the Falklands. The chant went up around the River Plate stadium that 'He who doesn't jump is an Englishman'. Everyone started jumping. I felt as vulnerable as my dad did when as a secretive English diplomat in Madrid during the Second World War he attended a bullfight where the German national anthem was suddenly played. Maradona has helped me understand why football should matter, and why it shouldn't, and how it can help one survive the most desolate of moments. I did not have the money, the patience or the gullibility that would have ensured hours of taped interviews with my subject. But halfway through my researches I was told by Maradona's psychoanalyst that I was in the process of finding out more about Diego than he knew himself. I was further reassured by Ossie Ardiles: 'The problem about writing a book about Diego is that the truth hurts,' he told me. Ossie was among a small minority of players, relatives and friends who subsequently refused to be interviewed for this book on the grounds that it was unauthorized and therefore disloyal to Maradona. I respect their attitude rather more than that of others whose reason for avoiding me turned out to be that they had too much to hide. This book would not have been possible, however, without the help of many more both within Maradona's intimate circle and outside it who provided much insight, comment and fact.

Several witnesses have asked to remain anonymous, while others I have openly quoted throughout the book. I am particularly grateful to Jorge Cyterszpiler, Carlos Bilardo, César Menotti, Marcos Franchi, Vincenzo Sinischalsci, Nicolau Casaus, Settimio Aloisio and Terry Venables for finding sufficient time for me in their otherwise hectic official schedules. Peter Parker helped with some invaluable early research, as did Maria Laura Avignolo, Marcela Mora y Araujo and Gabriela Cerruti.

Warm thanks also to the following, who in one way or another contributed to making this book possible: in the UK, Simon Kuper, Peter Aspden, Simon Greenberg, William Lewis, Clay Harris, Andy Anderson, Robin Pauley, Richard Lambert, Nina Higgs, Brian Glanville, Tony Mason, Alan Tomlinson, Esteban Cichello Hubner, and the ever helpful staff of the London and *Financial Times* libraries. In Spain, Tom Burns, David White and 'Isa' in the *FT*'s Madrid office, the press office and library of Barcelona FC, 'El Lobo' Carrasco, Paco Aguilar, Luis Fernando Rojo, Manolo Salcedo, José Manuel García, José Vicente Hernaez, and all the staff at *Marca* and *El País*; in France, Alejandro Valente and the staff of *France Futbol*; in Italy, Candido Cannavo, Andrea Bungiovanni, Eli Trifari, Rosario Pastore, Jennifer Grego, Gustavo, Angelo and all staff at *Gazzetta dello Sport*, Robert Graham, Bruno Passarelli, Julio Algañaraz, Franco Esposito, Martin Bokhart, Gerardo Kaiser and the staff of the British Consulate in Naples, Carlo Juliano and the staff of Napoli football club, the staff of the Hotel Paradiso, Cristiana Sinagra, Juan Carlos Laburu and Paulo Pauletti. In Argentina, Roberto Guareschi, Ricardo Kirschbaum, Mariano Hamilton, Ricardo Roa, Horacio Pagani, Nestor Straimmel and all the staff at *Clarín*, Guillermo Blanco, Jorge Ruprecht, Ernesto Cherquis Bialo, Amy Wright, Fernando Niembro, Ezequiel Fernández Moores, Judith Evans,

Mariano Grondona, Daniel Antonio Strada, Andrés Federman, Mathew Doman, David Pilling, Rogerio García Lupo, Silvina Wagner, Isidoro Gilobert, Pablo Llonto, Margarita Mitchell, Emilio Mignone and Oscar Davila.

In Buenos Aires, special thanks to Sonia de García and the Hotel Principado, Diana Tussie, John Fernandes and the staff of Aerolíneas Argentinas for a combination of hospitality and logistical support. Elsewhere, FIFA officials past and present including Andreas Herren and Guido Trognoni. In London my agent Caroline Dawnay was as always a source of encouragement, as were my editors Penny Phillips, Jocasta Brownlee, Caroline Taggart and the late Vikki Orvice.

I would also like to add a few names of people who have helped with the new closing chapter for this edition. I am indebted to Patrick O'Brien's article 'Close up with Maradona' in *Sport for Business*, 27 November 2020. I also thank Asif Kapadia, Angus Macqueen, Nicky Bolster, Maria Laura Avignolo, Fernando Signorini, Marcela Mora y Araujo, Annabel Merullo of Peters Fraser & Dunlop, the team at Bloomsbury – special mention to Nigel Newton, Paul Baggaley, Sarah Ruddick and copy-editor Catherine Best – and last but by means least Kidge, Julia, Miriam and Nadia.

DYING WITH DIEGO

T his preface is a story about two stories, or rather, about two stories that became one, thanks to my encounters with a tragic genius in the world of professional football.

It's about what Diego Maradona said and did once this (unauthorised) biography of him, *Hand of God*, was published; and the strange transformation that began to take place in my life as a result of writing about Diego Maradona. Along the way we each took a little bit of the other.

I blame Diego for wanting to get this story going by choosing to come to London in early September 1996 just as my book is beginning to find its way into the bookshops. Following a steady decline into drug-induced neurosis, Diego has temporarily rediscovered his zest for life just as I am sinking into a monumental state of depressed inactivity.

Someone rings me from Buenos Aires on the eve of Diego's arrival in the English capital to play me back a recording of a radio interview he has given. It is an upbeat Diego I am listening to. He and his wife Claudia are having another go at having their first son: 'I hope my sperm can get in there this time,' Diego tells a young Argentine reporter as they share pasta and a tomato salad in his flat. A few weeks earlier he had quit Boca Juniors amid fresh public admissions of his drug problem and after missing several penalties. I may not score goals the way I used to, he seems to be telling us, but I can still fuck and procreate.

In 1986, during that game with England, Maradona thanked God for his first hand ball. When he missed the penalties for Boca, Maradona blamed it on hell. 'It's the witches. They are against me,' he tells the local media. I guess I'm living under a kind of spell too, not a brilliant one. My star has fallen out of the sky, gone splat. I was brought up by the Jesuits, but not even they prepared me for Diego.

Just when I thought I had seen the end of him, crafted the final chapter, Diego announces he is coming to London as the star guest of an international football festival of school children sponsored by Eurosport and Puma. The English might still remember him for cheating them with his hand, but he speaks only fondly of them. After all, about this time, a year previously, he was enthusiastically received at Oxford University and given the honorary title of Inspirer of Dreams.

But I'm not only depressed, I'm also paranoid. I don't believe Diego's coming to London simply to kick a ball around in Battersea Park with a bunch of kids. Soon after the radio interview, I wake up in the middle of the night covered in sweat: a panic attack follows a nightmare about Diego chasing me round Trafalgar Square with an army of lawyers in pin-stripes and bodyguards carrying violin cases.

By then, nearly a year had gone by since I first appeared on Argentina's most popular TV chat show alongside Diego's manager Guillermo Coppola, and the former Argentine coach Carlos Bilardo, and announced that I was preparing a book about the life and times of Maradona. That flippant boast I now imagine has come back to haunt me. Diego is on his way to London, to beat me up, mentally, physically, and legally.

Then I remember some old advice from my late Spanish grandmother: the best way to deal with a striker is to strike first. With two aggressive women friends for bodyguards and armed with a copy of my book, I make my way late on a Saturday night to San Lorenzo, near Harrods in Knightsbridge, where I've been tipped off Diego is having supper.

Unless you're a journalist or happen to have written a book about Diego Maradona, San Lorenzo is the kind of place you can get into only if you've got money or you've got a title. Diego goes there to show that there is nowhere in the world that should be barred to him. He may not be an aristocrat, but he left the poverty of the shanty town behind him long ago.

Diego is sitting at the table with Coppola, his personal trainer, and Vialli. The Italian Chelsea player is silent and sober (he's got a match to play at Stamford Bridge the next day), but Diego's been drinking and who knows what else to help him along. He seems unable to focus on me or what any of us are doing there. He doesn't even seem to remember that we've been together before and that I've been following him all the way from Buenos Aires to Oxford via Naples, Barcelona and Paris, and that I've written a book about him.

I realise that it's the kind of state of mind that can lead to everything – a smashing of a glass, a broken bottle over the head, tables turning – or nothing at all. I hand him the book as one who hands his opponent a pistol in a game of Russian roulette. I would like to believe that I am handing him part of his soul. Scribbled into the inside cover is the dedication: 'To Diego, with a human sense of life'. What I mean is that I believe my biography to be critical but truthful. But then as Ossie Ardiles, speaking of Maradona, once told me: 'The truth hurts'.

Diego takes the book much as he had earlier taken the menu, overlooking the dedication, and flipping through its pages with the air of someone who hasn't got the stomach or the mindset here and now to get back into his soul. He pauses only to look at the photographs, chuckling like a naughty boy at one in particular – him posing with the Giuliano family (head of the Naples Camorra) in 1986.

If I too have said nothing until this moment, other than 'Here Diego, this is the book I've written about you!' – it's because my fear has given way to a form of fascination, as I wait for Diego's reaction. Diego continues to say nothing to me which is when I realise that he may be seeing me clearer than I had thought possible at first, and that he is not about to thank me or hit me but rather just ignore me.

He has taken the pistol, and shot, but he is alive and well and dining in San Lorenzo. As he closes the book and pushes it across the table at Coppola, a group of waiters come up and ask for his autograph in Italian. They are followed by the owner of the restaurant who embraces Diego like a long-lost brother. The whole restaurant now seems to be focused entirely on him. Somehow San Lorenzo takes on the aspect of a film set for *The Godfather*, with Italians kissing each other in a ritual of tribal complicity.

'You son of a bitch, Diego,' I think to myself. 'I've bust my ass trying to find out in a year what you've been hiding for most of your life and you haven't got a word to say to me.'

But in the restaurant this night, only one table looks on the whole scene not with adoration but with cool detachment verging on amusement. The men and women on this table are blue blood English, have gone to private school and inherited great wealth. They go shooting and hunting and play polo. They gave up shopping in Harrods the day it was bought by an Arab, but somehow San Lorenzo remains part of their social circuit. Tonight their territory is close to being invaded and they realise just how close when one of the women gets up to go to the toilet. She is tall and blonde and with the rose skin of the pampered English female – a kind of Lady Di look-alike. Diego gets half off his chair and speaking loudly and in Spanish asks her to join his table. Her boyfriend gets up and half aggressively says in English: 'Excuse me, Mr Maradona, but she is my fiancée, and she already has a table.'

And Diego bursts out laughing as the woman goes on walking past, and the waiters laugh with him, and he apologises in a way he knows no one will believe, least alone me. At that moment I hate and love Diego Maradona.

I may be nursing an obsessive melancholy still, but Diego at least makes it clear that this is not to be a night of revelations. We could have sat through it, drinking and maybe snorting coke together, going over each other's lives, but instead Coppola stops me from joining them in the taxi that takes them from San Lorenzo to the Ministry of Sound nightclub then back to the Dorchester Hotel, where the whores sometimes mix with the rich.

'You know Diego's not happy with that Englishman,' Coppola whispers menacingly to one of my girlfriends, pointing to me. I realise then the roulette is just beginning.

According to the *News of the World*, Diego, after San Lorenzo, arranges for several ladies of the night to join him back at the hotel. He picks on a Brazilian and snorts cocaine with her. I've no firm evidence that the newspaper's story is accurate, but I guess anything is possible in London's Mayfair in the early hours of a Sunday morning. I go to bed that night with a part of me nursing a strange kind of envy. Without anyone beside me I feel as abandoned in this city as a dog without his lead.

Then things start looking up for me just as they have been doing for Diego. Next day, while Diego is followed round Battersea Park by hundreds of adoring fans, I get a phone call from a TV station in Madrid inviting me to appear on their highest rated programme. It is just the escape I'm looking for. With the onset of English winter I suffer easily from light denial syndrome, and I need the warmth and light of Spain where I was born eight years before Diego.

But then he and I are beginning to follow each other like body and shadow as I discover when, four days later, I fly into Madrid.

Diego has flown from London to Alicante in southern Spain to submit himself to yet another drugs cure, as always administered by a specialist few other doctors have ever heard of. Diego believes in medicine men not the medical profession, in miracles and divine inspiration, and cheating life and death. It's September, a time when top footballers around Europe are cashing in on their latest massive transfer deals and engaging their talents in a new season. But in Alicante, Diego Maradona, the person once widely acclaimed as the greatest footballer of them all, mounts a scene which, had it been Chicago, might have been scripted by Norman Mailer.

It is Mailer who in his book *The Prisoner of Sex* has this to say about the price of fame: 'Fame is your phone ringing a few times more each week to request interviews you do not wish to give and don't, fame is people with kindly intentions interrupting your thoughts on the street, fame is the inhibition which keeps you from taking a piss in a strange alley for fear of cops and headlines on the dance floor. Fame is the inability to get boozed anonymously in a strange bar, which means it is the inability to nurse an obsessive melancholy through a night of revelations.'

Sure, I'm learning something about fame with Diego. In Alicante he pours out his latest confession about his drug addiction in a local radio interview before slamming my book as a crucifixion. 'Burns is really out of order, he's pissed all over me,' he declares before naming a list of players, managers and agents he threatens to take legal action against for the help they gave me in researching his life story. I know that of course he has not read the book because he speaks no English. However his personal trainer, who does, reads him the first couple of pages which are full of acknowledgements. Diego feels betrayed and claims that his friends are now enemies.

A few hours later he returns to his hotel and tells Coppola he wants to hit the night, starting off in a local nightclub which doubles up as a brothel. Coppola tries to restrain him at first but then, as managers have done throughout Maradona's career, gives in, lets him go, a necessary indulgence for he who is beyond good or evil, a demi-god of the sporting world. Diego arrives at the nightclub, spots some male clients talking to some women and gets the owner to pay them off – the men that is.

In the early hours of the next morning, Diego returns to his hotel a second time, this time in a state of mind a bellboy describes as 'very strange and exalted'. Together with two women, Maradona gets stuck in the lift when the electrics fail. I suffer from claustrophobia and panic attacks too, so I can understand something of what Diego now feels, but what happens next suggests the extent to which our separate existences have yet to fully coincide.

For Maradona the lift experience is not just a bit of temporary anxiety. It becomes a bad trip into hell and back, a feeling that has haunted him before, a suffocating sense of entrapment, of dreadful darkness, of inability to escape, like when, as a child, he falls into an open sewer of the shanty town and starts drowning in the communal shit before being rescued by his Uncle Cirilo. Now in Alicante, Diego lashes out with the frenzy of an animal brought in from a wild landscape and dumped in a sealed cage. In that scene in the lift, with Diego kicking until his foot bleeds and his body bathed in sweat, there is projected the enemy he has always carried without and within himself.

Afterwards, the hotel manager will discover the consequences of Maradona's rage which erupts once Diego is rescued by the local fire brigade. He kicks and hits everything he sees, breaks tables and chairs, cries into the night. 'Your work is a pile of shit,' he screams at the man from the insurance company who has come to assess the damage.

Alicante occurs exactly a year after Maradona returned in triumph to play for his old club Boca Juniors, having served a 15-month ban for failing a World Cup dope test in the US. There is a sense of *déjà vu*. Maradona's life has been helter-skelter, oscillating between stardom and disgrace. Those of us who have followed his career through the years are as wary about declaring him finished as we are of proclaiming his enduring success. And yet even close friends of Maradona are whispering in private what they are afraid to say in public: if Diego goes on like this, he's going to die soon.

I'm thinking on Diego as I sit on a chair having my face painted with eye shadow and blush in preparation for my live TV appearance. The pressures of fame, the distortions and disruptions to life that money makes . . . The TV programme is Spain's most popular, which is to say that I have made a pact with the devil. In return for a free return ticket to Madrid, and the chance to promote my book in Spain, I have agreed to appear in a programme that sandwiches serious reportage between crude comedy and soft porn.

In the waiting room I sit for a while with the other invited guest.

Her name is Lucia, a Catalan girl in her late twenties who looks and speaks as if she's had it tough. 'I'm here because I've been abusing my body since the age of ten,' Lucia says to me lifting her skirt and showing me two large burn marks on her thighs. Her wrists are scarred from an earlier attempt to experiment with profuse bleeding.

Lucia tells me she was abused as a child, and has been raped five times since puberty, the last time in the mental asylum near Barcelona from which she has escaped to appear on the programme.

'I do have another life you know,' she confides as the minutes tick away towards deadline. 'I like writing, particularly poetry. I guess it's my way of trying to discover love.'

I appear first on the programme. I find myself having to use twenty years of journalistic experience to anticipate and control an interview clearly set on bringing out only the most negative points about Diego.

Although I would not claim to see Diego yet as my best friend, I do try to paint a sympathetic picture of a victim of people who should know better than to wreck people's lives: so-called doctors and managers and politicians who have exploited Maradona in the course of his career. The interviewer wants me to deliver the final 'estocada' or sword thrust to a genius who may be mortally wounded, but I wind up the interview on a note of reconciliation.

'It's a pity Diego has lashed out at the book without reading it. We could have sat round and had a drink instead,' I say before the cameras move to Lucia.

Poor Lucia. No journalistic training there. Just a raw pathetic victim of life, pictures of her brutalised nakedness flashed across millions of TV screens as she tries to explain why she does what she does.

That night Lucia and I find ourselves being put up, at the TV company's expense, in the same luxury hotel in central Madrid. The concierge thinks I've brought her in from the streets and gives me a conspiratorial look as we ask for separate keys. Then, just as we are about to enter the lift, I turn to Lucia and ask if she'd like to come out with me for a late-night drink. 'There is nothing I feel like more,' Lucy says, all the tension of a ruined life somehow temporarily giving way to a totally innocent smile.

Diego returns to Buenos Aires, and I to London. Diego carries on with his drug cure – it seems eternal, this dealing with witches, trying to come to terms with getting older, never playing football the way he once did.

I feel we're struggling together – Diego and I – now that my dad's died and the book's written and there's a single postcard of some Vietnamese peasant sitting on my desk with the unsigned hand-written inscription 'Miss Saigon'. An ex-woman friend has gone off to Saigon of all places, leaving me with her ghost and Diego's shadow. My publishers are telling me there is huge interest generated by my book, but I can't bring myself to tell them that what I have written has become a terrible reminder of someone else.

'What do you feel like?' a male friend asks me one day as the winter chill grips London. I've taken to kicking a football around a piece of parkland near the river. 'I'm disintegrating, mate, I'm disintegrating,' I tell him.

I'm where Diego's been before, down in the communal shit of one's own existence. The memory of his Uncle Cirilo rescuing him from the cesspit served as a reminder of his ability to survive, to pull through, but in my case it's the inability to put my book behind me that really hurts.

Just when I thought I'd finished with promoting the book, the phone begins to ring. For nearly two weeks Argentine journalists pursue me asking me what I think about Diego's latest fall from grace. Interest in my book has been fuelled by the arrest of Coppola and the suggestion that he is part of a major drug-smuggling ring. Diego silently grieves the imprisonment of his friend and confidant, somehow gets himself to believe that it's all part of a great conspiracy against him which includes my book. By now letters from his lawyers have gone out to several individuals whom I interviewed, pressurising them to retract their statements.

The prosecution against Coppola collapses after it is alleged that police had planted cocaine at his flat and conspired with a series of false witness statements. By then Maradona has himself given a statement declaring himself and his manager innocent, in a brief appearance before the investigating judge that shows the enduring nature of his popularity. Clerks and other staff of the court beg for his autograph and pose for a 'team' photograph with the past.

Such adulation in the past has fuelled Maradona's sense of himself as above good or evil, has given him an extraordinary power in his own country. So why is it that when my Argentine publishers ring me to invite me for another promotional road show I jump at the opportunity?

Well, I'm still fascinated by the guy, something in me tells me we're getting level, somewhere, somehow, subject and biographer must have it out, not on anyone's territory but on his own where it all began, in a way neither he nor I chose nor could have even predicted.

So it is that on 2 April, preparing to board a British Airways flight to Buenos Aires, I can't help but ponder the significance of the date – fifteenth anniversary of my trial-by-fire as a foreign correspondent working in Buenos Aires for the *Financial Times*. 2 April 1982 – the crowds, with national flags and anti-British slogans, pouring into the Plaza de Mayo, the terrible sense of shock and apprehension I felt at the thought that Argentines and English could soon be killing each other over distant islands.

On the eve of the invasion I had gone to see Maradona playing in a friendly against the Soviet Union. The chant had gone up around the River Plate stadium that 'He who doesn't jump is an Englishman'. Everyone had started jumping. And yet Argentina's number one player, not I, was destined for failure – on the playing fields of Spain, the country where I was born. the Argentine media could lie about what was happening in the trenches, but there was little it could do about the football matches beamed live from Spain, short of blacking out the screens and risking a national riot. Glued to their TV boxes, millions of Argentines ignored the news that shells were falling on Port Stanley and that their troops were being forced to retreat. But they watched the national team go down 1–0 to Belgium and Maradona sent off in a game against Brazil – his blatant foul on an opposition defender, the humiliating climax to one of the worst performances of his international career.

Fifteen years on I'm not bouncing with a sense of commemorative celebration. Days before my departure, a veiled death threat to the English, addressed to me, is posted to my London office by someone claiming to be a Falklands War veteran.

When I lived in Argentina I used to get more threats than I care to mention. Some of them were hoaxes, but one had seemed potentially serious enough that the Foreign Office advised me to leave the country temporarily. So I ask a police contact for help: 'Can't M15 check it out before I fly?' I plead. 'That might take at least two months,' is the answer.

At the Victoria station Gatwick check-in desk, a BA employee looks at me strangely. 'I'm sorry sir, but the computer is telling us you will be requiring a wheelchair,' she says. I find myself having to argue with her that there must be a mistake. 'Can't you see I am standing!' I say at one point, although a part of me has begun to suspect that Maradona's cast some kind of mad spell of on me.

When I arrive at Gatwick, they are calling for Dr Burns over the loudspeakers. This time the airline employee asks me: 'Will you be requiring a wheelchair, sir?' By now I am convinced this is Diego's idea of a sick joke.

After I touch down in Buenos Aires, Ignacio, head of media relations for Planeta, my Argentine publishers, seems close to breakdown. 'I've never experienced anything like this. No one wants to touch your book. They say they won't want to get on the wrong side of Diego. It's like a Mafia out there.'

In fact, Ezequiel Fernandes-Moores, a sports columnist with *Pagina 12*, interviews me within hours. Ezequiel has been through a few rough rides himself as the unauthorised biographer of another Argentine hero, the boxer Oscar Bonavena, who was shot dead in a Las Vegas brothel. But nothing prepares us for what happens next.

While we talk over a cup of coffee in the lobby of my hotel, I catch sight of Carlos Bilardo, the former coach of the Argentine national squad. Some English fans may remember that Bilardo's roots in the tough, no-nonsense school of Argentine football – where anything is permissible as long as it secures victory – had an early example when he played for Estudiantes, the Argentine champions of the 1960s. In a game between Estudiantes and Manchester United, Bilardo head-butted Nobby Stiles, leaving it up to his mate, Carlos Pachame, to kick open Bobby Charlton's shin.

I hold no ill-feelings towards Bilardo. He had once given me an hour of his time, providing me with some useful perspectives on Mexico 1986. It's something Maradona does not like. He has got his lawyers to write a letter to Bilardo (and indeed all the others who were interviewed by me) threatening action unless he denies ever talking to me.

I want to say hello to Bilardo, thank him in some way for helping me out, but Diego has got to him first. Nobby never had it like this.

'Hi, Carlos. Remember me, Jimmy Burns who came to interview you about Diego?' I extend my hand in friendship.

Bilardo takes it, then pulls away when he recognises me. 'Yes. I remember you. You're a son of a bitch. Fuck off out of this country.' He seems as if he's about to hit me but decides on a final line of abuse before walking away. 'We should have cut your balls off.'

The exchange is described in censored form by Fernandes-Moores in his newspaper the next morning. 'Burns has been warned that launching *Hand of God* in Argentina is not going to be an easy task,' he writes.

Day 3. I'm beginning to feel like Diego does after coming down from coke, a sense of creeping paranoia, fuelled by the surrealism of the Argentine media. Today, a journalist begins a live radio interview with me by quoting from a Borges poem about the Falklands War. It's about a Brit and an Argie killed in action who were more like each other than they ever realised. 'They could have been friends,' says the poem, 'but they only saw each other's faces once, on some islands that were far too famous, each one was Cain, and each one was Abel. They buried them together. Snow and ashes know them. What I have just recounted belongs to an event we cannot understand.'

I'm thinking of the relevance of all this. Am I meant to be starting another Falklands War over Diego? Are we like the characters of the poem – Juan Lopez and John Ward – interchangeable, symbiotic, biographer/subject, subject/biographer . . .

'Mr Burns are you there? Can you hear me? Are you all right,' the radio interviewer asks.

I want to say 'You've thrown me, you fucker, just like you wanted to do.' But what I say instead is 'Yes I'm here, it's just that I was really moved for a moment there.'

Then the phone-in begins. A woman in a shrill voice says: 'I think Burns has come to rob us of the one thing that belongs to us.' Another contributor says: 'You're a son of a bitch.' Then enter stage right Guillermo Coppola, Maradona's manager recently released from prison. Coppola is live and dangerous. 'Burns is a liar, and everything in the book is lies,' Coppola declares to a prime-time national radio audience.

'Have you read the book?' I ask Coppola over the airwaves. He admits he has not.

At supper that night with some old Argentine friends, conversation revolves around the power of myths in contemporary Argentina. 'People here still think the topic of whether or not Evita died a virgin is a serious political issue,' a journalist working with an Argentine TV channel says.

Day 4. Maradona collapses during a TV show in Chile. Drugs overdose? Heart attack? No, it's all OK, says Coppola, just the heat in the studio. Ignacio finds more local journalists prepared to talk to me.

Day 5. A pre-recorded interview for one of Argentina's leading football programmes. The journalist asking the questions admits that most of my answers will be heavily edited. I ask him what the problem is? 'You've written a book about politics, about drugs, about Mafias. It's a touchy subject here. We won't broadcast it because Diego might react badly,' he says.

Another phone-in. My interviewer is a former female model called Tete, who now runs a very successful afternoon chat show. My book lies on the table in front of her, crisp and unread. She looks clearly bored with the subject of football, but declares her professional duty to tackle a subject that is causing a bit of domestic bother. Once again, Coppola is called upon live to give his expert opinion. Once again Maradona's manager accuses me of lying. He is followed by Maradona's former accountant, Marcos Franchi, whom I interviewed in October 1995. He accuses me of inventing the meeting.

I go and see Luis Moreno Ocampo, a local lawyer I had befriended during the trial of the military juntas for human rights violations after the Falklands conflict. He was then deputy state prosecutor.

He tells me he is now a TV star and offers to mediate between Franchi and me by having us on his programme. 'You'll do wonders for my ratings!' he quips.

Moreno Ocampo's show is called *Forum*; guests say what they like about each other after signing a statement that bars legal action. In a country where proving libel is lengthy and costly, the offer attracts me as a way of straightening the record. Franchi admits over the phone that I had interviewed him, but backs out of the programme.

Day 6. A photographer insists on having me pose, balancing a football on my head, just like Maradona. We are in the middle of Florida, Buenos Aires' main shopping precinct. I strike a ridiculous figure, a skinny, most unsporting figure in a suit, but the hand of God ensures that I hold the ball there long enough for the motor drive to click ten frames. But I'm getting tired now of all the circus, back to thinking on Mailer, *The Prisoner of Sex*, prisoner of Diego – 'fame was your phone ringing a few times more each week to request interviews you did not wish to give . . . fame was the inhibition of taking a piss in a strange alley for fear of cops and headlines . . .'

I am driven to a piece of open ground near La Recoleta cemetery, where parts of Evita's body have been buried from time to time over the years. There, a man with a baseball cap and a large microphone leads another strike on behalf of the Maradona camp. Questioning my right to write the book, he asks: 'How would the English feel if an Argentine turned up and wrote a book about Prince Charles and Lady Di?' I think they would love it, I answer.

Day 7. My last night in Buenos Aires and halfway through it I forget I have a last interview at breakfast time. You could say it's a typical Diego night. I'm surrounded by music, booze, women, joints, lines of coke dragged deep into the bright lights of the city from hell. A bunch of us end up in a hotel room, plundering the minibar, watching the dawn rise over the River Plate, and then it's the interview, just me and a microphone – silent and threatening – words failing me, trying to express the anger I feel towards the whole world ganging up on me, as Maradona's dad-in-law tells listeners to boycott the book.

Postscript. First day back in London. Spring is in the air but I feel wasted. An Argentine friend living in England receives a phone call from Coppola. 'Why did you give Jimmy such a rough time, Guillermo?' she asks.

'Why, all we want from him is a thirty per cent cut,' says Coppola.

And then I'm in some London bookstore clutching a copy of the paperback of my book that has just come out, feeling that a part of it belongs to someone else. I'm telling myself I've been reminded of the excitement and limitations of the game. I've loved and hated Diego. I'm coming out of the shit I was landed in by someone I loved. I'm going to tread more carefully alongside those who make football an obsession. I've thrown away the postcard from Saigon.

1

RESURRECTION

October 1995. Mid-spring in Buenos Aires. Amid the sweet scent of the jacaranda, heavy drum beats and frenetic flag waving, thousands of football fans are making their way to the Bombonera stadium of Boca Juniors. *Bombonera* means chocolate box in Spanish, but there is nothing sweet or contained about the scene. The masses shatter the quiet Sunday of Latin America's most sophisticated capital city, like a wild tribe let loose on a tea room. The men – for there are few women or children among them, so intimidating is the sport still – are bare-chested and wave their shirts like broken chains. They move relentlessly as if to war. Their chief, Diego Maradona, looks down on them from the top of a double-decker bus, dark eyes unflinching, hair cropped and dyed in the war paint of the Boca colours, clutching a mobile phone. The chorus is provided by a radio reporter whose voice is cracking with hysteria. 'Our idol is coming, our idol is coming,' he repeats, over and over again. Beyond the waste land and the rusting houses lining the River Plate, the frenzied cavalcade runs a gauntlet of riot police with their long batons and tear gas at the ready, before claiming the territory irrevocably.

Once inside the stadium, the fans pack the terraces. The high wire and moat surrounding the pitch concentrate their passion, accentuate it. La Bombonera vibrates with the sound of feet stamping and exploding gunpowder, a collective war dance that grows in intensity with every minute that passes.

In the middle of the pitch, there is a giant box, wrapped and ribboned, slowly girating on the back of a truck. But for a moment all eyes are on a long sausage-shaped piece of plastic from which emerge Maradona and the rest of Boca Juniors. A huge primeval roar greets him as he makes the sign of the cross and raises his arms triumphantly to the sky. 'Maradoona ... Maradoona ...'

the fans scream. A giant balloon descends, bearing the words 'WELCOME BACK, DIEGO!' For them, the *descamisados*, the shirtless ones who have never lost faith, it is a piece of instant magic. The idol takes the ball, flips it effortlessly from one foot to the other, brings it to his chest and down again. Then, still with the ball close to him, he skips over the paper ribbons which now criss-cross the stadium to where the box has begun to show signs of coming alive. Another explosion, the box opens like a broken cracker and out of it skip Maradona's two young daughters dressed in Boca colours – a surprise present from the master of ceremonies, Maradona's best friend, manager and night messenger Guillermo Coppola. A touch of reassuring innocence to dispel past nightmares seems to be the intention.

It is fifteen months almost to the day since Maradona exited in disgrace from the US World Cup after failing a drugs test. Many thought that that moment finally spelled the end of a career which had swerved between success and scandal. But today in La Bombonera the god is back, defiantly proving to the world that Maradona does not die so easily. He visibly lacks the acceleration to dribble through his opponents and score, but there is no doubting his near-faultless passing and depth of vision. Within minutes he imposes some sense of purpose on a scrap heap of a game, creating the few opportunities that Boca has to shoot at goal. When the goal finally comes, in the last minute of the game, Maradona plays no direct part in it. And yet such has been his presence throughout the game that no one among the 60,000 people crowded inside the stadium objects to him claiming it as his own. With the ball firmly in the net, Maradona turns and runs across the pitch, raising his arms in triumph to his family, to Coppola, to the TV cameras. The last time he ran like that at a camera was when he scored the third goal against Greece – his first goal in the ill-fated World Cup. Today, as then, he wants to tell people he is still the best, that he is not easily defeated. 'Olé, olé, olé, olé, Diego, Diego!' chorus the crowd. Yes, God is back.

That this resurrection, after what seemed the definitive fall, should be staged here in La Bombonera is a reminder that Maradona cannot really be separated in the end from the country in which he was born and brought up. The only certainty about Maradona is that when he dies, no matter how he dies, his funeral in Buenos Aires will be as big as Evita's and even then people won't believe that he is dead. If Argentina is football mad, it is nowhere more noticeable than in the impassioned rituals of the Boca fans, many of whom are drawn from the same poor immigrant-mixed-with-Indian stock as Maradona. Many of them live and breathe football because there is nothing else left to believe in. Argentina has a long history of churning out false prophets.

Every Argentine player worth his salt says that his one ambition is to play for Boca one day. Maradona said that when he was very young, but went one step further. He admitted to harbouring a second ambition: that of winning the World Cup. He helped win Boca a championship when he had just turned twenty-one. He has returned to La Bombonera after captaining his side to a World Cup victory. His outstanding performance in the World Cup in Mexico in 1986 earned him the title of the most talented footballer the world had ever seen. Standing at 5 feet 4 inches, and yet with the strength of will and balance in body to withstand an extraordinary catalogue of physical abuse, Maradona combined the skill and vision of a Pele with the versatility of a Johan Cruyff. But Maradona always seemed beyond comparisons. He defied categorizations as easily as he rejected the demands of club presidents and the discipline of managers. Therein lies his charisma.

It was the international projection of an Argentine success story that endeared Maradona to his fellow countrymen. To them he seems to make up for so many of the failings in their own history. Maradona has provided Argentines with a sense not just of identity but also of escape. They saw purity in his play and called it poetry.

Maradona's popularity among a wider audience has drawn its strength from the extent to which he epitomizes the prospect of achievement and recognition, thanks to nothing more than a natural gift for the game. The rags-to-riches legend of a genius whom destiny marked out for success has its poignant early image in the newsreel clip of the boy Maradona showing off his remarkable control of the ball in the dust-covered playing fields of the shanty town. It developed into the myth of the natural talent who, while determined to win, could still at times demonstrate that he was in love with the game. On a good day, Maradona forgot what he had become, and just went out and played.

Anecdotes which illustrate Maradona's universality are legion and usually tell one more about individual countries than about the man himself. But two in particular bear mentioning from the

outset. They underline the extent to which Maradona has managed
to cut across cultural prejudice and national boundaries. The first
involves a group of female Argentine tourists who on a visit to
the Pyramids found themselves harassed by some Egyptians. The
women were becoming increasingly desperate after their demands
to be left alone were repeatedly rejected. Then one of them suddenly
remembered something that her brother, a Boca fan, had told her
before her departure: that Maradona had played a friendly once
somewhere in the Middle East and helped inaugurate a football
school for young children. So the woman backed away yet again
and cried, 'Maradona!' On hearing the word, the Egyptians
checked themselves and, in an instant, had changed the focus
of their attention from sex to football, allowing the tourists to
beat a retreat, unhassled, a few minutes later.

The second story has Maradona on the London Underground,
disguised under a hat and in a long coat with a collar shielding
most of his face. On one of his rare visits to England – he has
just delivered a lecture to the Oxford Union debating society –
he is characteristically late for a plane he is meant to be catching.
He has been persuaded by his host, a young Argentine student,
that the tube to Heathrow is faster than a taxi. He agrees to the
ride on the condition of the disguise. He fears that he may be
held up or even assaulted if he is recognized. All seems to go as
planned until four stops from the end when a fellow passenger
recognizes Maradona and announces his presence in a loud voice.
Instantly everyone stops their conversation and looks up. Seconds
later the entire carriage has gathered round Maradona demanding
his autograph. The majority are English people. One of them says
he has not forgotten the Hand of God, but he also remembers
that other goal Maradona scored against England, one of the most
universally celebrated in footballing history.

The talent forms only part of the Maradona story. The
myth of Maradona as God has been fuelled and exploited by
economic interests and national and regional idiosyncrasies. From
an early stage in his career, Maradona was both commercialized
and politicized. His image set transfer records and encouraged
the spread of sponsorship and TV rights as crucial elements
in international football's growing engagement with the free
marketplace. There was a cyclical aspect to Maradona's return
to Boca in more ways than one. The TV-linked $10 million deal
behind his return was arranged by the same businessman who

signed one of the first sponsorship deals with the player in the late 1970s.

Maradona chose to play in countries where football is inexorably mixed up with politics of a particularly passionate kind and where media pressures on star players are enormous, without fully realizing that in so doing he would have to play a role that fell outside the strict demands of his sport. Some of the less edifying aspects of the outside pressures on Maradona have come from individuals claiming to represent the medical profession, who cynically put the short-term interests of Maradona the 'money machine' above the longer-term considerations of his survival as a stable human being.

The tragedy as much as the inspiration of Maradona's life has its roots in the poverty of his childhood. To be the first-born son and born an urchin was to be saddled from an early age with the burden of being the main breadwinner of his family through his football, without being given the time or education to consider or explore alternatives. I remember sitting beside Maradona's parents, Chitoro and Tota, during his season with Boca, and witnessing the obsessive way in which his mother in particular followed her son's performance on the pitch.

At the same time it is hard to imagine Maradona coming from a different background. From the shanty town came a hunger to succeed, as well as a somewhat tortured value system based on superstition and living by one's wits. Less clear is the extent to which Maradona's life might have turned out differently had he chosen a different set of friends and managers or played in different countries. Both his 'inner tribe' and some of his advisers share as much responsibility as his doctors for the personal and professional setbacks he has suffered throughout his career. Too many of the characters who formed part of Maradona's life seem to mistake subservience for loyalty, indulging his eccentricities when criticism might have been of greater benefit. In the wider spectrum, Maradona's repeated charges of hypocrisy against certain footballing authorities are not without some justification. Time and again, senior officials turned a blind eye to Maradona's personal shortcomings when it suited them, only to clamp down on them when they considered he had outlived his sell-by date. In this, officials of all the clubs for which Maradona played, national team managers, the Argentine football federation and last but by no means least FIFA, world football's supreme governing body, should share much of the blame. Their apparent desire first and foremost to exploit Maradona commercially has not always served the best interests of football.

And yet it is only too easy to portray Maradona as simply a victim of circumstances beyond his control. In fact he has carried within him both his worst enemy and his best friend. An inherent weakness of character has meant that he has been unable to handle the pressures that have ensued from his success and fame. He cannot bare to be touched in a crowd, and yet falls into deep depression if he considers that the crowd ignores him or turns against him. I have seen Maradona at his best when, alone with just one or two friends, he does something simple like sip a soft drink or eat a pizza. He seems relaxed, at ease with himself and the world around him, generous and funny. And I have seen Maradona at his worst, when not quite recovered from the night before, or still flushed with the frustration of defeat, short-tempered and sententious, playing the king to unquestioning subjects at a press conference. One can only speculate on how different things might have been if he'd gone to England instead of Spain, as Ossie Ardiles advised him to. He might have found less of a need to speak about anything other than football. He also might have led a quieter, less complicated personal life. And yet from Paul Merson's drug addiction to Eric Cantona's Kung-Fu kick, British football continues to spring controversial surprises.

Maradona remains a product of his country. His politics are a mish-mash of half-baked ideas which have never been tested in argument. A British TV documentary in 1995 tried to portray him as a radical revolutionary, but when Maradona praises Castro he does so on the grounds that he is the last remaining 'true patriarch with balls on'. Maradona's politics are little more than a crude but fervent nationalism which makes him vulnerable to any Argentine government in power, however unethical its practices.

In Argentina the English concept of fair play is not as popularly recognized or indeed applauded as that of *viveza*. The word literally means liveliness, but is used to mean craftiness or trickery, and is never used in a derogatory sense. Argentina's cultural hero is a gaucho called Martin Fierro who spends his time cheating and getting away with it. Maradona himself admitted in an interview in 1994 that he carried within him more of the *viveza* of the Buenos Aires shanty town than the straightforwardness of provincial Argentina.

One other aspect of the life of the *villero* or shanty-town dweller is loyalty to a very closely knit circle of relatives and friends – a tribal unit in effect – and a disdain for outside institutions. Thus, for a public figure, Maradona remains extraordinarily inaccessible. His press conferences are carefully manipulated affairs in which he gives only half an answer or only those that he feels like giving. On a one-to-one basis, he is highly selective of journalists to whom he opens out part of himself, and even then he does it only for limited periods.

All this goes some way towards explaining why his drug addiction has been much more long-running than was initially supposed. He admitted only belatedly that he had used drugs to cover up and hide the extent to which his life had fallen apart. Having consistently refused to confess himself on the subject, in early 1996 he granted a carefully arranged interview to the Argentine society magazine *Gente*, giving some details of his drug abuse and promoting better anti-drug education for youngsters.

For more than fourteen years Maradona had justified his refusal to discuss the subject on the grounds that the public should concern itself only with his footballing talent. He used similar arguments in refusing to acknowledge certain other aspects of his life off the pitch, such as his fathering of a child in Italy or his connections with the Naples Mafia. His position would be defensible if Maradona had not been Maradona. In other words if he had not, of his own volition, allowed himself to stray outside the confines of his professional career to inhabit a world that demanded a measure of social responsibility which he was unable and unwilling to assume.

It is here that Maradona's failings as a human being emerge most strongly. Those who praise him unquestioningly make much of his outspoken attacks on certain emblems of authority such as the leadership of FIFA, and his defence of the underprivileged. The reality is that Diego Maradona has spent rather more time on himself as part of FIFA's universal machinery for the exploitation of football than on his parents' poverty-stricken former neighbours in Esquina and Villa Fiorito, rather more time on defending his own right to be than on setting an example to future generations of footballers who may be tempted into drugs or abandoning the children they promised to raise or sharing a glass of champagne with an organized criminal because of his example.

Perhaps it is a symptom of the very commercialization of sport, that we expect too much of that most commercialized of all sports, football, and that footballers expect too much of themselves. This book no doubt would never have been written were it not so. Years ago Maradona might simply have passed into history as just one more self-obsessed and not very intelligent footballer who was nevertheless the best player the game has produced. But he has become a myth in his own time, carrying millions of people with him, and that requires accountability.

On one part of Maradona there can be no argument – the moments of magic he has brought to the game, and the way that this has, at certain moments of his career, been stifled by poor refereeing, the unprofessionalism of his opponents and the bad management of officials who should have known better. Yet Maradona's ultimate tragic flaw lies in the extent to which he himself has perpetuated, through his statements and conduct, the myth of his own god-like status, without fully assuming responsibility for his own failings. Too often has Maradona squandered his talent, denying not only his supporters but himself the chance to enjoy his football pure and simple, with God truly on his side.

2

A CHILD IS BORN

It was a star, glowing in the Southern Hemisphere and reflected on the cold slabs of the hospital floor, like a pearl, that announced to Doña Dalma Salvadora Franco Maradona the birth of her son Diego. It was 30 October 1960, a Sunday – a day for masses and football.

The precise circumstances of the birth, in the working-class Buenos Aires suburb of Avellaneda, in a hospital named in memory of Evita Perón, remain steeped in legend. However, a version, neither confirmed nor denied by Doña Dalma herself, has it that her first-born son came out into the real world kicking, not so long after she had felt her first pains on a dance floor. Doña Dalma, or Tota as she is more familiarly known, let out a cry that many years later would be echoed by commentators around the world. 'GOOOOOOOOL!' she screamed, before the doctor held up the bloodied Diego before her and said, 'Congratulations, you have a healthy son, and he is pure ass.' Thus did this macho child begin to achieve a kind of divinity.

When you're born into poverty, a toy, any toy, is steeped in magic. In the shack where Diego Maradona spent his childhood years, there were neither teddy bears nor electronic games, but there was a leather football. Diego was given it by his uncle Cirilo on his third birthday, soon after he had learnt to walk, and took to it as if it were a diamond. 'There are many people who are scared to admit that they came from the shanty, but not me,' he would say in a later interview, 'because if I hadn't been born in the shanty I wouldn't be Maradona. I had the freedom to play which kids in cities today find it hard to find. We had the space . . . to play what we liked.' He added, 'That first football was the most beautiful present of my life . . . The day I was given it I slept all night, hugging it.'

During the day he'd kick it about in the waste ground around his home in Villa Fiorito, a shanty suburb of Buenos Aires. There, as the ball bounced awkwardly over the dust and stones, the young Diego Maradona learned his first tricks, gradually turning his anarchic toy into a source of skill and inspiration.

Uncle Cirilo was to prove an important presence in Diego's life in more ways than one. While still a toddler, and living in that shack without running water or electricity, Diego lost his way in the dark one evening, and fell into a cesspit. To the cry of 'Diegito, keep your head above the shit', he was rescued by his uncle Cirilo, who pulled him from the family faeces and handed him to Tota so that she could wipe away the excrement and comfort the shocked and tearful child. Three decades later, as Diego Maradona, by then steeped in drug-induced depression and self-doubt, tried to make sense of his troubled life, that experience became a symbol of his emotions and behaviour. Immersed in the memory of that traumatic accident was the perception of an all too brief childhood, together with the reassurance that however deep one falls, there can be recovery.

Survival in the midst of adversity had characterized the Maradona family long before the star was born. On both the paternal and maternal side, Maradona's ancestral tree is obscured by illegitimate roots, with the name itself a mystery. Just two previous generations can be traced with some certainty to the somewhat primitive frontier town of Esquina in the north-east Argentine province of Corrientes, close to the Paraguayan border. It was here that Maradona's father Diego and his mother Tota were born and lived the early years of their adult life before moving south to Buenos Aires. The families of Diego Senior and Tota lived two hundred yards from each other on the banks of the River Corrientes in a hamlet little changed from the days before the Spanish conquest of America, when the semi-tropical province of Corrientes was populated by the Guarani Indian tribe.

Diego the elder came from Indian stock and was brought up, like his future wife, in a cramped riverside hut moulded with clay and manure and covered in reeds. It was a pre-industrial community of hunters and fishermen, struggling with pain and hardship well into the twentieth century. Diego Maradona's existence was little better than that of a slave, employed by a local transport company as a porter, loading fruit, rice and lumber on to small barges before these made their way downstream to the port of Buenos Aires. It was hard work for which one received little thanks. 'The *patrón* or boss paid you what he wanted when he wanted and that was usually close to nothing,' recalled 'Cacho' Galvaliz, who worked on the same shift as Maradona's father.

With his broad shoulders and strong stocky legs, Maradona senior earned the respect of his peers as a simple, hard-working man with a strong sense of solidarity and an ability to deal with adversity. He was nicknamed Chitoro, an amalgam of 'friend' and 'bull', soon after recovering from a workplace accident in which he broke three ribs while loading a crate of cotton. When there was no work available, Chitoro went hunting in the nearby plantations and hills for small deer, armadillos and snakes, or took a wooden canoe to go fishing for pike using the same traps as those used by the Guaranis. But it was a more contemporary sport, pursued religiously every Sunday in Esquina, which occupied Chitoro in his hard-earned moments of leisure: football.

Many years later the relationship between the name Maradona and the world of English football would be marred by controversy. But the football Don Chitoro played in Esquina took place in less conflictual circumstances. In South America the game had its origins in British seamen who came ashore at the ports of Montevideo, Santos, Rio de Janeiro and Buenos Aires, in the late nineteenth century, and kicked a ball around in their spare time while ships were loaded and unloaded. Similarly, in Esquina, Chitoro and his friends found pleasure in a game which cost not a peso to organize and which, on a good day, could provide the entertainment of an extended party. On a typical Sunday, round about midday, Chitoro and his brother Cirilo would gather with other relatives and friends and share a simple barbecue of salted beef or fish, home-made flower cakes and litres of wine. Then the two brothers, half drunk, would set off to play their afternoon match with the local team.

Juan Soto, another of Chitoro's childhood friends, recalls, 'Both brothers would drink well on Sundays before playing. Chitoro, even when drunk, didn't find it difficult to go straight into the game. He wasn't one of those who felt he needed to practise beforehand. Once on the pitch, he never played particularly well, but he worked hard at it. He played at right wing in the old five, three, two, one formation. I remember just one memorable goal he scored. He kicked the ball from the centre line, and the wind picked up behind it so that it caught the goalkeeper at the other end out of position and it swerved in over his head.'

Among the inhabitants of Esquina it is however Diego Maradona's uncle Cirilo, not his father Chitoro, who is best remembered for his skills as a footballer, as well as his courage. There survives an old and fading photograph of the San Martín football team which won a local championship for Esquina in 1952. Third from the left is an image of Cirilo in his early twenties. He is smaller, by far, than the rest of the row, and is standing somewhat defiantly, unshaven and with a beret perched precariously on his head. The image belies the vital contribution Cirilo made to his team's fortunes. He earned the nickname 'Tapón' or plug for his ability to block even the hardest-hit opposing strike at goal with a mixture of instinctive reaction and sheer tenacity. After each match, Tapón would lift his shirt up to reveal a chest bruised and cut from the many saves he managed to make.

Thus were the 'war wounds' of a generation of Maradona males earned with pride on the playing fields, while the women waited at home and laboured. Tota's domestic role and a somewhat basic religious devotion – based on holy water and prayers to the saints and the Virgin Mary – were passed down to her by her mother Salvadora Cariolochi, a descendant of poor immigrants from southern Italy, who had given birth to her illegitimate daughter at the age of seventeen. Tota was officially recognized by her father Atanancio Franco only when she was eighteen, and appears herself to have chosen to live with Chitoro, not bothering with a costly wedding ceremony until after she had borne him the first three – all daughters – of his eight children in Esquina.

In 1950, when she was twenty-one, Tota left Esquina and Chitoro for the first time, and travelled to Buenos Aires. The move formed part of the internal migration from the provinces to the capital that was encouraged in the post-war years by the régime of General Juan Perón and his mistress turned second wife, Evita. Perón was an admirer of the national socialism of Mussolini and Hitler, and of the way that sport could be used to suppress political life and fuel instead the concept of national union. He also believed strongly in the promotion of football among the masses, proudly proclaiming himself the nation's 'first sportsman' and channelling state funds into sponsoring teams at both national and local level. One of the main vehicles for this was the Eva Perón Foundation, over which Evita was given unrivalled powers. Initially drawing its funds from two days' wages subtracted from the annual salaries of all employees, the foundation later boosted its coffers by draining the budgets of other ministries and taking 'voluntary' contributions from individuals and businesses.

As amateur footballers from poor backgrounds, both Chitoro and Tapón were easily seduced by Perón's promise of a 'New Argentina' based on income redistribution in favour of the working classes. Their team benefited from the funds the foundation made available to youth championships up and down the country. They could also dream of better paid and better protected employment in the state enterprises which Perón was focusing on Buenos Aires. The Argentine capital, so the pledge went, was no longer the preserve of landowners, Englishmen and polo players, but a place of opportunity for the *descamisados*, the shirtless ones, whose cries of 'Perón, Perón' had swept the populist army colonel, as he then was, to power on 17 October 1945.

The move to Buenos Aires was nonetheless less tempting at first to Chitoro than to Tota. For Chitoro, the industrialized world of factories and urban transport seemed a planet away from the riverside rural existence with which he and his Indian forefathers had grown up. By contrast Tota thought there was little to keep her in Esquina. Her Italian ancestors had come searching for a better life in Argentina, and she had yet to find it. Now the example of Eva Perón herself encouraged her to move on. Evita was also from an illegitimate and provincial background, and had nevertheless managed to turn Buenos Aires into her glittering prize.

Tota found not so much fortune as drudgery in Buenos Aires, but better paid drudgery than the voluntary domesticity of Esquina. She was employed as a domestic servant in a rich family house, and paid the minimum wage guaranteed by Perón for washing other people's clothes and feeding other people's children. Within two years she returned to Esquina to find her husband's job prospects worse than they had ever been. Ironically, the fact that his employer was anti-Peronist meant that Chitoro was made redundant for political reasons. The 'boss' was constantly fined and harassed by the local authorities. This added to the difficulties the business was undergoing as a result of the declining commercial use of river transport. Tota was convinced that survival lay in having her whole family join her in Buenos Aires. She returned to the capital with her mother and her youngest daughter. Chitoro followed some weeks later with the rest of the family, having reluctantly sold his fishing boat.

He travelled downstream by river steamer, slowly leaving behind the natural world he respected and loved – a delta filled with reptile and bird life and a shore lined with willows, eucalyptus trees and floating flowers. When the boat reached the port of Buenos Aires, his eyes and ears struggled to make sense of the concrete and the noise. His prevailing sense of insecurity deepened soon after he had rejoined his wife. Tota had moved into temporary rent-free accommodation with some relatives. But the modest comfort of living in one of the few legally registered houses in Villa Fiorito was cut short within days when the relatives inherited a house in another part of Buenos Aires and asked the Maradonas to find alternative domestic arrangements.

The family became squatters in a shanty hut which Chitoro built with scrap metal, loose bricks and cardboard. The hut was about the size of the entrance hall of the house in which Tota had worked. It had three box-like rooms separated by doors made of sack curtains which gave little privacy. It was a cramped, basic dwelling where no member of the household could easily keep a secret from another, and where the roles of mother and father, woman and man, were acutely defined in the eyes of an impressionable young child.

By the time the Maradonas settled in Villa Fiorito, Perón had been overthrown in a military coup and Evita, riddled with cancer of the uterus, had died. Opponents of the Perón régime wasted little time in displaying the boxes of jewels and more than 300 lavish dresses Evita had worn during her short reign as vice-president. Perón was dismissed as a Nazi dictator. But the Peronist myth persevered. For decades, Argentina's working and destitute classes would revere Peronism as the dogma of hope, justice and liberation. The cries of 'Perón, Perón, Perón' and the anthems to his manly prowess would echo through the stands of the football stadiums. Evita would remain a saint in the popular consciousness, her death looked up to as a mystical martyrdom. Altars were constructed in her honour, prayers offered in abundance to Saint Eva; millions of Argentines went on dreaming of her, convinced that she would return. Evita had proclaimed that 'each Peronist woman will be, in the heart of her home, the sentinel of austerity, avoiding waste, diminishing consumption and increasing production'. Thus had the Argentine housewife, however poor, become the 'mistress of the national destiny'. Thanks to Evita, too, the passivity of woman became virtually complete in her role as wife and mother. True self-fulfilment lay in abnegation and sacrifice, and subjection to the will of the husband.

When Diego Armando Maradona was born, his fate was sealed by circumstances. Following the birth of his three sisters, Diego came into this world with all the weight of responsibility that is placed on first-born sons in Latin and Third World countries. His attitude towards life was further coloured by the particular social and political context in which his family moved. It is significant that throughout his life Diego Maradona has held one particular framed photograph in his room with as much reverence as a relic: it shows a grown-up Maradona side by side with General Perón. The former president and the footballer never met – when Perón died, Maradona was only fourteen years old, but the montage fixed the role model.

Diego spent most of his early childhood in the presence of his sisters and two like-minded, strong-willed adult women: his grandmother Salvadora and his mother Tota, who doted on him. They taught him to pray to the Virgin and certain saints and to make the sign of the cross, while instilling in him a sense of the responsibility which fate had conferred on him as the eldest son.

While the women were thus charged with Diego's basic education, Chitoro got a job at a place where his strength and innate stoicism – he was a quiet man who rarely complained – helped him to survive: the nearby bonemeal factory. Each morning at six o'clock, he would leave his sleeping family and walk along the dust track that led from the shanty huts down to the polluted canal known as the Riachuelo. The Riachuelo was the colour of dense oil, its stagnant water punctuated with brownish bubbles. It stank. No fish here. Just the accumulation of toxic waste from the nearby tanneries and pulp factories, and the putrid meat of cows and murder victims. Once, when Perón had come to power, thousands of shirtless ones had crossed the Riachuelo. But it has since returned to its previous status as the unofficial border separating the rich and the poor of Buenos Aires.

As he arrived at the factory each morning, Chitoro was left with no doubt which side of the divide he was on. At the time, Argentina was still one of the world's leading beef exporters and the meat trade one of the country's biggest employers. Bone-crushing, like tanning, provided some of the lowest paid and most unhealthy jobs in the industry. Health and safety precautions were kept to a bare minimum for the poorly educated, low-skilled work force. Conditions were appalling, according to Máximo Arumayo, a Bolivian sugar worker who migrated to Villa Fiorito soon after the Maradonas moved from Corrientes. Arumayo built a hut just opposite the Maradonas. He used to watch Chitoro set off in the mornings, and return exhausted when his ten-hour shift was over. 'It was hard, hard work in that factory,' Arumayo recalled. 'Very unhealthy. Officially, it was cattle bones you were crushing, but they bought all sorts of bones and more besides. It didn't matter if the bone came from a diseased or long-dead animal, or even if it had belonged to a human body. It was all pushed on to the conveyor belt. The noise was terrible, so was the dust. The majority of workers contracted lung disease before being forced into early retirement. But Chitoro was saved by his son.'

3

TO THE TEMPLE

Diego Maradona began his earning life as a street urchin. With other boys from the shanty town, he would play cat and mouse with the ticket collectors on the local train or hitch a ride on a truck to one of the city's main railway stations. There they would try and earn some pesos by opening the doors of taxis, or selling whatever scrap they'd picked up on the way. One of his more lucrative enterprises involved collecting the silver foil of used cigarette packets and then reselling it. The reality of life for those who lived in Villa Fiorito seemed far removed from the promises of Perón and Evita, although both remained venerated by the Maradonas in death as in life. The government no longer protected the poor. To survive meant living by one's wits. To be something more, to bridge that gap between mere existence and some kind of dignity, families like the Maradonas had few options. You could be a criminal, of course, joining, like some latter-day Artful Dodger, any one of the gangs that ruled over places like Villa Fiorito. The shanty town where Diego Maradona was born had a reputation as one of the most dangerous of the suburbs of Buenos Aires: a resting place for hired assassins, petty thieves and pimps.

That Diego Maradona did not sink immediately into criminality like so many of the other young boys in the area was largely thanks to his parents. Chitoro and Tota had been known from their early days as a couple in Esquina as honest, hard-working people. It was an unwritten creed in the Maradona household that while you might avoid taxes, you should never rob your neighbour. But most crucially, it was Chitoro and Tota who understood that the key to their future lay in that football Tapón had given to his nephew, and their son's natural ability to turn it into something magical. They seem to have grasped this while Maradona was still very young. From there on two factors ensured that the innate talent was fully exploited: a parental obsession with enabling their son to play and develop his football, and Diego's own determination to succeed. There is an early picture of Diego Maradona, scarcely past toddler stage, standing holding his football in the front garden of his home. He is surrounded by a wire fence, twisted and bent because of the battering received by these makeshift goalposts. The kid kicked with force and determination whenever his left foot tired of dancing with the ball.

It was a part-time truck driver with a good ear for neighbourhood gossip who gave Diego Maradona his first real break. José Trotta was driving one of his clients home when he was told that there was a boy in Villa Fiorito who, when it came to kicking a football around, seemed to have something rather special about him. Trotta's client, a man named Carrizo, was a neighbour of Chitoro, and his son Goyo played football with the young Maradona. Chitoro had started up his own local football team called Estrella Roja (Red Star) since arriving in Buenos Aires, but by the time he was introduced to Trotta, he was open to any offers that might be made relating to his son's future. His own salary was scarcely sufficient to cover the costs of the upkeep of his growing family. In Trotta's presence, Goyo and his father talked wonders about 'Diegito', and Chitoro offered no contradictions. Chitoro willingly acceded to Trotta's request that the young Diego should be introduced to Francisco Cornejo, the trainer of Cebollitas, the youth team of the first-division club Argentinos Juniors. Goyo took it upon himself to kick-start the promotion, for he himself had already been talent-spotted by Cornejo, and was keen that his friend Diego, a year younger than himself, should join him in this first step in a football career.

Cornejo recalls the first day that Goyo Carrizo tried to sell Maradona: 'I had been with Cebollitas for several years and was happy with the players I had. I wasn't particularly looking for new talent. Goyo came to me and said that he knew of this kid in Fiorito who played better than he did. At first I thought, so what? In the world I moved in, people came to me every other day claiming there was a kid they knew very well who was brilliant. But I thought, what have I got to lose? So I told Goyo that he might as well bring him along. And he did. That is where history began.'

On a hot, humid summer's day in December 1968, Trotta drove

the eight-year-old Diego Maradona through the dust of Villa Fiorito to his first encounter with Francisco Cornejo in the less squalid neighbourhood of La Paternal. 'No sooner had we arrived than Diego joined the other kids for a test training session. He seemed to come from another planet. From the start, he seemed to be able to do whatever he wanted with the ball. He dribbled better than the others, and showed equal control when stopped or turning. He'd hold the ball on his head or his left foot for ages.'

Diego Maradona was smaller than the other players – a strange, inadequate build, with an unnaturally large head. 'Squat, a little weird, almost dwarf-like,' was the initial image Trotta had of him. As for Cornejo, he had never seen a young boy display such skill in all his years in football. But he too was struck by Maradona's strange physique. He thought the boy was a runt, older than he said he was, and deliberately lying about his age in order to stand out among the less experienced players. He demanded to see Maradona's identity card before taking the matter further. This confirmed that the boy was indeed eight years old, as his father had told Trotta. Thus, amid early controversy, did the street urchin Diego join his first football team. It was a step that would in time abruptly end Diego's childhood, throwing him into a world of fame and the sort of money most men fail to earn in a lifetime.

The first game that Diego played for Cebollitas marked the start of a gradual but irreversible shake-up in the priorities of the Maradonas. Football, that game once innocently played on the waste land of Villa Fiorito, now became an obsession for a family bent on overcoming the poverty to which they had seemingly been condemned. A daily pattern soon developed whereby Chitoro, with Tota's blessing, would return from his factory, collect his young son before he had time to complete his homework, and take him straight to Cornejo's training ground. For a while, the Maradonas ceded control over their son's future to Cornejo, allowing him to become Diego's mentor and effective guardian. Cornejo had no trouble in obtaining their consent for an early visit by their son to visit 'Cacho' Paladino, a doctor of dubious reputation who had specialized in building up the bodies of boxers with a mixture of drugs and vitamins; he was also employed by the Argentine football team Huracán.

Of Maradona's visit to the doctor, where he was submitted to a course of pills and injections, Cornejo had this to say: 'Diego was so small when I took him on that he didn't seem to be strong enough. I wanted Paladino to round him off, get him fatter and bigger. So I asked the doctor to give him vitamins and other things to help him develop. Cacho, I said to him, you fix him. This boy is going to grow up to be a star.'

Paladino was a large man with a gruff no-nonsense approach to life that had endeared him to several players and managers in Argentine sport. He joined it at a time when no specialized training existed for the profession of 'sports' doctor, and when the footballing and boxing authorities of the country had yet to develop an effective policing role on the methods and prescriptions with which doctors treated the injured or underdeveloped. When I interviewed him, Paladino admitted that trial and error had surrounded the early practice of the so-called sports doctors, and that while he himself claimed a university degree in general medicine, much of what he practised he had learned by instinct 'in the dressing room'. As an example of how his instincts were usually right, he recalled with pride a typically robust conversation he had had with Cornejo soon after he had given Maradona his first injection. Cornejo had enthusiastically described the boy's footballing skills before asking Paladino for advice about the future. 'Listen carefully to what I tell you,' Paladino said. 'Don't give him to anyone, keep him for yourself, and when he's older, sell him and keep half the money. Best you do that, because you're going to be left behind.'

Paladino had not seen Maradona play but he thought, on that first visit, that the boy looked thin – not necessarily underdeveloped for his age, but lacking sufficient weight to be an effective sportsman and deliver what the boy, his mentor and family aspired to: football greatness. When I visited Paladino in his consultancy in October 1995, the doctor declared unhesitatingly, 'When I finished with him [Maradona] he was like a racing colt.'

There is an early image of Diego Maradona captured on film soon after the visit to Paladino – without a hint of hesitation the young player declares to camera his dual ambition in life: to help win the League Cup, and to help win the World Cup. Maradona speaks with the rough tongue of the shanty town. He is dark skinned, and his hair falls in ragged ringlets about his face. There seems a pure athleticism and raw energy to the boy.

The film clip survives as a memorial to innocence and unshackled talent, but its existence is also an early example of Maradona's commercialization. The young Diego had already been discovered by an Argentine TV producer with an eye for child prodigies. Maradona was asked to show off his skills on a popular entertainment programme broadcast on Saturdays. He was given a ball one week, an orange another and a bottle a third, and told to show viewers his mastery with all three. With the dexterity of a circus dog, Maradona balanced his playthings on his left foot for long periods, while periodically spinning them in the air. On Sundays his tricks, exclusively with a football, were repeated live during the half-time period of matches played by the senior club, Argentinos Juniors. Before the cameras, Maradona seemed a natural, and audiences loved him.

There were times when the whole stadium would react with more enthusiasm to that interlude than to any single move in the entire match. Such was the case during a game between Argentinos Juniors and their first-division rivals Boca in July 1970, when Maradona was ten years old. The match got off to a less than inspiring start, with little individual brilliance on either side, and teamwork reduced to a disorderly scrap. The half-time whistle blew and out walked the boy Maradona, clearly determined to make the most of the few minutes given to him. In perfect imitation of his elders, he limbered up by running with the ball, closely tracking it, zigzagging this way and that, delicately passing it from left to right and back again. He stopped and, with a back spin, brought the ball on to his head, where he held it with a gentle, almost imperceptible inclination of the neck. He let the ball drop, and then held it on his left foot before spinning it again and letting it fall back on to his chest. He repeated each trick at least a dozen times, now and then breaking into a sprint and showing extraordinary acceleration. Then the moment came when the players reappeared and the referee motioned to the young boy to kick the ball away and leave the pitch. But before the referee had even time to blow his whistle, the crowd in the stadium erupted spontaneously. 'Let him stay, let him stay,' the fans chorused over and over again, with all the enthusiasm felt for a prize fight. And the boy Maradona did stay, but off the turf, near the substitute benches, thinking for the first time about the nature of that demanding tribal cry emanating from the stands.

In later years it was the image of the God-given talent turned magician that prevailed in many newspaper accounts of Maradona, particularly in Argentina. And yet Maradona himself grew up never forgetting the social humiliation of being born into the shanty. This coloured his world view and influenced his hunger to prove himself in a world where the odds were firmly stacked against people of his background. As a child he discovered that his parents – Indian mixed with poor Italian immigrant – belonged to that sector of society disrespectfully referred to by the upper classes as *cabecitas negras*, little black heads, or simply Indians: landless, poorly paid, subservient peoples without firm roots; migrants and squatters. Of all South American countries, Argentina had been most successful in its ethnic cleansing: the blacks killed off by yellow fever; the Indians displaced from their homelands by conquest and civil war. In the eyes of the Establishment, to be truly Argentine was to be white and of pure, preferably North European stock, with a large estate on the pampa and an equally ostentatious house in Buenos Aires.

In Argentina, from the late nineteenth century, the élite attempted to control sport just as they had controlled politics and culture, with the Anglo-Argentine community in particular making sure that football remained an essentially British game. Only gradually, with the process accelerating under Perón, did football take on mass appeal, while polo retained its snobbery and exclusivity. The growth of football as a sport in Argentina reflected the changing composition of society, with immigration boosting the ranks of the working and lower middle classes, and the *cabecitas negras* converging on Buenos Aires to demand a greater say in national life. By the late 1960s and early 1970s there was hardly an Englishman to be found either on the pitch or on the terraces. Stadiums heaved and steamed with mass exuberance, the channel for pent-up frustrations and aspirations. Urchins emerged from the dust and were transformed into heroes on manicured turf.

Francisco Cornejo recalls a revealing exchange he had with Tota early on in her son's career. 'This kid is going to be the salvation of us all, Doña Tota,' Cornejo told the boy's mother. 'May God make it so,' she answered.

Cornejo was the son of a Spanish immigrant, whose fate was to have been born four hundred years too late. He was a man of dreams but limited circumstances who might have struck it rich had he arrived in Argentina as a Conquistador in the sixteenth century. Instead he worked in a bank as a cleaner for most of his adult life, scrubbing first the toilets and then, after being promoted, the desks and floor of the chairman's office after each directors' meeting. For the most part he witnessed other people making money, while having to content himself with picking up the crumbs.

Cornejo loved football and might have managed to join a team. But as a young man he injured his leg while playing, and a subsequent botched operation ensured he would never walk again without a limp. This did not stop him from offering his services free of charge as a part-time trainer of Cebollitas, the youth team of Argentinos Juniors. He'd work at the bank from six in the morning to two in the afternoon, and then make his way to the training ground.

By the time Diego Maradona was first brought to the ground, Cornejo was middle-aged, still cleaning at the bank and earning a token salary from Argentinos. But he had long believed that if there was a future for him it was in investing his broken dreams in others much younger than himself. In Diego Maradona he rediscovered all the energy and hope of his lost childhood. For his part, Maradona appears to have been touched and inspired by a man who contained within him both the workmanlike dedication of Chitoro, and the love for football of Maradona's uncle Tapón. On account of his work, Chitoro was partly an absent father figure, who would re-emerge from the bone factory only to bludgeon his son in the direction of the football pitch. While silent much of the time in the presence of strangers, Chitoro had a temper and could make his presence felt domestically, resorting to physical violence if he considered his son's rebelliousness warranted it. Tota was more obviously strong-willed, both overprotective and domineering towards her son. She was shaped psychologically by her provincial Italian roots, living out the matriarchal role that an essentially macho society demanded of her.

Chitoro and Tota both looked upon Cornejo not so much as guardian and friend of their son, but more importantly as the person who seemed most eager to harness the boy's natural talent and prepare it for greatness. Each afternoon the Maradonas, trailing their growing family behind them, would make their way to the training ground of Cebollitas. They trusted Cornejo up to a point, and willingly accepted his offers of hospitality. It was Cornejo who bought Maradona his first decent pair of boots, and who, together with Trotta, his driver, organized teas and suppers for the boy, his friends and family. In these comings and goings, the

Maradonas formed a friendship with Cornejo and Trotta, although this grew strained once it became clear that the family wanted to retain ultimate control over the son they saw as their salvation. Cornejo and Trotta did their best to hang on to the prodigy in their midst.

'At first Maradona's parents treated me very well, as if I was the boy's best uncle,' Cornejo recalls. 'For sure they never invited me to a meal. But I'd go along to Diego's home just the same. I wanted to keep an eye on him, make sure he didn't escape.'

On balance, Cornejo appears to have proved an effective first coach to Maradona, stimulating his talent and inspiring him to greater things. The coach was convinced from the outset that he had found the star he had always been searching for among his child players. 'At the beginning of any season I'd draw up two tables on a range of one to ten. One table was for skill, the other for commitment. Diego scored ten on both. Why else do you think I dedicated my life to him?' Cornejo said.

His high expectations appear to have been justified within months of Maradona joining Cebollitas. The following paragraph, which was published in the mass-circulation Argentine newspaper *Clarín* on 28 September 1971, is the first newspaper report ever to allude to Maradona, although his name appeared as Caradona due to a typographical error.

He is left-footed but knows how to use the right. Diego Caradona, ten years old, won warm applause at half-time in the match between Argentinos Juniors and Independiente, making a real show of his rare ability to control and dribble with the ball. His shirt is too big for him, and his fringe hardly allows him to see properly. He looks as if he's escaped from a piece of wasteland. He can kill the ball, and then just as easily lift it up with both his feet. He holds himself like a born football player. He doesn't seem to belong to today, but he does; he has a very Argentine love for the ball, and thanks to him our football will continue to nourish itself with great players.

Cornejo described Maradona as a 'great dribbler with an unrivalled touch' and liked to recall one particular match he played aged twelve during the Evita Championship which brought tears to the older man's eyes. Cebollitas was playing a team called Azul y Blanco in the old San Lorenzo stadium in Buenos Aires. 'Diego tackled an opponent in midfield, then ran with the ball, beating two other players, until he was just outside the box. The keeper challenged him. He side-stepped and pushed the ball ahead of him to his left. He ran after it, caught it on his left foot, and on the turn kicked it into the empty goal. I remember even the fans who had been backing Azul y Blanco passionately breaking out into unanimous applause.'

For all his forays into the Maradona camp, Cornejo's sphere of influence appears to have been largely contained within the football pitch itself. Whether on the training ground or during a match, Cornejo had a tough, no-nonsense approach to discipline and expected his young players to abide by his orders. With the evidence of hindsight, his success in coaching Maradona had less to do with his abilities as a teacher than with the fact that his pupil was green and uncorrupted and filled with youthful enthusiasm. 'I was very straightforward,' Cornejo recalled. 'I expected everyone to do their duty. If I said training begins at nine, training began at nine. Anyone who tried to play tricky with me suffered the consequences. I never had any problem with Diego. He loved football, and it seemed to me at the time that it was because of that he was never absent. Whether he came by bus or train or on the back of a truck, he was never late for a training session or a match.'

And yet some of the more idiosyncratic characteristics, the mixture of indulgence, narcissism and rebelliousness that was to mark later stages of Maradona's life, had begun to emerge unchecked around this time, the product of family, society and a less readily identifiable enemy within. One of Maradona's earliest football colleagues, and a person who went on to become one of his few close friends, was Adrian Domenech. He joined the youth team of Argentinos Juniors a year after Diego, although he was a year older. 'When I arrived on the scene, everyone was talking about Diego, saying that he was something special, that he was different from the other players. I soon realized why. To watch him play was to be part of something astonishing. He showed enormous talent in spite of being small and skinny for his age. He didn't seem to have the height to head the ball, but he sure knew how to run with it, and to strike it at the end.'

Domenech was witness to an early example of how Maradona's talent and promise set him apart from the other more mortal beings, and how authorities and players conspired to make it so. Under the rules of the Argentine Football Association, Maradona was not allowed to play in Domenech's team. He was not old enough. In practice, however, Cornejo and the other players agreed on a plan whereby Maradona was signed on to the team register before some of the games with the false signature of a player called Montanya. Domenech recalled, 'I remember one game, against Boca's youth team in the Candela training ground, in which Diego, having signed his false signature and had it accepted as genuine by the referee, sat for the first half on the bench. By half-time we were 3–0 down, so we decided to bring Diego on. We drew after he scored a hat-trick. In the heat of the game and the excitement of seeing it turn in our favour, one of our players forgot about the Montanya deal and shouted out "Diego" instead. At the end of the game, the manager of Boca came over to Cornejo and said, "If this is Montanya I'm a Chinaman. You've slipped Diego Maradona in."'

Cornejo stood his ground and said nothing, while the manager stared at him. Then the manager broke into a smile and gave Cornejo a friendly slap on the back. 'Don't worry, I'll let it go this time. The kid was bloody marvellous. I won't make a fuss. How can you when you watch football played the way he did?'

Maradona's first international encounter was in 1971, when he was eleven years old, in a youth championship in Uruguay. He found the experience humiliating. While most of the team, from better backgrounds than himself, were put up in spacious middle-class homes, he was sent to a small shack without running water owned by an unemployed negro. Two years later, a trip to Chile with the Argentine youth team proved more gratifying. As a guest of the newly installed military government of General Pinochet, Maradona joined his team mates in the capital's five-star Hotel Carrera, from where Western journalists had witnessed the Pinochet coup just three months earlier.

From the window of the small suite in which Maradona was installed, you could look out across Santiago's main square to where the presidential palace, once occupied by the democratically elected Salvador Allende but bombed during the coup by the air force, still lay partly in ruins. To the youthful Maradona, as indeed to the rest of his team mates, the ongoing repression of political opponents by Pinochet appears to have been of little or no concern. Instead Maradona was an excited teenager, looking forward to his first exhibition game in Santiago's national stadium, and prepared to make the most of his free holiday. On the first morning in the Carrera, Maradona refused to go down to the hotel restaurant, and insisted instead that room service bring breakfast to him in bed. He went on that day to score four goals for his team.

Back in Villa Fiorito, Maradona enjoyed few such luxuries or successes. On the contrary, even while being turned into a great footballer, he could not escape from the reality of life in the shanty town. So dangerous did the authorities consider the inhabitants of Villa Fiorito that they refused to build a permanent police station in the area, thinking it would become the object of regular assault. Instead, police travelled in and out of the area in a fortified Leyland bus.

Maradona may have been more protected by his parents than most children of his age, but there is some evidence that he was not immune to the rougher expressions of social deprivation and frustration. Later, when he reflected on his childhood, he would compare the harsh world of Villa Fiorito with Corrientes, the land of his forefathers. While in the first, 'one had to live by one's wits and instincts . . . and there bad things happened', in Corrientes Maradona continued to draw comfort from nature and the essential underlying sense of an uncluttered, honest community.

One of the 'bad things' that happened was an incident in the early 1970s when a group of Maradona's male friends surrounded, kidnapped and sexually assaulted a seventeen-year-old girl. The victim, a migrant from the north of Argentina who had moved to the capital in search of work, initially considered pressing charges, but decided instead to leave Villa Fiorito and subsequently disappeared. It is unclear whether this was the result of intimidation or financial recompense, but the incident has remained for years a closely guarded secret.

Whatever Maradona's feelings about the incident may have been, it appears to have had little impact on his growing success as a footballer. Thanks largely to him, Cebollitas became one of Argentina's most successful young teams, with its star number 10 attracting the increasing attention of the outside world.

It was earlier, at the age of twelve, that the boy Maradona got his first approach from a first-division club, the Argentine champions River Plate. It was promptly turned down by Cornejo with the strong support of Diego's parents and the directors of Argentinos Juniors, who saw that the best investment lay in keeping Maradona to themselves and selling him only when his value had become greater. To them it seemed a certainty that the colt, moulded by the good Dr Paladino, would soon become a racing horse, capable of big prizes – but they wanted to keep control.

Their faith in Maradona proved well founded. Osvaldo Dalla Buona, a childhood friend of Maradona who played alongside him in Cebollitas, summarized the collective enthusiasm that soon began to grip the team in the presence of the rising star. 'It proved fortunate for the other kids in Cebollitas that we didn't lose Diego to River Plate. We were given the opportunity of assisting in the birth and early formation of one of the greatest players in the history of football, watching the extraordinary things he was capable of: before him, ten opponents seemed as vulnerable as skittles; thanks to him there were seemingly impossible goals scored, amazing passes. And yet for all his brilliance, he still behaved like a good team player, capable of encouraging and supporting his colleagues. You could see a champion in the making in those days, particularly in his capacity not to let a match day go by without making his evident superiority felt both on and off the pitch.'

And yet the boy Maradona was already beginning to show the propensity for high drama and indiscipline on the pitch that was to mark his later career. He proved himself a better winner than a loser. Once, when Cebollitas lost a game, he threw himself down in the middle of the pitch and wailed. The reaction seemed typical of a spoilt brat for too long used to having it all his own way. But thanks to the writings of one of his apologists, the Argentine novelist Alicia Dujovne Ortiz, the incident was glossed over and turned into part of the legend. According to Ortiz, the distraught Maradona was approached by a man who comforted him and said, 'Quit crying, kid. One day you're going to be the best number 10 in the world.' Maradona immediately fell silent, and the anonymous witness disappeared, like a guardian angel. During another match, there was little comfort to be had when Maradona lost his temper with the referee and promptly was expelled from the game.

In 1973, Cebollitas was runner-up in the youth championship finals played in the northern Argentine city of Córdoba. The following year Cebollitas won the championship. Within months, the directors of Argentinos Juniors had drawn up Maradona's first contract, promoting him to the main club side. In spite of its name, the club had traditionally sat awkwardly with the English origins of Argentine football. It was formed in 1904, as increasing numbers of local teams were created to accommodate the growing popularity of the sport among the working class, many of whom, employed in such British-controlled areas of the economy as the meat trade, looked on the English as arrogant colonialists with a penchant for exploitative capitalism, when not drinking tea. The club's founding motto was 'United Libertarians'. Considered too political by the nascent Argentine Football League Association, the motto was subsequently changed to the more esoteric 'Martyrs of Chicago' – a reference to a group of anarchist workers shot in the US.

In the early 1970s the actions of the club's management focused firmly on Maradona and seem to have had little regard for the rest of the players. Settimio Aloisio, the club's vice-president at the time, recalled, 'The only player we felt was emerging as a real class act was Maradona. All our hopes were focused on this one kid who with every match that he played seemed to get better and better. It was of no worry to us if other team players fell by the wayside through lack of encouragement.'

It was on the occasion of his fifteenth birthday that Diego Maradona received a symbolic and financially significant token of the special status his club had reserved for him: the key to his first apartment, large enough to accommodate his family. Only a few weeks earlier, Maradona's first discoverer, Trotta, had visited Cornejo and suggested that the two men elaborate a binding contract bringing Maradona formally under their personal control. The project got as far as a lawyer's draft, but was abandoned, on Cornejo's insistence because he feared it would undermine what he liked to believe was the special relationship of mutual trust he had developed with the boy.

Both Cornejo and Trotta were to live to regret that decision. For once the directors of the club, with the approval of the player's parents, had set their sights on maximizing the commercial benefits surrounding Maradona, the two early mentors became as dispensable as a used football ticket. Cornejo will never forget the day when the manager of the club, Juan Carlos Montes, came to tell him that Maradona was wanted by the main team. He had hoped to have at least another year with Maradona. And yet, in the manner of one involved in a passionate love affair, he seems to have given little thought to the longer term. Cornejo told Montes the boy was not for grabs, and decided to appeal directly to the president of the club, Prospero Consoli. It was a strained encounter in which Cornejo, with tears forming in his eyes, pleaded, for the good of the boy's future, to let him stay in the youth club a little longer, and Consoli talking the language of a hard-nosed financier.

'There I was, the man who had devoted his life to the kid, who had trained him through his formative years, who knew him better than anyone, begging . . . and Consoli having nothing of it. He said, "I am the president of the club and you do what I tell you." And that is how they signed up Diego Maradona.'

4

FIRST LOVES

The handing over of a rent-free apartment marked a key point in the life of the rising star: the abrupt end of adolescence and the enforced entry into adulthood. From that moment, the pampered first-born son became the main bread-winner of the family. The family for its part began to see Diego as the main point of reference for their existence. Within a year of moving into the apartment in Villa del Parque, a comfortable working-class neighbourhood well removed from the horrors of Villa Fiorito, Chitoro had given up his work in the bone-crushing factory, and instead devoted himself virtually full-time to watching over his son's affairs. The change in circumstances left Chitoro's personality virtually unchanged. He continued to keep to his factory hours, partly out of habit but also out of a sense of self-discipline. He welcomed the invitation to the new apartment, not because it ushered in a period of financial well-being, but because he thought it would bind the family together into its natural tribal unit and in particular bring him closer to his son. He remained essentially stoic, longing in his darker moments to return to his native Corrientes whenever he could, so as to be closer to the elemental life.

As for Tota, the new arrangements intensified her possessiveness. She developed a mistrust of people beyond a very close circle of relations and friends, spoke rarely to strangers, and when she did so made it clear that her main concern was not to lose what had been gained.

Tota appears to have consented to Diego first official girlfriend only after assuring herself that she posed little threat to her own matriarchal control over the Maradona family as a whole and the emotional interdependence that had set in between the parents and their eldest son. Claudia Villafane was the girl next door passively prepared to wait for the day when the boy of her dreams would consent to marriage. Her introduction to the Maradonas came one day when she happened to bump into Tota in the local supermarket. Tota was at the cash counter having problems finding the necessary money to pay for her purchases. Claudia was a few steps behind. The timid young girl of small stature and plain looks stepped up and offered to help her out with some loose coins. Tota accepted the offer and, having taken the girl's name and address, promised to repay the debt that day. And so she did, sending her son Diego to his first encounter with his new neighbours the Villafanes.

The apartment where the Maradonas now lived belonged to a typical tenement building of the kind increasingly occupied by the upwardly mobile members of the Argentine working class. Bedrooms, kitchen and bathroom all gave on to a common corridor. New and old arrivals, wherever they came from, seemed destined to form a community of extended interests. In the case of the Villafanes and Maradonas, the bonding appears initially to have been encouraged by Claudia's father.

Coco Villafane was a part-time taxi driver and the owner of a local canteen. While coming from a slightly higher social strata than the Maradonas, he appears to have staked his future on what he perceived from an early stage as the inevitable commercial success of his daughter's boyfriend. Soon after Claudia and Diego had met, Coco began actively to foster closer links between the two. Diego became a regular visitor to the Villafane household, causing occasional rows with Tota when she discovered that the two young friends had been left, with Coco's consent, alone together in Claudia's apartment. It was not quite a picture-book courting. The concept of male fidelity did not form part of Argentine culture, and Diego, exceptional as he might have been on the football pitch, appears not to have acted very differently from most of his friends when it came to dealing with the opposite sex. Once installed in his new apartment he took to enjoying the bright lights of the city after playing football. As one of his friends at the time recalled some years later, 'Sometimes we'd go out in a group, sometimes in couples, Diego and Claudia, and I and my girlfriend. But then there were times when we'd drop our girlfriends and just go out as bachelors to one of the dance halls downtown. We'd dance, pick up a girl, depending on what was on offer, and then Diego and I would leave together or else one of us would stay behind with the girl. It depended on who had more success. When together with their respective girlfriends, Maradona and his male friends liked to share a meal of seafood and frogs' legs. But on the bachelor night out, the favourite venue was one of the looser joints along a sophisticated red-light district in Buenos Aires called La Recoleta, a few yards from the cemetery where the country's good and great are buried.

By all accounts this was one of the rare stages in Maradona's life in which his professional and private life appear to have followed their course without impinging negatively one on the other. These were days of commitment in the field, and youthful longing for life off it, all largely consented to by family, friends and the directors and managers of the club.

Exactly at what point it was judged that a formal education as much as fatherhood could only get in the way of Maradona's career as a footballer is not clear. But Maradona himself has admitted that from an early age his studies took second place to his training sessions, and his parents do not appear to have opposed him in this. On the contrary, Chitoro and Tota have spent most of their life fuelling their son's ambition to be a great player, making it their goal as much as his. Jorge Trotta, the van driver and assistant coach at Cebollitas, recalls that Maradona had an increasing pattern of absenteeism at school from about the age of fourteen onwards. At one point Trotta felt so guilty about the way that he and his friend Cornejo's training sessions appeared to be undermining Maradona's formation as a student, that he personally went to see the headmaster.

'I knew the headmaster because he had once played in a local football club and liked the game as I did,' Trotta recalls. 'I told him, "Look, I'm really sorry about Diego going absent, but you should see how he plays football." I invited him to come and see Diego the following Saturday and promised he would see something special. Well, he came. We won 4–0, and Diego scored three. With one of the goals he ran rings round several players, including the goalkeeper, and kept the ball with him until he was inside the net. After the game was over the headmaster said he had never seen anything like it. The following Thursday, Diego passed all his exams, and the headmaster gave me three books for him so that he could keep up his studies without bothering to turn up at school. Diego never read them.'

Among Maradona's close circle of friends in his teenage years, few were to play such a critical role in promoting the success of the footballer as Jorge Cyterszpiler. When Maradona was first taken to play for Cebollitas, he and the boy who was destined to become his first agent/manager had yet to meet. Cyterszpiler was two years older than Maradona and lived in a different, more comfortable neighbourhood a block and a half away from the stadium of Argentinos Juniors. The son of first-generation Jewish refugees from Poland, Cyterszpiler was fat and walked with a marked limp, the result of having contracted polio at an early age. As a young boy he had become the official mascot of Argentinos Juniors. He had a habit of dumping his crutches and standing precariously behind the goalpost, while his athletic brother Juan Eduardo, ten years older, ran up and down the pitch. When Jorge was twelve, the twenty-two-year-old Juan Eduardo accidentally took the full force of an opponent's kick in his testicles. He developed a haemorrhage and died. Jorge entered a period of profound shock, abandoning his regular visits to the football pitch and staying at home with the blinds shut. Friends and family made various attempts to lift the boy out of his depression, and failed, until the day, six months after Juan Eduardo's death, when Jorge was told by a friend that there was a boy playing for Cebollitas who created magic out of a football. Jorge was sufficiently intrigued to want to see for himself.

At that first encounter the boy Maradona cast an instant spell over Jorge Cyterszpiler. His bursts of speed, his control of the ball and the unexpected little touches he would produce to set up a movement towards goal brought back to Cyterszpiler all the enthusiasm and joy he had experienced when watching his brother. Cyterszpiler's love of life was rekindled by this short dynamo of a boy from Villa Fiorito who outshone players much bigger and more experienced than himself with his tricks at half-time and his pieces to camera. Soon afterwards, Maradona found himself invited to the Cyterszpiler household, where he was fed well and introduced to other middle-class comforts, like running water and kitchen gadgets, absent from the primitive shack in Villa Fiorito. Maradona was further impressed by Cyterszpiler's seemingly instinctive kindness towards him, which seemed to transcend his physical disability. Seeing how these Jewish refugees had managed to establish themselves in Argentina, and how their son was managing to live life to the full, was for the shanty-town dweller a reassuring reminder that it was possible to overcome the most adverse circumstances.

As well as organizational skills, Cyterszpiler brought some spare cash into Maradona's circle of friends. He'd invite Maradona to the cinema or foot the bulk of the bill at the local pizzeria. On the days Maradona played football he'd bring him tins of coca-cola and biscuits. There were other times when he'd use family contacts and arrange for tickets at the capital's Luna Park stadium to watch some of Dr Paladino's patients slog it out on the boxing canvas. These were fun days, easily funded, for the movies and food were cheap, and the boxing tickets were cut price because Jorge's father knew the promoter. Maradona and Cyterszpiler shared in the Argentine love for the cinema, particularly films made in the US and Europe, places where dreams could be seen being realized, and points of reference for future action easily established. Movies like John Travolta's *Saturday Night Fever* and Paul Newman and Robert Redford's *The Sting*, which Maradona and Cyterszpiler watched together, sank easily into the subconscious of any Argentine with an eye for the chance.

When Maradona gave up his secondary education to concentrate on football, Cyterszpiler was still firmly focused on his studies, investing in reading and writing the time he would probably have devoted, like his brother, to playing football had he not been physically handicapped. While Maradona got himself into Argentinos Juniors, Cyterszpiler won a coveted place at Buenos Aires University to study economics. Far from separating them, the different pursuits of the two friends drew them into a joint business project which would break new ground in footballing history. For, by 1976, Maradona and his family had begun to detect that the world was changing around them. Money was beginning to be made on their account, over which they appeared to have little control, and the loyal shields of men like Cornejo were being sidelined by men of more cunning ambition and business acumen. In Cyterszpiler, the Maradonas saw a friend to their son who apparently knew about money.

Cyterszpiler, for his part, was not blind to the changes that were affecting the Maradonas. The growing buzz in footballing circles, the first tentative signs of popular adulation and media interest, the granting of the keys to the new apartment, were all evidence of a star in the making. While still at school, Cyterszpiler had worked part-time in the administrative offices of Argentinos Juniors and gained an insight into the way a football club was managed and its relations with the outside world. From that time he began to imagine making a living out of football, an ambition that he soon saw could be best realized through his friend Diego. Late in 1976,

Maradona and Cyterszpiler paid a well-publicized visit to *Clarín*, the mass-circulation daily. In an interview Maradona described Cyterszpiler as a friend and went out of his way to emphasize that he was not his manager or in any way representing him. In fact the interview was a carefully orchestrated piece of misinformation which Maradona and Cyterszpiler believed was necessary to stop any negative reactions undermining their partnership. Several weeks beforehand, Maradona had formally asked his friend to look after his financial affairs, and Cyterszpiler had agreed.

Cyterszpiler recalled, 'It was difficult starting up in those early days. The concept of an agent did not exist in Argentine football, although it was a recognized profession in other countries. Diego and I were sensitive to the fact that there were people who didn't like the idea of it, who were suspicious about the way we might set out to make money.'

And certainly there were friends and acquaintances of Maradona who did mistrust Cyterszpiler's motivation: a mistrust based partly on envy for a person who apparently was more worldly-wise than they were, and partly out of fear that their idol and benefactor was being distanced from the informal tribe to which he had belonged since Villa Fiorito days and would soon restrict the scope of financial rewards emanating from his success. As one of Cyterszpiler's detractors and a childhood friend of Maradona put it, 'Cyterszpiler had his eye on the big chance from an early age. His ambition was to find the best footballer to make money on, and in Diego he thought he'd found him.'

Cyterszpiler preferred the word 'vocation' to opportunism when referring to his role, taking pride in claiming to be Argentina's first football agent and bringing to the career of Maradona some tried and tested expertise. He underwent no formal training, but studied closely newspaper clippings and articles on agents such as Mark McCormack, who has made millions from looking after the interests of such sports personalities as Jack Nicklaus. Naturally affable and an enthusiastic linguist, Cyterszpiler went out of his way to pick the brains of other agents and personalities in the international sports world, building up a dossier on how best he could serve his friend and client, as well as himself. In order to improve his knowledge of accounting, he took on advisers trained by firms such as Price Waterhouse and Arthur Andersen. 'My aim,' he said, 'was to form the first company ever devoted to promoting the image of a footballer.'

5

THE KILLING FIELDS

O n 20 October 1976, Diego Maradona, ten days short of his sixteenth birthday, became the youngest player in footballing history to play in a premier-division match. The entire Maradona family turned up to witness the latest confirmation of divine destiny, in a match between Argentinos Juniors and Talleres of Córdoba. Of the event Maradona would later recall, 'I always knew I would become great one day, but not so quickly . . . I've been asked what did I feel being confirmed in that way. Well, I was confirmed the day I played my first game in the premier, because that is what I dreamed I would do when I was a child playing in the waste land of my beloved Villa Fiorito.'

The decision by Argentinos Juniors' manager Montes to give Maradona his first real break in professional football came halfway through the second half. Argentinos Juniors were losing 1–0. Maradona was sitting on the substitutes' bench when Montes unexpectedly told him to start warming up. The young player may have dreamt about the moment all his life, but his initial reaction to it was one of vertigo, of staring out into a stadium filled with angry, frustrated fans and thinking about how he couldn't allow himself to blow it. Glimpsing a momentary hint of panic in his young player, Montes told Maradona with paternalistic firmness, 'Don't worry, you just get in there and play as you know how to. Just enjoy yourself.'

Maradona got an early touch to the ball, leaving an opponent, with several years more footballing experience, with no time to think how he'd even lost it, as the newcomer swerved past him. The move changed the whole tenor of the game, with Talleres focusing their efforts from then on on an unimaginative if solid defensive play, based on a leech-like marking of Maradona. Diego was badly supported by the rest of the team, which was unable to exploit the few openings he managed to create. At one point, a cross by Maradona was blocked just inside the ten-yard box by a defender. Maradona went moaning to the referee, claiming that it was hand ball and demanding a penalty. His team captain pulled him back and said, 'Shut up, boy, and just do what your elders tell you.' Talleres survived the game with its 1–0 lead.

It was an inauspicious rite of passage for a player destined to be king, although the general consensus among the local footballing press the next morning was that here was indeed a genius in the making. Only the mediocrity of a team which had largely been ignored by the directors of the club had let him down. *Clarín* summed it up: 'The use of the boy Maradona gave his team more offensive mobility, but it was insufficient to stamp his team's control on the game; the reason was that Maradona, a very smart player, had no one to pass to. His efforts generally ended up frustrated by Talleres' steely marking.' It would take several more matches for Maradona's 'smartness' to instil some imagination into his team's play, a period during which the unique skills of the young player continued to impress. Newspapers began to extend their sports columns so as to accommodate glowing references to the emerging star. The experts compared notes and were united in their praise. Settimio Aloisio, Argentinos Juniors' outspoken Italian-born vice-president, who would later become one of Europe's top agents, never forgot watching Maradona take the field for the first time as a first choice for his club. The match, played towards the end of the season, a few weeks after the Talleres débâcle, was against Newell's Old Boys of Rosario. Again Argentinos lost, but Maradona scarcely put a foot wrong. Aloisio recalls, 'In that game, Maradona did things which very few players were capable of doing. But what really struck me was the joy there seemed to be in his playing. What seemed unique was that he didn't seem to have any fear, he was so self-assured, so determined. It was the first time he played the full ninety minutes in a premier-league match, and he did it with all the confidence of a player who had been playing top-class football for at least six years.'

The enthusiasm which Maradona was beginning to generate among his people seemed a world removed from the darker realities then gripping the country. Two weeks before Maradona's début against Talleres, the Argentine foreign minister Admiral César Guzetti had found himself angrily barracked by the world media while he attended a meeting of the United Nations General Assembly in New York. Foreign journalists, basing their views both on first-hand experience and on the testimony of refugees, held the Argentine government responsible for an appalling record of human rights violations. Since taking power in March of that year, the military junta led by Generals Videla and Lami Dozo and Admiral Massera had embarked on a systematic annihilation of political opponents. Initially justified on the grounds of the growing brutality of extreme-left terrorism, the repression had within a matter of weeks extended to blanket censorship, the curbing of parliamentary and trade-union activity, and the torture and disappearance of many thousands of innocent victims.

Priests and teachers were among those tortured or 'disappeared'. So were shop stewards, doctors and journalists. Those abducted included children rather younger than Maradona, some of them still in their mother's womb. Throughout the worst period of the repression, football went on being played much as it had been for years, although there was a tension lingering beneath the surface.

In May 1976, two months after the coup, two premier-division Argentine teams, Estudiantes and Huracán, played in La Plata. Huracán was enjoying one of the most successful seasons in its history with the talents of players such as Ossie Ardiles and René Houseman. Among the thousands in the stadium that day was Gregorio Noya, a thirty-eight-year-old public auctioneer, and his sixteen-year-old son, both Huracán fans. At the start of the game a group of sympathizers of the anti-government Montonero guerrilla organization hung one of their banners at the end of one of the stands occupied by Huracán fans and released balloons bearing their colours. The banner was ripped down by security guards, and at half-time the police moved in on the stadium with live fire. A bullet fatally struck Noya, puncturing his lung. The police blamed the death on left-wing terrorists, a version contradicted by witnesses, including the dead man's son.

Two days later Noya was buried with only a few relatives and close friends attending. The 'accidental' death of a football fan as a result of a clash between the 'forces of order' and an 'illegal organization' was barely mentioned in the Argentine media. The national game continued to be played as if nothing had happened, with its officials and players seemingly either ignorant of or simply indifferent to what was happening to the 'disappeared'. Maradona seems to have suffered from both ignorance and indifference when it came to the military repression, although he exaggerates the extent to which he was in the dark about what was going on. By his own admission, Maradona had 'no time' for politics then, while claiming that he only found out about the nature of the repression later after the collapse of the régime. Even after the return of democracy following the Falklands War, Maradona's political statements remained poorly formulated and unconvincing. He lacked the intelligence, let alone the education, to move much beyond a crude kind of populist rhetoric. And even this seemed too often to be undermined by his inability to practise what he preached.

Maradona's political passivity was reflected in his lack of public comment on the disappeared during the years of the military régime. This is not to say that he was either inactive or silent. Both in his conduct and in his statements he still made himself vulnerable to manipulation by the military junta. And there was no doubt that in spite of Noya's death, and occasional acts of political defiance by fans, the junta was determined to permit football as long as it served their political interests and could be controlled. They were handed this control on a plate by FIFA when it was confirmed that Argentina would host the 1978 World Cup, an event that was destined to have the whole world watching.

The man picked to manage the Argentine national team, César Luis Menotti, seemed at first sight an unlikely ally of the junta in such an enterprise. Menotti had grown up in Rosario, a town with a tradition of radical politics matched with stylish football. In the 1960s he had become something of a hippy both on the football field and off it. Tall, long-haired and with sleepy good looks, Menotti developed a free creative style of football, based on a slow tempo and elegant touches. It did not fit easily with the heavy marking and kick-and-run playing that characterized the two Argentine teams he played for during those years: Racing and Boca Juniors. In 1967 he opted for temporary exile, playing first for the Generals in New York, and then in 1969 with Santos of Brazil. After a brief career as a journalist he returned to football in 1973, when he was appointed coach of Huracán. His year there coincided with a period of growing political upheaval in Argentina. Menotti gained a reputation as an articulate public figure, with contacts in radical university circles and sympathetic to left-wing causes. When Huracán won their first championship in 1973, members of the Montoneros waved their flags unrestricted as team members made their traditional triumphant walk round the pitch.

Menotti was appointed as a national coach soon after Argentina's failure in the 1974 World Cup, and following the return to power of General Perón with huge popular backing in 1973. By then, he had become widely known in Argentina for his philosophy of football, defending a style which, he claimed, was an original native creation responsible for producing some of his country's best players, such as the Real Madrid star Alfredo di Stefano and Omar Sivori of Juventus. The focus was on a mixture of elegant technique and instinctive daring, with the emphasis on dribbling and great offensive vitality. In his writings and public utterances, Menotti spoke with passion of his mission to restore Argentina's superiority as a footballing nation. It was the kind of language the junta wanted to hear. The military came to power, pledged, in the words of one of its own manifestos, to 'extirpate the influence of subversive foreign ideas on Argentine society, and of resurrecting the concept of a superior nation state'. What better way to do this than through football?

As the main inspiration of a team that could win the World Cup, Menotti was viewed by the military not so much as an opponent as a tactical ally. By contrast Maradona did not slip easily into the scheme of things. In his search for a national team capable of the international superiority to which the junta aspired, Menotti was aware of a rising star. Soon after he was appointed national coach, information reached him about a little big man from the shanty, who at the age of fifteen was showing unrivalled brilliance for someone of his age. Within weeks Menotti decided to judge for himself, and watched Maradona play in his first-division début against Talleres, in October 1976. The next morning, the media coverage was sufficiently enthusiastic to convince Menotti that Maradona was not a player who could easily be left out of the grand scheme.

In late February 1977, nearly a year after the coup, Menotti included Maradona among his substitutes in a friendly between the national team and Hungary at Boca Juniors' Bombonera stadium. Two days earlier, Menotti had held a private conversation with Maradona after a training session involving the youth and senior teams. The coach had insisted that Maradona spend the weekend avoiding the media so as to remain calm. He also promised that if the game looked like going well for the Argentines, he would have a strong possibility of playing. Maradona did as he was told, sticking firmly to a very ordinary pre-match agenda, well removed from the public limelight.

Maradona later gave this account of that Sunday, which shows how uncomplicated and uncorrupted life still was for him. There is no hint here of personal problems. Just a footballer like any other preparing himself for the game: 'Menotti's words had made me really happy and I felt calm . . . I wanted to rest as much as possible, so I got up at eleven o'clock. I had a bath and then watched TV in my hotel room until midday. Then I went down and talked with the mates until lunchtime. I went back to my room and then watched a little more TV. Then at 3.30 p.m. we set off for the Bombonera.'

Only when the team coach reached the stadium and the fans crowded round the players did Maradona admit to the first hint of pre-match nerves. 'It's unbelievable the fear that crowds make you feel sometimes,' he admitted later.

Argentina dominated the match from the outset and by half-time had a commanding 4–0 lead over the visitors with goals by Bertoni and Luque. From the stands the fans began to react intuitively, chorusing, as they beat their drums and waved their shirts, 'Maradooona, Maradooona, Maradooona!' Menotti waited. Two minutes into the second half, Luque scored again. Twenty-five minutes from the final whistle, the Hungarians scored their first goal. By then Menotti had nothing to lose, and played the hidden card that would win over the stadium completely. He brought on Maradona, as substitute for Luque. It was a tough act to follow, but Maradona had been waiting for the moment all his young life, and the fans' enthusiasm for him had reached fever pitch. 'Play as you know you can, keep cool, and move all round the pitch,' were Menotti's final words of advice as Diego Maradona entered an international match for the first time.

The young player made his presence felt from the outset, launching a series of moves from deep inside his own half, manoeuvring through the Hungarian defence and delivering to Ardiles and Houseman when not having a crack at goal himself. Five minutes from the end, he passed to Houseman, ran forward and picked up the return pass just outside the ten-yard box before narrowly missing a thunderous strike at goal. At the end of the match, Maradona was hugged emotionally by his colleagues and cheered enthusiastically by the crowd. Then he went home with his father and Cyterszpiler and watched the match replayed on TV. He felt it didn't look so good.

In a post-match conversation with Carlos Ferreira, a reporter with *El Gráfico*, Argentina's leading football magazine, Maradona gave his first-ever detailed international match postmortem. 'I made a series of mistakes. I passed to Bertoni, when it was Felman who was unmarked on the other wing; I tried to dribble past a Hungarian and didn't hit the ball in front of me enough; I saw how I was kicked by a Hungarian when I didn't even have the ball . . . but then that's one thing that hurts less when you watch it on TV. Afterwards I went to sleep. No, I didn't dream about anything, I just slept like I'd never slept before.'

Such self-effacement, such apparent calmness, proved short-lived. The huge coverage given to Maradona by *El Gráfico* in a three-page report headlined 'Young enough for bedtime stories, but he listens to applause' hinted at Maradona's immaturity. It also marked the player's definitive passage from the private enclave of domesticity to the public world of media attention, with its ensuing pressures and demands.

Maradona himself alluded to the pressures building up around him in another of the numerous interviews that followed the Hungary game. In it he showed both a determination to make his career a success and an apparent refusal to allow himself to be spoilt by it: 'When I was younger I trained once a day. Now I train all day long. I don't want people to think that I've abandoned my friends, but the fact is that since I was picked for the Hungary game, I haven't had a free moment to spend in the neighbourhood. I don't want it ever to be said of me that I'm getting too big for my boots, that I'm boastful.' The interviewer, noticing a certain tension in the voice, asked the player if he was beginning to get tired of journalists. 'No, it's not that,' came Maradona's reply, 'it's just that since I played those few minutes against Hungary, it's all come on top of me, the magazines, the TV channels, the newspapers, with everyone asking the same questions. That is what I find really tiring. I'm no one really, and the only thing I can talk about is about my childhood and about my idol, Bochini . . .'

And yet there was still an innocence about the emerging star that left him unruffled by the glare of publicity. In most of his early interviews, he speaks with the same untutored language, in the same subdued voice he had used when first facing the camera with his bag of tricks. He expresses himself without pretension in short sentences that never veer away from a somewhat basic assessment of his game. But such modesty belied the latest ambition which Maradona had begun to nurture: that of playing for Argentina in the 1978 World Cup, thus becoming the youngest player to do so in the history of his country.

Choosing the national team did not prove an easy task for those most closely involved. Following the last World Cup there had been an exodus to Europe of some of the country's top players and Menotti was faced with the difficult choice of either moulding his new philosophy around local players, many of whom had yet to prove themselves of international quality, or to risk recalling some of the big names from abroad and having them accommodate their play to the national team effort. During some of the early trial friendlies in 1977 and the early part of 1978, Maradona himself was excluded from the team. Instead Menotti put him in the national youth team and watched him from a discreet distance. The youth team played a bad season, with Maradona uncharacteristically unable to inspire either himself or his colleagues above a generalized mediocrity. The team did not qualify for the finals in Tunis, after failing to win a match against other South American teams in the qualifying round.

Maradona went on to recover some of his reputation after returning to premier-division football with Argentinos Juniors. He remained immensely popular with the fans, and the focus of unrivalled media attention. Among those taking a keen interest in him was Ezequiel Fernández Moores. A young and articulate graduate, Moores was pursuing his other natural talent as a sports reporter. He found himself among the select group of local journalists following Menotti's final preparations for the cup:

There was no doubt that Maradona's reputation was already of such a nature as to eclipse most of his rival candidates for the final selection. The only thing that really interested us in the media was Maradona. We were waiting for him to play, to see if he could really prove himself at an international level. He was among the players that Menotti gathered around him at a special training camp outside Buenos Aires before he made his final decision. I remember how intense those days were. It was as if football had suddenly become the centre of everything that was happening in Argentina. One couldn't, because one wasn't allowed to, talk or write about anything else. There we were, in a dictatorship, with footballers surrounded by soldiers.

It was in such an atmosphere of raised expectations and tension that Maradona learnt from Menotti that he had not, after all, been picked for the final twenty-two. For the child prodigy who had for so many years been bent on winning the approval of his elders, the feeling of rejection by this latest of a series of father figures in his life was profoundly shocking. Without waiting for Menotti's explanation, Maradona locked himself in a room and wept uncontrollably. It was at least the second time in less than a year that he had thrown a tantrum. A few months earlier he had accompanied his mother's tears when told he had not won a prize in the national Sportsmen of the Year awards. Now as then he sank into a deep hole of desolation mixed with self-doubt, in which some of the most extreme thoughts crossed his mind. He vowed never to forgive Menotti for the betrayal, and to quit football altogether. He felt physically as well as mentally sick, as if a loved one had suddenly lashed out and hit him. It took the encouragement of his father Chitoro, always present whenever his son's career reached a new crossroads, and of his childhood friend and emerging business partner Cyterszpiler, to pull him out of the waste land. Cyterszpiler knew instinctively that on an empty stomach nothing could seem gloomier. So he bought several pizzas and the three men sat commiserating with each other till five in the morning. Amid more tears, hugs and passionate exchanges, father and friend persuaded Maradona that it was simply a battle lost, on which Menotti would look back with regret. And there were many more lucrative battles still to be won. He was young and a life of fortune and success lay ahead. Moreover, the heart of Argentina remained behind him. A few days later, Maradona rejoined his club and scored three goals, including the winner, in the next league match against Charait.

So why was Maradona excluded from the World Cup at such a critical juncture? Menotti told me he didn't pick Maradona because he believed he was still too young, both physically and emotionally, to deal with possible defeat – an assessment which appears at first sight to have been confirmed by Maradona's reaction to his exclusion. 'Can you imagine what would have happened if we had lost, given the pressures that had been building up? And

I think it could have happened because we had a very difficult draw in the first round, against the France of Platini, Italy and Hungary.' Menotti claimed, moreover, that medical advice was that Maradona's muscular structure was still in the process of development, and that, as he put it, 'He risked suffering a bad foul and being crippled for the rest of his career by it.' Finally, Menotti felt he was spoilt for choice when it came to selecting the team. There was no shortage of talent from which to choose and Maradona, in his view, had yet to prove himself the best.

Menotti's favourite 'star' at the time was not Maradona but Mario Kempes. When Kempes left Argentina to play for Valencia in August 1976, Menotti bemoaned the loss of what he described as the 'only indispensable member of my team'. He went on, 'Argentine football will feel his loss. It will be almost impossible in the two years we have left before the World Cup to invent a player who can match his youth, his potency and his experience in the national team.'

By the time the World Cup came round, Menotti's glowing assessment of Kempes remained undiminished, to the extent of eclipsing any rational thought that Maradona was ready and willing to take up the mantle. In the weeks previous to the World Cup, Menotti met for lunch with Alfredo di Stefano. The former Real Madrid player with enormous international prestige told Menotti that it was many years since he had seen a player with such a capacity to play creative football as Kempes. He had saved Valencia from relegation and taken it within sight of the Spanish championship. The club's own manager had said of his star player, 'He is the most beautiful football machine there is at the moment.'

Apart from Kempes, there were other good, experienced players picked for the team, such as Villa and Alonso. And yet Menotti's decision to exclude Maradona initially cast a shadow over the World Cup. Settimio Aloisio had been so certain that Maradona would be picked that prior to the final selection he had visited the national team's training camp to press the player to renew his contract with Argentinos Juniors. 'I believed he was going to play, that his performance was going to be outstanding, and that consequently he would come back from the cup demanding the kind of money which we just wouldn't be able to pay for him. I had to get him there and then before he got beyond our reach.'

Aloisio turned up at the training club to have his access to

Maradona blocked by Ricardo Pizzarotti, the team's trainer and Menotti's effective number two. Aloisio, however, had a secret ally in the Argentine camp, Dr Ruben Oliva, the team's doctor, and managed to talk to him while Menotti, Pizzarotti and the team were in a closed training session. 'Doctor, I told him, you've got to do me a big favour. Figure out how to get Diego away from Pizzarotti and to a room where I can talk to him. Otherwise it's going to be disaster for my club.'

The request was music to the doctor's ears. Oliva owed no special allegiance to Argentinos Juniors, and had no pronounced opinion on Maradona. However, during the World Cup preparations he had developed a visceral dislike for Pizzarotti, arguing over training methods and the physical fitness of the players. Oliva also saw Pizzarotti's appointment as a challenge to his influence over Menotti. The doctor, a left-leaning intellectual, claimed to be Menotti's philosophical mentor, instilling in the Argentine manager his flirtation with radical politics and his vision of a new dynamic Argentine football. Aloisio's little conspiracy offered him the opportunity to get his own back on Pizzarotti, and regain his influence. Oliva approached Maradona while Pizzarotti was talking to some of the other players and, in a break in the training session, led Maradona secretly to a meeting with Aloisio. There the player agreed to extend his contract. Thus did Maradona involve himself in the first of many intrigues, large and small, surrounding his career.

A week later, Aloisio met Menotti and discussed the choice of players for the World Cup. Aloisio argued strongly that Maradona was the player with the greatest potential individual talent, who had already proved himself as a top-class player, and would do so even more brilliantly in the cup. Menotti was unconvinced, insisting that Maradona was too immature and arguing that the man he would pick instead of him as substitute, Alonso, was a much greater potential crowd-puller by virtue of playing for a bigger club, River Plate, whose stadium had been chosen for the finals.

According to witnesses who monitored the Argentine team closely at the time, Menotti had other, more personal reasons for excluding Maradona. The manager had approached the World Cup confident that he would win it. A man of enormous ego, he was obsessed with the glory that victory would bring, and feared that any rival would eclipse him. Still fresh in his memory was that friendly against Hungary in which he had found himself almost bulldozed into bringing out the young player to the tribal cry of 'Maradoona, Maradoona.'

'Menotti saw the World Cup as his big chance. He couldn't conceive of anyone being bigger than himself, and he feared Maradona, and the effect he might have had on the team,' Fernández Moores recalled.

The view is supported by someone who had first worked with Menotti at Huracán, and who was subsequently appointed as a key member of the World Cup '78 enterprise. Dr Ruben Oliva recalled, 'Menotti was paranoid about Maradona. He didn't want any important person near him, or assuming the role of number one. Nor did he want anyone imposed on him. Menotti felt that if he ceded to that kind of pressure, he would lose his authority.'

In the end, the 1978 World Cup survived the Maradona controversy and became one of the most politically exploited events in sports history. Employing the services of the US PR company Burson & Marsteller, and relying on the silence and acquiescence of a nation subdued by terror, the junta made every effort to turn Argentina's World Cup performance into an image of national self-discipline and superiority. In a country as fanatical about football as Argentina, the junta managed to channel emotions behind a team and a manager. Only afterwards, when the killing was over and the junta long gone, did Menotti offer his excuses for winning for the generals. In 1986 he wrote the following valedictory note on behalf not just of himself but of all the Argentine footballers he had managed, including Maradona:

Many people could say that I have coached teams during the time of dictatorships, in an epoch when Argentina had governments with which I had nothing in common, and even more, they contradicted my way of life. And I ask what should I have done? Coach teams to play badly, to base everything on tricks, to betray the feelings of the people? No, of course not . . . We were conscious and we all knew at the time that we played for the people. A people that, in the moment in Argentina, needed a new point of departure for doing together something different . . . We tried to play in the best way because we understood that we were obliged to give back the spectacle of football to the people. To give it back through victory, if this was possible, but, after all, in the pleasure of playing honest football. Each of us had an order when we entered the field the day of the final: to look at the people in the stands. We are not going to look at the stage-box of the authorities, I said to the players, we are going to look to the terraces, to all the people, where perhaps sits the father of each of us, because there we will find the metal workers, the butchers, the bakers and the taxi drivers.

What Menotti did not mention was how his players prepared for the World Cup, thinking on how best, if at all, to kick out old habits. One medical source told me that in 1978 the 'whole of Argentine football was doping itself . . . I started a big fight to break the trend.' He appears to have been only partly successful. Argentina had players who had been regularly provided with amphetamines while playing for their league teams, and who found in this World Cup a suitably lax régime when it came to urine samples. FIFA had yet to develop an efficient system for controlling the taking of drugs during the competition, while for political reasons Argentine officials appear to have ensured that none of their own players were shown positive in the periodical testing that did take place. The sacrificial lamb of the competition was the Scottish player Willie Johnston, who was sent home in disgrace and banned from international football for a year after his dope test had proved positive. He had taken two Fencamfamin pills to accelerate his play. According to other reports, Kempes and Alberto Tarantini were so 'high' after playing one particular World Cup match that they had to keep on going for another hour before they came down again. But one of the most extraordinary episodes of the World Cup involved the pregnant wife of the Argentine team's waterboy. Her urine was used as a cover for on Argentine player's in one of the competition's dope tests. When I put these allegations to Menotti in November 1995, he was indignant, denying that his team had taken any banned substances during the 1978 World Cup. He described Kempes as 'one of the purest players I have known in Argentine football', and listed others in the 1978 team, like Ardiles, Bertoni, Galvan, Olguin, Luque and Pasarella, who went on with successful careers. 'When a player is into drugs, he doesn't last three years. After three years he's destroyed, poor kid, pure garbage. My team played better than any other Argentine team in the history of international football.'

6

THE JUNTA'S BOY

Argentina's victory in the 1978 World Cup fuelled the ruling junta's illusion of its own invincibility. Generals and admirals developed a keen sense of the potential control football could give them over people. In the aftermath of the World Cup, no player caught their attention as much as Diego Maradona. Although he hadn't played, he was fast becoming a national institution, with his name echoing ever louder across the stands and a revived stream of enthusiastic media reports. The depression which gripped Maradona following his exclusion from Menotti's World Cup squad proved short-lived. With the extraordinary will power that was to rescue him time and time again throughout his career, Maradona put the disappointment behind him and set his sights instead on proving that he could achieve the success that had been marked out for him since childhood.

In striking contrast to the previous disastrous campaign, a more confident and physically mature Maradona led his team through a successful qualifying round for the Youth World Championship. In one match closely monitored by the South American media, Argentina beat Peru 4–0. Brazilian journalists present declared for the first time that 'not since Pele' had they seen a player of such quality.

Menotti, a national hero following the World Cup win, was sufficiently relaxed to set aside any personal prejudice. Again he took note of the child prodigy he had so ruthlessy kicked in the stomach. Only six months on from the World Cup, he brought Maradona back into the national squad for a series of international friendlies, after informing the media that over the last year the kid from Villa Fiorito had 'developed the maturity he needed and he now has the potential to be a great player'. He saw no contradiction between this and his previous decisions, and has since insisted that he never for one moment doubted Maradona's potential to be one of the greatest players in footballing history. 'From the age of sixteen, the dauphin of football had made his appearance. There was no doubt in my mind that he would one day inherit the title held previously by Di Stefano, Cruyff and Pele.'

This potential was revealed to British journalists for the first time in a game at Hampden Park, Glasgow, in June 1979. Playing only his fifth international at the age of eighteen, Maradona helped Argentina to a 3–1 win over Scotland. The *Sun*'s Alex Montgomery described the goal that amazed 62,000 Scots that day and in his view confirmed Maradona not only as the outstanding player in the Argentine squad, but as Pele's natural successor at the top of world football: 'Maradona had the ball to the left of the Scotland goal, with three Scots, including keeper George Wood, in a semi-circle around him. He produced a series of feints and dummies, and as Wood prepared for a chip, he whipped the ball between the keeper and his left-hand post.' Former Scottish international Denis Law called it the cheekiest goal ever scored at Hampden, and went on to comment, 'Maradona has everything. There is no department of his game you can fault. He is strong, brave and skilful. He's an individual who works for the good of his team.'

Later, with the Argentine youth team, Maradona won his first World Youth Championship cup in Tokyo. He celebrated with Cyterszpiler and Chitoro, who had accompanied him to Japan. All three considered the victory a major breakthrough in Maradona's footballing career, and one that would greatly enhance his commercial value. It was also an event which was exploited to the full by the military régime. The tournament in Tokyo coincided with a visit to Buenos Aires by a group of delegates from the Organization of American States on a fact-finding mission to update themselves on the country's human rights record. While officials warned journalists not to look too sympathetically at the OAS visit, they encouraged renewed nationalistic fervour around the championship in Tokyo which Argentina was favourite to win. Because of the time difference, the final whistle on the match was blown just one hour before the OAS had been given permission to open its temporary offices a few blocks away from the Plaza de Mayo, where the presidential palace stood. As the OAS prepared to take evidence from relatives of the disappeared, across the state TV there flashed an old graphic headline from the 1978 World

Cup: 'ARGENTINA CHAMPIONS!' it proclaimed. An official commentary urged all loyal citizens to take to the streets and demonstrate how 'happy' they were.

Journalists from *La Razón*, the leading afternoon newspaper, which was firmly controlled by the army at the time, were promptly dispatched to the Maradona family home, to interview Tota before her scheduled appearance on state-run TV. Surrounded by crowds of neighbours, Tota proudly proclaimed that her son had rung her every day of the tournament. 'The last time was to repeat what he had been promising me all along. Don't worry, Mama, we are going to bring the cup back with us,' said Tota. By her side, a more withdrawn and shy Claudia Villafane declared, 'I know Diego very well, and I know how much he suffers if he doesn't win. But I can imagine how they are celebrating now.'

Tota had made an appointment at the hairdresser prior to her TV engagement. Only when the journalists pursued her there did she display the potential for emotional eruption that she had passed down to her son. Sitting under a hair-drier, Tota sobbed uncontrollably before shouting to a journalist to get out and leave her in peace. Later that afternoon, composure restored, she appeared live and smiling on one of the country's popular chat shows. Her main contribution was to lift up a glass of champagne and toast to her son with the air of a proud queen.

Another key participant in the officially promoted Maradona 'show' that day was José María Muñoz, a journalist with Radio Rivadavia, the country's most popular radio station. Muñoz was not only sympathetic to the régime to whom he owed his job, he also had a wide audience. His breathless match reports and his technical knowledge of the game were respected by thousands of listeners. On the day Argentina won its latest cup, Muñoz took to his microphone like a man possessed, urging his listeners to converge on the Plaza de Mayo, and 'show these men from the Commission on Human Rights what is the real Argentina'. His message touched an immediate chord among the fans. No sooner had he spoken than some of them had gathered outside his offices, chorusing his name. Muñoz joined them and was carried, shoulder high, on a triumphant jig round the block. By the time he returned to his office, other radio and TV channels, alerted by their military minders, were echoing Muñoz's call. Those inciting the masses to celebrate 'this magnificent victory for the nation' included José Gómez Fuentes. Three year later Fuentes would still be at his microphone, leading the junta's propaganda efforts in the Falklands War.

The thousands who converged on and around the Plaza de Mayo that day in 1979 included secondary school students and workers given the day off and free transport, waved on by policemen. By contrast, mothers and grandmothers of the 'disappeared' who with their distinctive white bandannas had been patiently queuing to give their evidence from the early hours of the morning, found their progress obstructed, in the midst of the hooligan fever of Argentine flags, backed by a cacophony of rattles, bugles, drum beats and 'Maradooona, Maradooona . . .' The event was described by one observer, the French journalist Jean-Pierre Bousquet, as 'one of the most shameful episodes in the annals of Argentine radio and TV journalism'.

It did not end there, however. The junta's allies wasted little time in getting Maradona on air, warmly thanking the nation for its enthusiasm and seemingly content with the drooling messages of support from a line of generals. On his return to Buenos Aires, Maradona and the rest of his team were invited to the Casa Rosada and, in a gesture dutifully recorded by the state-controlled TV, warmly congratulated by the head of the junta, General Videla.

Just in case there was still any doubt about Maradona being part of the national enterprise, the army chief of staff sent him and Menotti a public telegram reminding them that Maradona was due for national service and was expected to continue his duty as a conscript once the celebrations were over. Maradona duly complied, cutting his hair, putting on a uniform and swearing his allegiance to the flag before being drafted. His stay in the army was brief. The military judged he would be more useful to them on the pitch than in the barracks. They released him after yet another military ceremony of appreciation. Handing Maradona his special conscript's savings book, his commander-in-chief barked the following words: 'The nation needs you, the youth, who are of such an example in the sporting world, that you should take on the mantle of hard work and effort as part of the great enterprise . . . You, the young player, can and should become an example. You can, because of your popularity, and you should, precisely because your status as a public figure carries with it the responsibility of being a good example.'

Soon after Maradona's triumphant return from Tokyo, a new

slogan joined the growing list of officially inspired soundbites so beloved of the military régime. It took hold in the packed terraces of some of Argentina's leading football stadiums, and was nowhere chorused with such apparent enthusiasm as in Maradona's own club, Argentinos Juniors. Against the pounding beats of drums, it emerged, with regimental precision, from the tribal war dances of the most fanatical fans, painted with their club colours and stripped to the waist. 'Maradona, no se vende, Maradona, no se va, Maradona es Patrimonio Nacional' – 'Maradona isn't for sale, Maradona is going nowhere, Maradona is part of the National Heritage.'

The most vociferous in the crowds belonged to the so-called *barras bravas*, the 'wild terraces', Argentina's own contribution to the hooligan culture. With the phenomenal growth of football as the country's most popular sport, the *barras* had emerged as a violent group of unemployed, rootless yobs, willing to be rented out by club officials and men in government to push particular interests through intimidation. In return for doing as instructed, members of the *barras* had food and transport expenses covered and were given free tickets to football matches, or to any other event where forceful persuasion was deemed necessary. Among the early targets of such intimidation following the 1976 coup were some of the mothers and grandmothers of the 'disappeared', who chose to defy the government's ban on public demonstrations. They were constantly harassed to the point of physical abuse by paid members of the *barras*, posing as enraged members of the working class.

There is no doubt that the *barras* were brought in to play their part by vested interests of the Argentine footballing world who were determined to ensure that Maradona was not transferred abroad. These interests surfaced publicly with a determined effort by the president of Argentinos Juniors, Prospero Consoli, after the Youth Championship in 1979 to lock Maradona into an extended contractual agreement with the club. Consoli had spent most of his working life as the official tailor of the Argentine armed forces, reaching the token rank of corporal and earning a handsome package of salary and perks. By this time he was officially retired from 'military' activity, but playing a more useful role as one of the army's stooges in the football industry. He had recently appointed General Guillermo Suárez Mason as titular chairman of Argentinos Juniors, with overall responsibility for the club's financial affairs. Suárez Mason's credentials for the job did not include a particular knowledge of or love for the sport. In the *barras*, however, he found a natural ally. As the head of the country's army corps, Suárez Mason had a record of human rights violations second to none. He was also financially corrupt. He had appointed himself to the boards of several state companies, including the oil monopoly Yacimentos Petrolíferos Fiscales and the domestic airline Austral, from where millions of dollars of taxpayers' money were secretly funnelled into private bank accounts or into prestige projects whose only justification was the amount of backhanders they generated.

In the aftermath of the 1978 World Cup, Suárez Mason had no qualms about pursuing his 'football interests' on the back of his expense account at YPF. Travelling in the company's helicopter, the General was a regular visitor to the offices of Argentinos Juniors, ensuring that he kept the management of Maradona's career closely monitored. Suárez Mason was a demagogue, with a penchant for pre-emptive strikes whenever he felt his power base was threatened. After the Youth Championship in Tokyo, he delved into the budget of Austral and diverted $250,000 to Argentinos Juniors to help the club meet their contractual obligations with their star player. As part of the deal, Austral provided Maradona with a T-shirt and baseball cap emblazoned with the airline's logo which the player agreed to wear at pre-arranged photo-opportunities, including a widely publicized signing ceremony.

There is little evidence that this particular publicity stunt, the first of its kind into which Maradona allowed himself to be drawn, dramatically increased Austral's sales revenue. As for the player himself, it appears not to have enhanced his image as one of Argentina's most popular sportsmen. *Crónica*, Argentina's mass-circulation afternoon tabloid, was so incensed by the Austral deal that it ran a full-page feature attacking it. To avoid the risk of closure or the murder of any of its journalists, the article made no attempt to link the deal with Suárez Mason. But no one reading it was left with any doubt as to the extent to which the military had manipulated Maradona. Under the headline, 'The Angel of football does not deserve to be forced into fancy dress', *Crónica* said Maradona looked not like a football player but like an astronaut or a racing driver, made to play the clown for a few dollars more. 'No one is to blame except the consumer society which wants a return on its investment. Maradona remains as clean and pure as ever . . .'

This was true, but only up to a point. For as *Crónica* itself pointed out, Maradona had begun to make pronouncements on matters which strictly speaking had nothing to do with the game itself, but more to do with the footballer's duties as a conscript soldier. Soon after signing the Austral deal, Maradona said, 'Now that I am also lucky enough to serve my country as a soldier, I am beginning fully to understand what is the meaning of national sovereignty. It is everything. It is my country and my country is like my family to me . . . And if one day our armed forces have to defend our country, there will be soldier Maradona, because first and foremost I am an Argentine.' It was a script straight out of the junta's manual, as written by army men like Suárez Mason and Consoli. At the time, the Argentine armed forces were still rattling their sabres over a territorial dispute with Chile in the Beagle Channel, while continuing their 'internal war' against political dissidents.

The Argentine military had also become deeply divided within itself. The rivalry between the army and the navy extended to football, where Suárez Mason found himself having to defend his hold on Maradona from the approaches of a navy rear-admiral, Carlos Lacoste. Lacoste had increased his power base within the régime as chairman of the main organizational arm of the 1978 World Cup, the EAM, doubling up as vice-president of FIFA at the same time, a post FIFA allowed him to retain until 1982. Lacoste was also on the board of River Plate, one of the top clubs, and following Argentina's World Cup victory, tried to persuade his club to buy Maradona. River Plate never came up with a convincing offer. Ironically it was pipped at the post in 1980 when Maradona was transferred on a one-year loan agreement to rivals Boca Juniors after Lacoste had strongly and publicly backed a regulation of the Argentine Football Association which restricted the transfer of footballers abroad. Boca went on to win the championship, much to the personal chagrin of Lacoste. The rear-admiral had declared, 'I'm not convinced by the argument that footballers don't earn as much as they should in our country. There are other values which we must keep in mind. We've organized a World Cup with the consensus and recognition of everyone and we are not going to throw away what we have gained as a result of it.' The message was only too clear. Maradona was to be kept in Argentina as long as the military thought they could make political use of him.

A revealing insight into the extent to which the Argentine military régime invested in the emerging career of Diego Maradona was provided to the author by Settimio Aloisio, the vice-president of Argentinos Juniors. Aloisio detailed publicly for the first time the problems he faced in ensuring that the relationship between his club and Maradona was based on firm financial considerations and not political ones. Following the 1978 World Cup, Aloisio had become privately convinced that his club could no longer afford to hang on to Maradona. The club's revenues – its real income as opposed to the hidden subsidies obtained by Consoli from his military friends – barely covered the mounting costs of extending Maradona's contract. The budget was not only weak, it was also inflexible. For it did not make any funds available for spending on other players and developing the team. Aloisio wanted to sell Maradona and use the proceeds to restructure the team, improve the club's facilities (thus drawing in more fans) and ensure long-term financial stability.

'The problem I faced within the club,' Aloisio told me, 'was that Consoli and Suárez Mason were just playing politics. Maradona was the teat on which everyone sucked. It wasn't just Consoli and Suárez Mason, but everyone in the military who wanted him to stay in the country. Maradona was a good diversion when things were difficult for the régime. He kept people happy. The Romans used the circus, our military used the football stadiums.'

7

HARRY GOES TO BUENOS AIRES

Just before Christmas 1978 (the summer season in the Southern Hemisphere), one of the most adventurous managers in British football, Harry Haslam of Sheffield United, flew across the Atlantic and into Buenos Aires determined to strike a deal. The groundwork for the visit had been laid at a series of secret meetings in Sheffield between Haslam and Antonio Rattín, the former captain of the Argentine national side. Rattín was best remembered by British fans as the tall, tough half-back who had defiantly made the long circuit of Wembley, exchanging insults with the crowd after being sent off in a bruising quarter-final encounter with England. The occasion was the 1966 World Cup, which England went on to win under the captaincy of Bobby Moore. Twelve years later, the man the British tabloids had branded 'the animal' had returned to enemy territory extending a commercial olive branch. Retired as a player, Rattín had used his extensive network of contacts both at home and internationally to establish himself as a part-time agent or go-between for Argentine football interests. He carried with him a list of largely unknown Argentine footballers who had yet to find a permanent place is the national squad and who were thus uncovered by Argentina's restrictions on transfers abroad. The list included the eighteen-year-old Diego Maradona, who, for all his emerging star status within his own country, still remained a relatively unknown factor internationally.

The city of Sheffield may have seemed a long way away from Buenos Aires, but United had been looking for an imaginative solution to their problems since being relegated in 1976. In Haslam the club had a manager with a reputation for risk-taking, nowhere more so than in the unpredictable world of transfers. Haslam felt his club was ready for remodelling and that the arrival of an Argentine player could be the harbinger of just the kind of energizing shake-out he was seeking. Together with Rattín and Oscar Arce, another former Argentine player who had an informal contract with Sheffield United as a coach, Haslam prepared his trip to Argentina. Initially he planned to travel with Keith Burkinshaw and Terry Neill, the managers of Spurs and Arsenal respectively, who also had an interest in buying Argentine players. Haslam appears to have convinced them that the only way into the heavily protected Argentine market was with Rattín and Arce acting as middlemen. While Haslam was manager of Sheffield United, he also doubled up unofficially as a 'Mr Fixit' for some foreign deals, but appears to have taken the precise financial details of this informal arrangement to his grave.

On the eve of the trip to Argentina, Terry Neill decided to stay behind in England. With Haslam's approval, his place on the aeroplane was taken by Tony Pritchett, a veteran Sheffield football reporter who had covered the club's fortunes for most of his professional life.

Burkinshaw was to use the trip to pave the way for the eventual purchase of Ossie Ardiles and Ricardo Villa, the two Argentine World Cup stars, but from the outset Haslam was clear which player he wanted to bring home with him: Diego Maradona. While the Argentine football world had yet to shake off its hero worship of those who had won them the World Cup, the buzz among the media, managers, agents and players was now firmly around 'El Pelusa', the straggly long-haired one – as Maradona was popularly known – whose physical immaturity belied play of extraordinary self-confidence and inspiration. Maradona's multiple skills as creator, organizer and striker were personally witnessed by Haslam both on Argentinos Juniors' home ground and during an away match in the summer resort of Mar de Plata.

Of his visit to Argentinos Juniors, Haslam would later recall, 'Rattín drove me to this poorish, non-league ground with only a bit of cover and no directors' box. We had to watch through glass from a clubroom. This was Maradona's club. He did some ball tricks before the kick-off and then started playing. I just couldn't believe that a mere kid would have so much all-round ability. Thanks to Rattín I had the field to myself and I knew this compact little boy was worth a million. And it didn't exactly lessen my interest when they said, "And wait until you see his two brothers!"'

It was in Mar de Plata, against the backrop of rolling Atlantic breakers and a holiday atmosphere graced by uninterrupted sun and some of the best wines and seefood in South America, that Haslam met Jorge Cyterszpiler. The two men shared a natural ebullience and struck up an immediate rapport. Like many of his countrymen, Cyterszpiler had been brought up with the idea that Englishmen were stiff, arrogant and snobbish, but he found in Haslam a man of disarming enthusiasm for life in general and a particular passion for football. 'I remember eating with Haslam and thinking, "This guy is OK after all,"' Cyterszpiler recalled. Haslam also went down well with Settimio Aloisio, who had given his formal blessing to having the young Maradona included on Rattín's potential transfer list, in apparent defiance of both the club's president and members of the armed forces. Haslam's presence in Argentina went unnoticed by the local press, although it was closely monitored by the military régime. Haslam was told by his Argentine hosts that the question of whether or not Maradona could be transferred out of the country had become such a politically charged issue that the veil of secrecy around the negotiations had to be maintained at all costs. The interests at stake were considerable.

As Tony Pritchett recalled, 'The boy was the prince, the greatest player in South America. It became obvious from the moment we arrived that for him to leave Argentina would quickly become a national football scandal. Haslam's Argentine contacts made it clear that if we wanted Maradona, he would have to be smuggled out of the country, and there would have to be extra payments for those involved.'

Such intrigue appears to have left Haslam's enthusiasm for Maradona undiminished. 'I remember when Haslam saw Maradona play for the first time, he got terribly excited,' Aloisio says. 'At one point, he turned to me and said, "Settimio, there is no doubt in my mind that we are in the presence of a great player with tremendous talent."'

It was a similar impression to that once given by Tony Currie, who had so captured the imagination of Haslam's predecessor, John Harris, and many English football fans over much of the previous decade. Currie, too, had been eighteen years old when he was bought from Watford by Harris for £26,500 in 1968. He went on to lift Sheffield United to promotion and within a whisker of a place in European competition, proving himself an instinctive entertainer and a magician with the ball. Sheffield supporters recall that when Currie was at his peak, it was a joy just to see him pass the ball. As Tony Pritchett put it, 'He didn't kick it, he caressed

and cajoled it and, long pass or short, he put it on a plate . . .'
The same was now being said of the young Maradona who, like
Currie, revelled in expressing his talents to the adoring fans with
gestures that verged on exhibitionism. While Currie blew kisses
to the terraces after scoring, Maradona ran diagonally across the
pitch before suddenly packing a victory punch into the air with a
clenched fist.

Currie agreed to a transfer to Leeds United when Sheffield
United was relegated in 1976. His price had risen to £240,000.
When Haslam watched Maradona play, he saw clearly how the
young Argentine could fill the gap, regenerating the excitement
of Currie, and bringing Sheffield United back into the forefront
of British, and international, football.

Haslam's was the first formal approach Maradona had received
from abroad and the Englishman's enthusiasm touched the player,
who was still smarting from the public humiliation of being left out
of the World Cup squad. In private conversations with Aloisio and
Cyterszpiler, Maradona said he was excited by the idea of playing
for an English team, and felt honoured that a man like Haslam
had let his eye for the spectacular fall on him. He would have
preferred an offer from one of the better-known premier-division
clubs like Manchester United or Tottenham Hotspur, rather than
one recently relegated, but was sufficiently well briefed on the
history of Sheffield United to realise the club's potential.

The problem lay in reaching an agreement on Maradona's worth,
given that he had never played for a non-Argentine team and was
relatively untested at international level. Without huge financial
clout behind him, Haslam had to try to strike a bargain that was in
his club's best longer-term interests. This was not fully appreciated
by the Argentines, who considered Haslam's offer of $900,000 as
simply the opening card in a lengthy negotiation process in which
the price would gradually be raised. Only Aloisio was prepared to
take the money there and then to use on refinancing Argentinos
Juniors. He also felt that Maradona would mature playing in
English football: 'I thought the deal Haslam was offering was
fabulous. It was good all round, for his club, for our club and
for Maradona himself.'

Aloisio was, however, overruled by his club's board and forced,
with the apparent blessing of Cyterszpiler and Maradona himself, to
make a counter offer of $1.5 million. To Haslam the figure seemed
astronomical. He had hoped to secure backing for his purchase

of Maradona from one of Sheffield's richest directors, the gold
bullion dealer Albert Bramall, but the money that Maradona was
asking for, together with the plethora of commissions that were
involved in the deal, proved too hot for the Sheffield board to
handle. Reluctantly Haslam abandoned the idea of ever buying
Maradona, and instead secured the transfer of Alex Sabella, a
left-side midfielder he had seen playing for River Plate. Haslam
later used his contacts with Argentina to help Spurs complete their
negotiations with Ardiles and Villa.

With the evidence of hindsight, one can pause to reflect on
what might have happened to Diego Maradona, and indeed to
British football, had Haslam's negotiations proved successful.
Sabella had mixed fortunes at Sheffield. He was popular with
the fans, but his self-discipline let him down when it came to
dealing with the harshness of a Sheffield winter and the rigours of
orthodox training methods. Ardiles, by contrast, greatly improved
as a footballer while playing at Spurs, and became so integrated
with the English way of life that he stayed on, becoming manager
at Newcastle, Swindon and Spurs.

Whatever might have been in Sheffield, the Haslam episode did
make an impact on Maradona's career. Once pitched on to the
international market, Maradona was there to stay, one of half
a dozen players who generated huge interest across the world.
While the negotiations with Haslam were going on, a 'flyer'
that Maradona wanted to play for Arsenal was launched by
Cyterszpiler. It was dutifully picked up in the UK, where press
reports suggested that Haslam had been acting as an Arsenal 'spy'
in South America. Haslam strongly denied this and there is no
evidence that the transfer of Maradona to Highbury was ever
seriously discussed. But the flyer served its purpose by boosting
Maradona's overseas profile. For the next three years Cyterszpiler
ducked, dived and negotiated for the most lucrative deal possible
on behalf of his friend and client, skilfully playing one offer off
against another. Maradona meanwhile enhanced his own star status
at home, helping Boca Juniors to win the championship. His transfer
abroad continued to be blocked by a conspiracy of national football
interests which included the Argentine Football Association, major
clubs like River Plate, Boca and Argentinos Juniors, the *barras
bravas*, certain military figures and César Menotti.

The Italian club Juventus was among a handful of leading European

clubs to express an interest in Maradona following Sheffield United's frustrated bid. With the blessing of their powerful owner, Fiat
boss Gianni Agnelli, club president Giampiero Boniperti and coach
Pietro Giuliano flew to Buenos Aires for a meeting with Cyterszpiler
and representatives of Argentinos Juniors. They were accompanied
by Omar Sivori, the veteran Argentine-born international, who was
well qualified to persuade his countrymen about the advantages of
quitting Argentine football. In 1957 Sivori, with his deadly left
foot, had been, with Maschio and Angelillo, one of the so-called
'Trio de la Muerte', or Death Trio – the stars of the Argentine
team that won the South American championship in Lima. A
year later all three players were scooped up by Italian clubs,
leaving the Argentine national team devastated but European
football greatly enhanced. Sivori subsequently pursued a highly
successful career playing in the Italian league alongside Giampiero
Boniperti at Juventus, before his appointment a decade later as
manager of Argentina. Sivori, like Maradona a poor Argentine
of Italian ancestry, had become a millionaire and had no doubt
that the emerging Argentine star would thrive in Italy just as he
had done. He also believed that the objections being thrown up to
his transfer did not have Maradona's interests in mind, but merely
responded to internal politics. No club or grouping in Argentina,
Sivori believed, could realistically give an Argentine footballer of
the star status of Maradona the financial benefits which a club
like Juventus could, being the footballing arm of one of the most
powerful family-run business corporations in the world.

Maradona's talents had been shown off at first hand to the
Juventus scouts during a friendly Argentina played against Italy in
Rome's Olympic stadium on 26 May 1979. The match ended in a
2–2 draw after turning into a gladiatorial duel between Maradona
and the gifted Italian defender Marco Tardelli. Maradona's ball
control, electric change of pace and sure touch on several occasions
brought the Olympic stadium to its feet, with the Argentine
outclassing Tardelli as man of the match. Sivori had no doubt
of Maradona's brilliance. Boniperti was a little more cautious.
As one source close to the Juventus talks recalled, 'As far as
Juventus was concerned, money was no problem. But Boniperti
had some doubts about Maradona. He thought he had all the
qualities of a great player, but that he was still in the process
of formation, and that there was a risk these qualities would
diminish with maturity. He regarded Maradona as unpredictable

and felt he needed more time to consider whether the club should sign him.'

Nevertheless, Boniperti did come up with what he believed was an imaginative offer in an attempt to get round domestic objections to Maradona's transfer abroad: the player would be loaned to Juventus for a season, after which he would be given the option of returning to Argentina, in time for the 1982 World Cup scheduled to take place in Spain. The talks with Juventus were tentative on both sides. However, their importance was inflated by the Maradona camp in a tactic clearly intended to reinforce their bargaining position vis-à-vis other more serious bidders. Thus in a cable widely picked up by the Argentine media the Italian news agency ANSA reported that Juventus was prepared to pay $10 million – when in point of fact, if figures were discussed at all, they pointed towards a more modest sum.

Whatever Juventus's real intentions, the club's approach failed to match the sheer persistence of the bid for Maradona made from 1979 onwards by Barcelona, which ended, after one of the most tortuous negotiations in footballing history, in Maradona's record transfer in 1982. Indeed, according to Sivori, the Juventus approach was handicapped from the outset by the knowledge that Barcelona had already sent one of its top negotiators on a scouting mission, in defiance of the Maradona-is-not-for-sale camp inside and outside the Argentine Football Association.

Sivori recalled, 'We had frank and open discussions, but in the midst of them Maradona himself clearly seemed awkward and embarrassed. He realized that he (or Cyterszpiler on his behalf) had subscribed to what in effect was a letter of intent with Barcelona; he also felt unsettled, almost threatened by the fact that there were other circumstances which seemed to be out of his control. Everyone in Argentina seemed to be fighting to ensure that he didn't go anywhere.'

The first toy.

Conscript days, 1979.

Signing up for Barcelona FC, 1982.

With the Giuliano family, Naples, 1986.

With his mother, Tota, and father Chitoro.

Naples San Pablo stadium 1984: the saviour arrives.

Diego and Claudia at the Vatican.

Fouled by Panagiotis Isalouchidis (Greece); World Cup, USA, 1994.

World Cup triumph, Mexico, 1986.

The Hand of God: Maradona vs. Shilton.

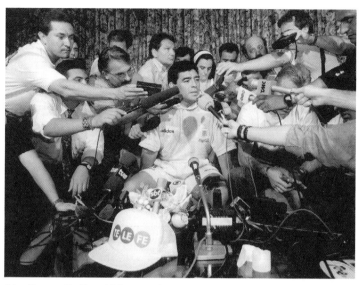

It's all over; Dallas, 30 June 1994.

Master inspirer of Oxford
dreams, 6 November. 1995.

The family man, Seville, 1992.

The People's Player: Maradona meets Castro.

Maradona with Lionel Messi of FC Barcelona, another legend.

8

MONEY, MONEY, MONEY

The story of Maradona's first record transfer shows the world of football in its most commercial and cynical light, but its beginnings were simple enough. It was early in 1977 that Nicolau Casaus, the veteran vice-president of Barcelona with a special responsibility for co-ordinating the club's *peñas* or international network of supporters, received a phone call from the Argentine resort of Mar de Plata. Casaus, a genial, cigar-smoking teetotaller with a knack for quiet diplomacy, was used, in an average working week, to fielding hundreds of calls from fans living as far apart as Tel Aviv and the North Pole, with polite but non-committal responses. But the call from Argentina struck him as deserving special attention. Argentina had the largest number of *peñas*, Casaus had a sentimental bond with the country, having been born there, and the caller, by the name of Beltrán, was a friend of his whose football expertise he respected.

Beltrán was the son of Catalán immigrants in Argentina and ran a cake shop. Although fanatical about 'Barça', he was an avid follower of the local football scene, and what he had just witnessed had left him in a state of high excitement. He had watched Maradona play in one of his first premier-division matches, helping Argentinos Juniors to a spectacular win against the local team. 'This Maradona is an absolute genius,' Beltrán told Casaus. 'You've got to come and see him for yourself.'

Casaus was given the opportunity to do just that during the 1978 World Cup when he was sent by his club on a general fact-finding mission. He was unimpressed by much of the quality of the playing, but his imagination was quickly captured by the boy Maradona, whom he observed from a distance playing club football.

'When I returned to Barcelona I told everyone, "Look, I've just seen this wonderful player. I think he is going to be as good as di Stefano or Pele." I was basically told to shut up. The feeling inside and outside the club was that the vice-president had gone over the top on this one. They felt that Maradona was too young, too untested and that I was deceived,' Casaus recalled.

Yet Casaus, for all his modesty, was not a man to be easily ignored. A retired businessman, he was widely respected in democratic Spain as a man of courage and conviction. During the Spanish Civil War he had been sentenced to death by General Franco for his Catalán sympathies. His close contact with Barcelona FC's international fan club had since provided him with an important power base inside Catalonia's most popular and influential institution.

Casaus was not demoralized by his board's initial reaction. He was prepared to wait, confident that Maradona was not a one-day wonder. He was soon proved right. In December 1978, Spain's hugely influential mass-circulation sports daily *MARCA* ran its first detailed coverage of Maradona, a full-page feature with an interview, facilitated by Cyterszpiler, headlined 'The New Argentine Star'. The piece confirmed what Harry Haslam was forced to find out the hard way – that Maradona was not going anywhere for anything under at least one million dollars. *MARCA* reported, 'This is a transfer figure which surpasses what was paid to Ardiles, Villa and Tarantini, and who are we talking about? They call him El Pelusa, the straggly-haired one. He's short, stocky, with an Afro hairstyle which hasn't seen a pair of scissors for months. He is a mere eighteen years old and yet he is potentially the most expensive player in Argentine football. The market seems overstocked, but Maradona seems to have something special to offer.'

Within a month of the *MARCA* article, Casaus was back in Buenos Aires, gathering further intelligence on Maradona. When I interviewed him in Barcelona in early 1995, Casaus recalled with warmth his early meetings with the player: 'My first impression was that here was a marvellous, simple kid who had become famous much too soon. He had the huge handicap of having been given money, status, popularity without being given the time to mature fully. I also felt that he was very rooted in his country and his family. When I went to his home, his whole family was there – parents, brothers, sisters, cousins – and I said to myself, this is a commune. Something in me made me think of trees and the dangers of uprooting them. Maradona seemed to owe his existence to his country and his family as a tree owes its existence to the earth.'

Casaus did not like Cyterszpiler, however. He thought the manager, like Maradona's father Chitoro, was in too much of a hurry to talk money. 'Cyterszpiler struck me as all head and no heart. It was all numbers. All that mattered was money.' That was perhaps hardly surprising, for Cyterszpiler had correctly identified Casaus as a stalking horse, with the undeclared motive of smoothing the way for the tough bargaining team that was following close behind. As Casaus himself later admitted, 'The directors of Barcelona FC, after their initial reticence, were no longer sceptical about signing Maradona. What they wanted was to negotiate hard and get the best deal possible ... we wanted Maradona cheap. Cyterszpiler wanted to sell him for as much as he could get.'

Over the next two years, negotiators travelled backwards and forwards between Barcelona and Buenos Aires. What began as a simple tip-off from a fan with a love of cakes and a good game of football developed into a revolving bargaining table involving an increasing number of people. It ended in the kind of sharp practices that were to become the stamp of more and more transfer deals in the 1980s and '90s.

Along the way, various vested interests struggled for hegemony over the life of Diego Maradona. Within Argentina, the efforts of one football executive to sign and seal an early contract between the player and Barcelona were met by a campaign of public vilification and mobster-style intimidation. As early as March 1979, Settimio Aloisio, having secured majority backing of his club's board, initialled an agreement in the Catalán capital with Barcelona. The agreement was immediately and publicly disowned by the club president Consoli, with the backing of sectors of the military. Aloisio returned to Buenos Aires to be confronted at the airport by a hired demonstration of the *barras bravas*. He later received a series of death threats. When he appeared at a home match accompanied by the treasurer of Barcelona, Carlos Tusquets, the *barras bravas* rose in unison to scream, 'Maradona no se vende' – 'Maradona is not for sale.' Aloisio was subsequently forced to resign after Consoli manoeuvred a board coup against him.

Among those most outspoken in the campaign to have Maradona stay in Argentina was Menotti. The national coach had used his success in the World Cup to pursue his idea of 'pure' Argentine football focused on a reborn nationalist identity. Looking back at the history of Argentine football, Menotti noted how the opening of the world market following the Second World War had led to a drain of some of the country's best young players. The most talented among them, players like Sivori (Juventus), Angelillo (Inter-Milan) and di Stefano (Real Madrid), achieved victories at European club level, leaving Argentine football back home to walk through a long march in the desert.

Menotti had overcome his initial reservations about Maradona. He now had no doubt of the player's value to his own future ambitions. In May 1980 Menotti was asked to describe what it meant to him to see Maradona in full cry on the field. 'It is like being a classical music fanatic alone in a private room with a symphony orchestra performing Beethoven just for you,' he replied, going on to describe Maradona as 'the nearest thing to Pele you'll ever see', and warning that he would turn his back on an international career if he went to Barcelona. 'Fans would hate him for it. It would look bad,' Menotti said.

Undeterred, Barcelona pushed on with its efforts to sign Maradona, but the club's negotiators, eager to drive a hard bargain, met their match in Jorge Cyterszpiler. Maradona's manager used his country's rules and regulations restricting transfers to string the negotiations along. At the same time, the extended publicity given to the talks – with speculative figures of what might or might not be on offer faithfully reported by the local press – gave Cyterszpiler the leverage he needed for dealing with Argentinos Juniors and other officials who were reluctant to see Maradona transferred before the 1982 World Cup. Cyterszpiler was not working for himself. He was doing no more and no less than his childhood friend expected of him: making as much money for Maradona and his family as possible so that they would never again experience the poverty and humiliation of Villa Fiorito, while allowing Maradona the freedom to get on with what he knew best: winning at football.

It suited some of the Barcelona camp to paint Maradona as a naive, ignorant kid who had fallen prey to the manipulation of an unscrupulous agent. But the reality was more complex than that. While the negotiations were underway, Maradona remained deliberately ambiguous in public. In statements to the Argentine and Spanish press, he spoke of his love for his country and his loyalty to his family, while reserving the right to choose to go abroad if he was not adequately rewarded at home. In his contacts with Italian and Spanish managers, he toyed with apparent enthusiasm with the thought of being poached by a leading European club. When talking to fellow countrymen like Menotti, he left the impression that his only real ambition was to play in the national colours. But Maradona was not working to a script prepared for him by Cyterszpiler. His dealings with the press were instinctive. They reflected the self-confidence of someone who had entered at a very early age into the hall of fame and felt that the world, by divine order, was at his feet, in more ways that one.

In financial terms, Cyterszpiler's strategy proved hugely successful. Barcelona's interest in Maradona was kept alive, its offer doubling with every year that passed. Back home, the Argentine football industry bent over backwards to match it, the value it put on Maradona far outweighing any economic rationale. Thus a debt-ridden Argentinos Juniors was salvaged by a subsidy of at least $400,000 from the Argentine Football Association so that it could make Maradona's contract more attractive. At one point AFA looked like reneging on its commitment, but fulfilled it when Maradona threatened the organization with a suit for breach of contract, and AFA with quitting Argentina. Quite where AFA generated the money for this has never been properly explained, and the suspicion remains that Maradona may have been paid with state funds diverted by Consoli's friends in the government. At the time the subsidy was granted, Consoli insisted that Argentinos Juniors would become self-financing, paying for Maradona with funds raised from a special 'raffle' and an increase in membership dues. Within a year, he had conceded publicly what he had known all along, that his club couldn't afford the player.

Instead, on 13 February 1981, a deal was signed with Boca Juniors whereby Argentinos Juniors loaned out Maradona until 30 June 1982 (the eve of the World Cup in Spain) with Boca maintaining an option on extending his contract. Boca paid $4 million in addition to assuming $1.1 million of Argentinos Juniors' debt. By agreeing to pay Maradona in dollars, Boca gave him the status he was seeking, but left the club vulnerable in the country's highly volatile foreign exchange market. In June 1981, only months after the deal had been signed, Argentina was in the midst of one of its regular financial crises, with the government forced to announce a 30 per cent devaluation of the peso. Boca was submerged in debt, its gate receipts and other income unable to meet the cost of Maradona, and having instead to increase its borrowing.

While two of Argentina's leading football clubs were thus financially crippled because of their involvement with Maradona, a third institution flourished: Maradona Productions. This off-shore company registered in Liechtenstein had been set up by Cyterszpiler early in 1979 with the approval of Maradona and his parents. The aim was to use the company as a vehicle for negotiating and channelling funds traded on the name of Maradona either in sponsorship deals or in merchandising. The choice of Liechtenstein had the double advantage of avoiding Argentine and European taxation and of protecting the emerging Maradona empire from financial scrutiny. Between 1979 and 1981 the company signed a series of lucrative sponsorship deals, the proceeds of which were instrumental in persuading Maradona to go on playing football in Argentina.

One of the first of these was with Puma, whose Argentine arm was headed by one of the country's leading entrepreneurs, Euneklian. Another was with Coca-Cola. In dealing with that company's local executives, Cyterszpiler and senior officials of Argentinos Juniors co-operated in a piece of tactical misinformation. Early in May 1980, Consoli announced to the Argentine press that Barcelona had bought Maradona for $6 million, making him one of the highest-paid players in the world. Although senior officials from Barcelona were in Buenos Aires at the time, no such deal had in fact been signed, pending an AFA decision on Maradona's transferability. The story was leaked with the apparent intention of further raising Maradona's international image and thus securing the contract with Coca-Cola. Subsequently, the story, reproduced in the Spanish press, was exposed for what it was – a flyer – but only after Maradona Productions had got its contract.

In the selling of his client's image, Cyterszpiler set himself few limits. The name Maradona found itself attached to every kind of commodity, regardless of the remoteness of its connection with football. Thus Maradona, smiling like a movie star, lent his teeth to a commercial for a new toothbrush which, the commercial assured consumers, would ensure oral hygiene at work and at play. The theme of cleanliness and self-pampering was continued in the soaps and other cosmetics to which Maradona's name was also attached. There were Maradona exercise books – a small irony here, given Diego's record of school absenteeism as a child – and a Maradona doll, 'Diegito', both cuddly and animated. Each contract was signed with the approval of Maradona. Only occasionally did he draw the line on 'social and ethical grounds'. A non-smoker, he turned down an offer to promote a brand of cigarettes. He also refused to lend his name to a wine commercial, believing that it might encourage alcoholism. These exceptions were drops in the ocean in terms of the overall revenue that Maradona was beginning to generate, but they did demonstrate a measure of moral rectitude absent in later years.

The concept of Maradonna Productions – with the player having a direct share in the resources generated by his own image – set a benchmark for other players in the future, offering them an alternative or additional source of income. While he was in Argentina, it certainly brought the Maradonas tangible economic benefits, although to this day the family have jealously protected the secrecy of their real net worth. According to Cyterszpiler, Maradona by 1982 was being paid about $65,000 per month before bonuses, and his annual income from 'other sources' was around $1.5 million. In 1979, using funds negotiated through Maradona Productions, Cyterszpiler had bought Maradona a country house near Buenos Aires for $350,000. It had a swimming pool and a specially constructed training area with a metal figure encrusted in a concrete wall against which the player could practise his passing. The following year over $1 million were spent on a house for Maradona and his parents in the Buenos Aires suburb of Villa Devoto. A string of apartments were subsequently purchased for other relatives and friends.

It was the purchase of the large house in Villa Devoto which generated the most publicity, much to the annoyance of the Maradonas' new neighbours. They feared that life in the once quiet residential quarter would never be the same again. And they were right. While TV cameras and paparazzi set up positions outside the new house, *Crónica* risked provoking the envy of its mainly working-class readership by running a full-page spread, together with photographs, on the luxuries that lay within. These included a dining room decorated in marble, a cascade and swimming room, sophisticated audio and kitchen equipment, and numerous rooms, among them a maid's quarters. The Maradonas had come a long way since the days when Cyterszpiler bought his friend Diegito the bottles of Coke he couldn't afford, Chitoro pounded cattle ribs and Tota handwashed her family's clothes near the cesspit.

Crónica, forever claiming to be the voice of the people, marked the event with an open letter to Maradona which said:

You know only too well, Diego, that envy is very common among us, and that nothing provokes envy more than success, money and contentment. But this hasn't stopped you, Diego, making it as a footballer and pursuing your dream of bringing happiness to your family. For some time now your genius has filled stadiums, and you've driven Argentines wild. And you have become the King of Football. But to be a good king, it is not sufficient to be able to dominate the ball, but also to have a throne worthy of its occupant. You need and deserve a palace like this . . .

While congratulating Maradona, the letter was also a veiled warning of the dangers of success and fame. At one level, the Maradonas had 'arrived' in social terms, proving, to even the most downtrodden, just as Evita had done, that with determination and with God on your side you can overcome poverty.

And yet the Maradonas risked driving a wedge between themselves and the world they had left behind, fuelling the mistrust of friends and relatives, and losing out on loyalty and solidarity. The world may have become materially more comfortable, but it was also becoming colder, more remote. At home Tota and Chitoro tried their best to carry on with some of their more uncluttered family traditions. She cooked the pasta and the empanadas as she had always done, gathering Diego and her other children round the family table as often as she could. Chitoro still got out of bed each morning soon after dawn, choosing not to break a routine that had been with him since his working days. But the strain of seeming different to much of the outside world began to show soon after they moved to Villa Devoto. So fraught did Tota's relations with some of her neighbours become one day that she ran out screaming on to the pavement and collapsed with an attack of nerves. In her ears resonated the gossip of those who claimed that money had gone to Maradona's head. Insults against the family began to be echoed in some football matches. On one occasion they became so vociferous that Diego issued a statement warning football fans that unless they showed more respect to his loved ones he would abandon the game and leave for Europe. The Barcelona talks were continuing.

The tension surfaced again before one of the last matches that Maradona played for Argentinos Juniors. As he entered the stadium, a fifteen-year-old fan jostled him slightly before asking him for an autograph. Maradona turned and punched him. Charged with assault, Maradona was given a two-month suspended sentence but subsequently had the incident wiped off his record by a friendly judge.

The pressures that fame had begun to put on Maradona personally were mentioned by the player himself in a series of candid interviews. In one published as early as December 1979, when he was only nineteen, he described the difficulties of making everyone happy – and meeting his contractual obligations – while keeping a sense of control over his own life. He spoke with pride about a football festival in which he had participated to help raise money for needy children, and his efforts to reply to letters from his fans and sign autographs. But he contrasted this with the people he claimed had begun to try and take advantage of him. He gave as examples a woman who had asked him to buy a house, and a man who had asked for a pair of sunglasses. As bad, Maradona thought, were the growing number of people totally unknown to him who were asking him to be the godfather of their newly born child.

'If they send me three thousand school books to autograph I'll do it, but what I can't do is also give three interviews at the same time. It's the kind of thing that is driving me crazy,' he told the Argentine magazine *Goles Match*. 'Whenever I've got a free moment I try and stay at home, because if I go out, I'm surrounded by people.'

In fact Maradona, like most footballers of his age, was not inclined to domesticity. Football, by its very nature, produces periods, during training and matches, of intense concentration and adrenalin in high doses, but also many periods of idleness, when a player seeks distraction in pleasure rather than in anything intellectually taxing. There were evenings when Maradona chose to do what he had done from his early teens, have a night out with his mates, while Claudia stayed at home. The difference was that now he could rarely do this in secret. If he wasn't actually snapped in the act, there was a growing list of women prepared to kiss and tell. One of the earliest such betrayals involved a well-proportioned brunette known as the 'Argentine Raquel Welch'. Although she indeed resembled the American actress physically, it was a somewhat misleading nickname for one Norma Moro, a woman of mysterious origins who claimed to be a former bullfighter while working in a strip joint in downtown Buenos Aires. Norma talked of how she had developed a relationship with Maradona after he had come one night to see her perform in a show entitled 'Circus Sexy'. She wore leopardskin bra and panties and matching boots. 'I've been a few times to watch him play football, but I had to stop going because he gets very jealous, and in a stadium, someone like me attracts a lot of attention,' Norma confessed.

The attentions of women like Norma – real or imagined – were at this stage in his life the least serious of Maradona's problems. Unmarried, without children and with a girlfriend confident enough about the long-term future to be able to turn a blind eye, Maradona played the rogue and got away with it. What was beginning to trouble him was the fear of social displacement and threatened identity as he struggled to pursue his assumed divine calling to football greatness amidst the growing pressures of contractual obligations.

To play football and win remained, as it had from early childhood, his key motivation. And yet his ability to perform had begun to be undermined by a problem that was to dog him for much of his career: his susceptibility to injury. By the age of twenty, Maradona's body was already suffering the consequences of an artifically enhanced and accelerated physical development. Once injured in a match, Maradona lost more than the use of his foot or leg. He lost his life blood, or thought he did.

9

BOCA CHAMPIONS

It was soon after signing the transfer agreement between Argentinos Juniors and Boca Juniors that Maradona began to show the first signs of his susceptibility to injury. On 20 February 1980, he had agreed as part of the contract to mark his transfer by playing in a match between the two teams, changing from one to the other at half-time. Seventeen minutes into the game, Maradona strained a muscle in his left leg and was forced to abandon the pitch. After half-time, he reappeared in the Boca colours with both sides level. Since his temporary absence, the match had deteriorated. Now the Boca fans chanted his name while officials looked on, expecting him to do what he had been paid to do. He did just that, shouting to the terraces at one point, 'I'm not leaving', and struggling to the end of the game. To the thousands watching that day, Maradona's performance seemed heroic. They were unaware that he had only been able to go on playing after a doctor had administered a strong dose of painkiller. Maradona later admitted that following the match he hadn't slept for three days, so great was the pain that returned to haunt him after the effect of the injection had worn off.

With Boca, Maradona went on to win his first league championship. Like so many stages in his career, this one appeared preordained by divine intervention and resolved through sheer will power. From childhood, Maradona had made playing for Boca his ambition. He had also predicted that his two younger brothers would end up playing for the team, but they never shared in Diego's gifts and ended up settling for lesser teams.

Boca had sprung out of the working-class Italian neighbourhood near the old port of Buenos Aires. Here the early immigrants had made their home and achieved a collective sense of identity with their tango bars and cantinas. Boca had become one of the best-known clubs in South America, its position at the top of the Argentine league usually challenged only by its historic rival River Plate. To play for either club was considered a privilege, although in the Maradona family there was never any question that Boca was the natural place to be. In the team, Maradona returned to his maternal roots. And each time he walked by the huge mural that covers one of the galleries leading to the changing rooms, he thought of his father too. For there depicted were the port workers, lugging their cargo, just as Chitoro had done so many years ago. The Maradonas may have grown rich, but Boca gave them an opportunity to be once again with the people.

At the start of the 1981–82 season, Boca was struggling. It had had a bad run lasting four years in which it had failed to win the championship. It now had a new coach, Silvio Marzolini, a former Boca player. The arrival of Maradona formed part of a major shake-up of the team, with Maradona one of four newcomers. Among the players who remained – they included the extrovert goalkeeper Hugo Gatti – there was initially some resentment of the star status that had been accorded to Maradona, and of his salary. There was also some concern within the management that the team effort would be undermined by rivalry up front between Maradona and Miguel Angel Brindisi, Boca's main goal scorer. Brindisi, a midfield inside right, was one of the veterans of Argentine football. Formerly with Huracán, he had played for Argentina in the 1974 World Cup. Conventional, by nature self-effacing and unambitious, and on the pitch hard-working if somewhat unimaginative, he was in both style and temperament the complete opposite of Maradona. The differences between them had been underlined by Maradona's growing commercial success as a national figure who seemed prepared to play for Boca one day and for Barcelona the next, depending who paid him the most. In the early 1970s, Brindisi had proudly accepted a medal from General Perón for refusing the blandishments of foreign clubs and staying at home.

The amiable and diplomatic Marzolini was sensitive to the inherent tensions and tactfully made it clear to Maradona that he expected him to play as one more member of the team, and to submit himself to the same discipline as everybody else. It was a tough request for a personality like Maradona, whose arrogance and pride had been growing in leaps and bounds. There were heated exchanges, Maradona instinctively reacting against being subjected to control on the football pitch. Miraculously, the tension dissipated by the time Marzolini faced his first real test.

Recovered from his latest injury, Maradona played a full game with Boca for the first time against Talleres of Córdoba. The match against this traditionally tough, hard-tackling northern team was one of the key encounters of the season. In the run-up to the match, it seemed as if the Roman circus would once again be gathering to see Maradona win or die. As it turned out, his reception in the impressive Bombonera stadium that day confirmed the very special place he had in the heart of the Boca fans. But more important was the degree to which he had become a symbol of his country's footballing success. As a journalist present at the match recalled later, 'The whole of footballing Argentina wanted to be in the Boca stadium that day. A small sector of that country – 65,000 – vibrated with a fervour rarely seen in the history of the sport. They were in the terraces and in the stands. Everyone without exception was attracted by the magnet of a name that today in the world is football itself: Maradona.'

As the ticker tape cascaded down the terraces, and the stadium was bathed in the blue and yellow colours of Boca, a collective tribal roar greeted Maradona. The Boca fans were there to pay allegiance to the king. Out on the pitch, Brindisi and Maradona could not have seemed more different. The first, well-groomed, narrow-shouldered and mechanical in his movements; the second, from the moment he stepped out on to the pitch, a visible loose cannon, long hair flying in the wind, body a powder keg of energy and strength, instantly ignited by the hurricane force of the Boca fans.

And yet Maradona played the kind of game that Marzolini expected of him. He avenged fouls against his colleagues by kicking two effortless penalties with his left foot, one in each corner of the net and both sending the goalkeeper diving hopelessly in the wrong direction. But the most brilliant of the four goals scored by Boca that day involved Maradona in a combined effort initiated by his extraordinary speed of thought and movement. Picking up the ball at the halfway line, he ducked his way through a couple of opponents before reaching the edge of the area. There, with perfect balance, he held himself back, keeping the ball close to him while Brindisi ran down to his right. With perfect timing and control, Maradona beat another defender and tapped the ball with his left foot, leaving Brindisi to complete the move with a thundering volley.

Tota witnessed her son's brilliance that day. She was also among the 60,000 fans who packed La Bombonera on the night of 10 April 1981 for the most emotionally charged of all the clashes that decided the championship. It was pouring with rain, but the stadium was boiling with excitement in anticipation of the classic derby between Boca and River Plate.

The potential rivalry between Maradona and Brindisi had by now been replaced by an effective partnership, Maradona proving his talent for facilitating moves as well as leading them, and often timing his passes for Brindisi to finish off. This, however, was the match in which Maradona established himself as the superior player. Boca thrashed River 3–0, with Maradona scoring all three goals. Of the three, one went down in the annals of Boca history as one of the most brilliant ever seen. Maradona took the ball from inside his own half and kept it close to him as he ran down the middle of the pitch, leaving opponents, including class players of the ilk of Passarella and Gallego, one after the other outmanoeuvred along the way. He then came face to face with Fillol, the international goalkeeper. Instead of striking the ball, Maradona cheekily dribbled it round Fillol with his right foot, leaving him looking like a collapsed scarecrow on the ground. Miraculously, one of River's defenders, Tarantini, had managed to get in behind Fillol and now stood determined to play second stop. Making an undignified dive, Tarantini, another experienced international, was left spread-eagled. Maradona side-stepped one more time before taking the ball with him into the net, his tongue out as always when he moved in for the kill.

In seconds, Maradona had made two of the country's top players look like amateurs, while crowning himself unrivalled king. Any uncertainty that might have lingered in the minds of his officials and team mates dissipated in an instant as La Bombonera erupted with cries of 'Diego, Diego' and 'Maradoona, Maradoona'. The euphoria was no less on the Boca bench. Marzolini and Cyterszpiler rose spontaneously to their feet, Marzolini holding his arms out to embrace Maradona while Cyterszpiler turned to absorb the roar from the terraces behind. The sheer emotion and excitement of watching Maradona that day proved too much for Marzolini. A few hours after the game he had a heart attack.

Marzolini survived. The celebration continued. Nothing perhaps summarized the collective sentiment better than the headline of a leading Argentine tabloid the next day. Occupying a whole front page, it proclaimed 'BOCA IS GARDEL!' By invoking the figure of the late Carlos Gardel, the newspaper had identified Maradona's performance with the joy and inspiration of Argentina's most celebrated tango singer, and the maximum cultural expression of a whole people.

In the following matches, Maradona's star rose in direct correlation to Brindisi's falling, the twenty-one-year-old soon overtaking the veteran as the team's main goal scorer. Maradona himself underlined the extent to which the team had moved from a position of scarcely suppressed envy to one of necessary dependence. With Marzolini convalescing and the fans overwhelmingly behind him, there was no one able or willing to contradict him. After another inspired performance in May 1981, Maradona commented, 'Today I played much more than before. And that's because my team mates now have confidence in me. They know that they can pass me the ball even if I've got someone marking me. They realize that I can get round an opponent and create a favourable situation. Silvio [Marzolini] now tells them they needn't fear passing the ball to me, I won't let them down. And I can't think of anything that I want more than to have the ball at my feet. It's the most beautiful thing that football can give one!'

Two months later, on 4 August, Boca was within striking distance of the championship. Facing Central of Rosario in an away match, Boca needed just a draw to confirm its leadership of the league. One goal down, it got its first and last opportunity at goal when in the seventy-sixth minute a penalty was awarded in its favour. It was taken by Maradona, and wasted. The ball curved upwards off his left foot, hitting the crossbar before bouncing over and out. Maradona screamed, his eyes shut, his face contorted, as if he'd been struck by the devil.

A week later, destiny was at his feet again in a match against Racing. Another penalty, this time struck with confidence straight into the net just before half-time, proved decisive. Maradona celebrated by looking up at the sky, giving thanks to God and blessing himself. At the end of the match, the champions made their triumphant progress around the circuit amid an unprecedented delirium of exploding fireworks and chanting which echoed across the waterfront and the centre of Buenos Aires. Ahead of the other players ran Maradona, half-naked and surrounded by fans, including his kid brother Lalo who had put on Diego's number 10 shirt. Jostled and pushed, his head arched back and his arms outstretched in a pose of semi-crucifixion, Maradona seemed voluntarily to have delivered his very self to the people. He would later reflect, 'At that moment I understood that Boca is pure devotion, that people live by and for Boca. I see the fans reflected in the eyes of Antonio Labat, an old man who works as a parking attendant down in the city. I promised him that I would give it my all. I hope I made him happy.'

The championship was won with blood, sweat and tears. And yet for all the euphoria, the honeymoon between the young Maradona and Boca did not prove open-ended. Three weeks later, in the midst of a deepening economic crisis, the club found itself unable to pay the latest instalment of its transfer agreement with Argentinos Juniors and was thrown into a highly publicized court action for alleged breach of contract. At the same time Boca's bank accounts were frozen by order of the Central Bank after a series of cheques bounced. They included one written out to Maradona Productions. Foreign interest in Maradona, still tactically dominated by Barcelona, revived as San Pablo of Brazil made an offer of $7 million for the player.

Maradona returned from an exhausting and uninspired twenty-day European tour with Boca to find that he no longer commanded the veneration of his people. Envy and suspicion simmered beneath the surface, as did the thought that Boca would not have found itself in such financial trouble had it not been for the exorbitant price put on the head of its star player.

Seemingly overlooked as people debated the financial crisis were the records which Maradona had set. Still only twenty years old, he had played 200 first-division matches, in addition to internationals and friendlies. He had scored nearly 140 goals, an average of 0.68 per game, although this figure underestimated his contribution to the game, taking no account of the goals he created for others. In thirty-three games played for Boca, he had scored twenty. When he scored a goal in his 200th game, he celebrated the occasion with a characteristic *coup de théâtre*, jumping across the moat that separates the pitch from the terraces and throwing himself like a delirious monkey on to the wired fence. This display of solidarity with the fans cost him a one-match suspension from the AFA, but made him hugely popular. It was the second week of October, and Boca's financial problems were yet to be exposed.

Maradona was already suffering from the pain of an on-off

injury to his left thigh. It was treated again mainly with pain-killing injections because of the pressure to have him playing continuously. Contractually he was committed to playing a minimum number of games, in addition to attending to the advertising and other public engagements signed through Maradona Productions. Abroad, in particular, he found just how commercially dependent Boca, and to a lesser extent the Argentine national team, had become on him. The presence of Maradona was made a necessary condition of most fixtures.

By 19 October Maradona could no longer hide the fact that he was feeling the strain. In an interview with *Clarín*, he begged for the first time to be allowed to take a break from football: 'I want a break not just from training and matches, but from travelling. People are talking a lot about me, and in the process they are deforming Maradona the human being, and I've got to avoid that . . . sure it's true that everything I have I owe to football. But I need to be able to go on enjoying the game and not feel it like a weight that tortures me.'

It seemed a long time since Marzolini's statement that all players were equal. Too much was at stake, not least Argentina's prospects in the forthcoming World Cup, for Maradona to be told to shut up and get on with it. He was allowed to take a break, but it was not easy to find a place to escape to. His leisure, like his football, has become the copyright of the nation. Maradona longed to wake up and feel that he was still the poor kid from Villa Fiorito simply graced with a mystical touch at his feet. He wished only for the protection of his family and the loyalty of close friends, to be considered by the rest of the world as just one more Argentine who loved his country.

The previous summer he had returned with his parents to Esquina. There he struggled to find himself along the river bank where his parents had been born, living the uncomplicated rural life. He went fishing and hunting, camped under the stars on a remote island, sang songs with friends round a log fire. The football he played was the football his father and uncle had played: kicking a ball around with the other men of Esquina for the sheer enjoyment of it. For a short spell, Maradona rediscovered the basic humanity he thought he had lost forever.

While he was there the town's local historian, with a love of the people and the place, passed Maradona a sheet of paper and asked him to write down why he had chosen to spend his holidays in Esquina with Claudia and his family. Maradona's reply was simple, written with the basic vocabulary and strained grammar of someone whose formal education had been cut short: 'I came here because Esquina is beautiful, because I have relatives and friends here, because it is where my parents were born . . . I love the river . . . and the women are so straightforward and warm. They are happy, too, and know how to respond to friendship when it is deserved . . .' The original of the sheet of paper with Maradona's childlike scrawl was shown to me when I visited Chitoro's home town fifteen years later. The local historian had kept it among his most precious mementos, like a relic.

Yet even in Esquina, Maradona was denied his idyll. His visit coincided with the town's annual carnival. On the main night, Maradona became the focus of attention as he danced in the streets with the protagonists, his moves, among the frilly-dressed local girls, captured by local photographers. Later in the evening the Maradona family were given VIP treatment, as officials led them to the presidential platform at a charity dance where the presence of the footballer had been billed as the main attraction. Maradona was asked to make a contribution to the local old people's home.

Maradona didn't return to Esquina the following year. When he was given his leave of absence by Marzolini, he chose instead to go to Las Vegas to watch one of his favourite boxers in a title fight. He was followed by journalists and their cameramen. The image captured and relayed back to Argentina was one not of escape but of conspicuous consumption: Diego alongside a swimming pool at Caesar's Palace.

In January 1982, Maradona gave one of the more revealing interviews of his career to Guillermo Blanco, a journalist with the Argentine football magazine *El Gráfico*. His statements threw light on a number of aspects to his character. Firstly it was clear to what extent he had lived and continued to live for his parents: 'I always felt that if I became a good player my parents would feel good and I would be able to give my family things which they had never had . . . I want to be El Pelusa, the boy that my mother loves, and loved by his family. That is my truth. That is my life.'

At the same time, he saw in the poverty of his background a justification for what he had become: 'I can talk about poverty because I lived it. Because my father worked much harder than I do and earned the bare necessary so that we wouldn't starve.

That is why I can say that poverty is something ugly. One wants a whole lot of things and yet one can only dream about them.' And he talked about the 'nostalgia' he felt for Villa Fiorito, 'because it was there that I did some beautiful things and some ugly things'. He confessed to having friends there who had not been as fortunate but made no excuses for having become rich. 'I'm happy with what I'm paid and I would like them to be happy too.'

So what made Maradona so different that he had succeeded where others hadn't? Did he feel privileged? 'Sure, I am. But only because God has wanted it to be so. Because God makes me play well. That is why I always make the sign of the cross when I walk out on to the pitch. I feel I would be betraying him if I didn't do that.'

Maradona spoke to Blanco towards the end of an international tour in which Boca had played several friendlies in the United States and the Far East. By then his escapade to Las Vegas and a subsequent refusal to train with the national team had been forgiven by Argentina at large as an unfortunate but temporary flip. The tour had confirmed that in countries where football was adopting an increasingly commercial edge Maradona was becoming eminently saleable.

In the United States, Maradona was already in that small privileged group of international football players who had been noted by those vested interests with an eye to the future. In 1980, the strange US hybrid of semi-retired or retiring millionaire 'stars', Cosmos, had arranged to play a friendly against Argentinos Juniors, on condition that Maradona's presence was guaranteed. Two years later Maradona was thought of by some in the US as an indispensable long-term investment, a key element in any future plan to ensure the commercial success of a World Cup held in the country. Boca was invited to Los Angeles, where they played against El Salvador. Maradona was in his element playing before a largely Latino crowd.

In Japan, where football was becoming an increasingly popular sport through the medium of TV, Maradona was followed everywhere like a superstar. The Japanese had not forgotten his performance in the 1979 Youth Championship. Forever looking towards the West for material that could be copied and improved upon, the Japanese footballing authorities and the advertisers linked to them had no doubt that Maradona was the role model for guaranteed excitement and skill. The Argentine media glowingly reported on the adulation with which Maradona was followed by his Japanese fans. The Japanese snapped him incessantly with their cameras, pestered him for autographs, begged him for sample locks of his hair. They bought T-shirts in his honour, and watched him live and on TV. Maradona shot a commercial and played with Japanese children in a couple of exhibition play-arounds. With Boca, he appeared in two friendlies against the Japanese national team, one in the Kobe Chua stadium, another in Tokyo's Olympic stadium. The Japanese loved him, not least because he was short and stocky like so many of them, thus proving that football can be played by anyone. It's just a question of copying.

10

THE FALKLANDS FACTOR

On 21 February 1982, General Leopoldo Galtieri visited the Argentine World Cup squad in the training ground near Buenos Aires. There, in the presence of TV cameras, he singled out Diego Maradona and embraced him. Since the early half of the twentieth century, when football had begun to be a hugely popular sport in the country, successive Argentine presidents had ignored it at their peril. But Galtieri had a special interest in making sure that the symbol of Argentina's footballing success was on his side.

Soon after coming to power in a bloodless coup at the end of 1981, Galtieri had begun secretly planning the most ambitious political project in Argentine military history: the recovery by force of Las Malvinas, the British-owned Falkland Islands which Argentina had claimed as hers for over 150 years. The military régime had become convinced that the move would unite the nation and neutralize the first signs of real political opposition since the coup. Among those who had spoken out against the junta was César Menotti, the Argentine coach. A virtual untouchable since winning the 1978 World Cup, Menotti risked little by criticizing the régime's poor economic and social record.

In Maradona, the régime still felt they had a star they could manipulate. He seemed, in his public statements, to be either politically naive or simply disinterested. A month earlier, he had expounded at some length on his life and football generally, but when asked the question, 'What about politics?', his reply had been, 'I don't know, I wouldn't know who to choose . . . All I want is for my country to be the best in the world.'

Maradona seemed certain that he could contribute to making his country just that. He was, he assured the interviewer, ready to give his whole being to ensure victory in the World Cup. 'I'm going to get ready so that I won't disappoint anybody. My dream is that Argentina comes out champion again.' Galtieri liked that. Equally welcome was Menotti's decision to reconcile himself with Maradona after relations between the two had hit their lowest point since 1978. Menotti had suspended Maradona when he returned from his holiday in Las Vegas because of his refusal to train. By the time of the Galtieri visit, however, Maradona was back in the team. 'Maradona may not be 100 per cent fit, but he is the only key player we have covering 75 per cent of the pitch,' Menotti said in justification for his indulgence.

Both Galtieri and Menotti hoped that Maradona would buckle down. He didn't, at least not to the extent expected of him. In the months leading up to the World Cup, Maradona showed himself to be utterly unpredictable. He still refrained from overtly political pronouncements, but he was becoming publicly critical of some of the vested interests behind the football industry. By so doing he was threatening to undermine the tactical, political and commercial alliances which had built up around his star status. He spoke out against club officials 'who seem more concerned that enough photographs are taken of them, than with making their clubs better'. On 28 March, as ignorant as the rest of the world that Galtieri had just given the secret signal for the invasion of the Falklands, Maradona also complained about the long training sessions to which members of the national squad were being subjected, arguing that the players would play better if they were given more time to be with their families.

Just four days earlier, while Galtieri and his generals were locked in permanent session Maradona had given a less that inspired performance during a friendly match against West Germany before a crowd of nearly 80,000 people at the River Plate stadium. The match was witnessed by British journalist Hugh McIlvanney. Writing in the *Observer*, McIlvanney commented that Maradona was 'deservedly recognized by just about everyone from here to the Angel, Islington, as the most exciting talent in football'. Yet during the match, Maradona had easily been upstaged by the twenty-one-year-old German midfielder, Lothar Matthäus. 'There was no evidence on the pitch,' McIlvanney reflected afterwards, 'that Maradona's pace or agility had been dramatically impaired. What counted was that his opportunities to exploit those and his other assets were deliberately and drastically limited.'

In fact, McIlvanney had underestimated the extent to which the young German had undermined Maradona's psychology by some tough tackling which left the Argentine's priceless left foot heavily bruised. Maradona missed further training sessions. He was given more injections. He went on playing. In the next friendly, against the Soviet Union in Buenos Aires, Maradona seemed so unfit that some fans whistled at him and shouted, 'Why don't you train?', as he was substituted well before the end. A few days later, he temporarily abandoned all thoughts of the World Cup and took off with Claudia on another voyage of escape and rediscovery – back to the fishing and hunting grounds of Esquina.

Unlike his previous trips to his father's birthplace, Maradona on this occasion acted like a man on the run, limiting his contact with the local population and aggressively rejecting any approaches from the local or national media. And yet even in moments of crisis, he could count on a sympathetic journalist to whom he could seemingly open his heart. Once again the journalist picked for the job was his old friend Guillermo Blanco of *Gráfico*. The conversation Blanco had with Maradona on a remote island led him once again to mediate between the footballer and the outside world. He had held Maradona in awe since first befriending him as a young player with Argentinos Juniors, and he wanted to see his idol back where he belonged, with the Argentine nation behind him.

The conversation that Blanco and Maradona had as they shared a barbecue round a camp fire revealed the symbiosis between journalist and player, but more importantly the fraught relations between the star and the nation that had created him:

BLANCO: I'm here because I'm looking for an answer that you can give the people, since lately there doesn't seem to be that communion that existed before. Tell me how you feel?

MARADONA: Firstly, what I feel, I tell my parents, my girlfriend, my brothers, and my friends. I don't want newspaper stories, regardless of whether I'm paid for them or not . . . With you I can talk because you're you . . .

BLANCO: I'm grateful for the deference, I really mean it, but without wanting to intrude on your life, I think that in some way you owe it to the people. Because the people have given you a lot . . .

MARADONA: Sure. I'm grateful to them for that. But sometimes people make mistakes . . . people shouted at me that I should train after the match with the Soviet Union . . . maybe they are the same people who think that I don't give my all, that I don't want to do things well . . .

BLANCO: I think the majority of people don't think that way, Diego. I think what the people want is for you and the rest of the team to give them good football, and happiness. I don't think there is any malice intended.

MARADONA: But people can't go on pressurizing me the way they do in this country. It's impossible. I don't understand it . . .

BLANCO: I want you to tell me what you feel, what state of mind you're in, that's why I've spent an hour and a half in a canoe trying to find you . . .

MARADONA: I'm calm enough. But be sure of one thing, I'm not going to take the applause the way I did before, because the people did not know how to wait for me . . . I'm going to score goals for my team mates, for those who love me, and nobody else . . .

BLANCO: I respect your opinion, but I don't know up to what point it is wise to have such an attitude. You have deservedly earned a name for yourself on merit, a personality which because of your public standing you should strengthen. I'm worried that you don't seem to know how to deal with this . . .

MARADONA: I do know . . . The only thing that I want to do is give a good life to my children, and to my mother. I'm very clear about that.

BLANCO: You seem to me to be trapped in a corner, and yet out there there are a whole lot of beautiful things which maybe you don't fully appreciate. Among them the huge wish people have that you give them a little more, to make them happy when they watch football.

MARADONA: What the people have to understand is that Maradona is not a machine for making them happy. He is not a machine that gives kisses and smiles. I'm a normal bloke, common and down-to-earth who happens sometimes to make people happy, sure, and that makes Maradona happy too. But the fact is that people think differently if Maradona doesn't do things right sometimes or has one or ten bad games. And why can't they forgive Maradona? It sometimes takes just one game in which Maradona doesn't play well or doesn't score a goal, and all hell lets loose. Firstly because Maradona is fat, then because he should cut his hair . . . and it's at that point that you feel rotten inside. That's the truth.

While Maradona and Blanco were thus engaged in contemplative discourse in the outback of Corrientes, thousands of young Maradona lookalike conscripts forcibly recruited from the province and other backward areas of northern Argentina were beginning to discover for the first time the reality of war after being sent to the Falkland Islands. At the beginning of May, a British submarine torpedoed the Argentine battle cruiser *General Belgrano* with the loss of 365 lives. Argentine retaliation, in the form of a devastating Exocet attack on HMS *Sheffield*, quickly followed. The Argentine World Cup squad, once Maradona had rejoined it, did their bit for the cause by posing for a team photograph behind a banner which said 'LAS MALVINAS SON ARGENTINAS'. In the UK, feelings about the war had their way of expressing themselves. Argentines playing for local clubs found themselves jeered by groups of Union Jack-waving hooligans. The English Football Association subsequently thought it both prudent and sensitive to recommend that Ardiles and Villa be left out of the Tottenham side in the FA Cup final at Wembley.

Yet Maradona continued to pursue his own agenda. Behind the scenes, he authorized Cyterszpiler to resume transfer negotiations with Barcelona. The talks now involved more 'negotiators' than a European summit. They included Helenio Herrera, a man with an impressive football career: he had managed Barcelona and Inter Milan to various cup titles as well as the national teams of Spain, France and Italy. Never one for quiet diplomacy, Herrera emerged in Buenos Aires halfway through the Falklands War and confirmed publicly what Guillermo Blanco had gathered from his campfire therapy session, that Maradona was fed up with the pressure of Argentine fans and couldn't wait to escape to Barcelona.

The deal was finally reached in Buenos Aires over four days of talks at the end of May. While Argentine conscripts, faced with an approaching Antarctic winter and a British advance, dug deeper into the trenches, the wily president of Barcelona, José Luis Nuñez, judged that the time was right for his *coup de grâce*. Taking advantage of a generally confused political situation and the deepening financial crisis of Argentine football, he flew into Buenos Aires to set his seal personally on the Maradona transfer in joint talks with officials of Boca Juniors and Argentinos Juniors, the two clubs who still theoretically 'shared' the player. As César Menotti later recalled, 'When Nuñez arrived in Buenos Aires he finished the whole thing off. He put the money down, dealt with the two clubs and proved that he was more intelligent than anyone.'

In fact the negotiations were as bruising and acrimonious as a prize fight, with the tension focused on a clash of characters between Nuñez and Cyterszpiler. Nuñez came with a considered view of Maradona's agent as an Argentine upstart, uncouth and unqualified to deal with the sophisticated world of top international football. For his part, Cyterszpiler thought Nuñez – no taller than he was, and only slightly less plump – an aspiring dictator who with his arrogance and inflated sense of superiority personified the worst aspects of the Spanish Conquest of America.

Cyterszpiler liked to poke fun at a peculiarly Nuñez habit. During the talks, Nuñez would pace up and down the room with his hands behind his back, like Napoleon. So affected was he by the experience of dealing with the Cataláns, that when recalling the talks thirteen years later Cyterszpiler was still not short of expletives: 'Nuñez . . . what a son of a bitch, what a bastard of a dwarf. He was terrible!' he told me.

In the talks, Nuñez gave the impression that he was doing the Argentines a favour by taking Maradona off their hands. He started off by offering $6 million, a similar figure to that which had been paid a year earlier in the Argentinos Juniors/Boca transfer but which in real terms considerably undervalued the player given the devaluation of the Argentine peso. Cyterszpiler, with Maradona's blessing, held out for what he considered the player's real value as an international star: $7 million. 'I told him if he didn't like it, I'd go to Juventus instead,' Cyterszpiler said.

In the end Nuñez caved in, in return for a stipulation that Maradona would stay with Barcelona for at least six years, during which he was expected to play an intense programme of matches. The talks had taken place in countless venues and extended, off and on, over nearly four years. In their final stages, they were thrashed out in Cyterszpiler's house and in the Hotel Plaza, where once an innocent, wide-eyed young Maradona had been entertained to lunch by the sweet-talking emissary from Barcelona, Nicolau Casaus. When they had concluded, Nuñez and Cyterszpiler temporarily set aside their mutual antagonisms and treated themselves and the other negotiators to a blow-out dinner at Au Bec Fin, one of Buenos Aires' most exclusive French restaurants. It was all done in secret. There was, after all, a war going on. 'We wanted to get away from the press,' Cyterszpiler recalled.

They also all wanted their slice of Maradona. They were all there, the denizens of big-buck football, for that final round of negotiations: the agents, lawyer and bankers. One witness who had been with the negotiations from their first tentative beginnings put it to me like this: 'In the end, Maradona's transfer to Barcelona turned into a Persian market with everyone trying to make money out of it . . . hundreds of thousands of dollars were paid out. It was such a degrading spectacle. I thought to myself, all that work I've put into it, all that sacrifice, and it's come to this: everyone dividing up their little bits. I suppose, though, it was a good deal for Maradona. Barcelona paid well.'

During the Falklands War, the Argentine government underlined once again the close connection between politics and football. The heavily censored Argentine TV interwove nationalist slogans backing the junta's invasion of the islands with scenes of the country's 1978 World Cup victory. The theme was echoed in the football stadiums, attended by many of the same hired hooligans who were used to bring a popular feel to the anti-British demonstrations in the Plaza de Mayo. During the 1978 World Cup final between Argentina and Holland, the most popular chant had been 'He who does not jump is a Dutchman'. Under Galtieri, it became 'He who does not jump is an Englishman'. The chant reverberated around the River Plate stadium when Argentina played the Soviet Union in the early stages of the war. Among the many leaflets devised by and printed with funds from the Argentine intelligence services, was one of a cartoon baby gaucho – not unlike a child Maradona – dressed in football kit and accepting the surrender of an imperial British lion.

In the aftermath of the invasion of the Falklands, Argentine journalists were encouraged to disconnect with the reality of war and to confuse soldiers with footballers. A memorable example was provided on 1 May – the day the British bombed Argentine troops for the first time – by the commentary of Nicolas Kasanzew, who reported from the islands for one of the military-controlled TV stations. The occasion, representing as it did the first outbreak of serious hostilities on the islands, involving numerous casualties, should have been a cause for reflection. Instead Kasanzew described the advance of the British planes and the response of the Argentine artillery as if what was at stake was nothing more than an advance up the middle ordered by Kevin Keegan, and an equally speedy reaction led by Maradona. For Argentina's military junta, football was, as it had been in 1978, part of its political design; only this time it was to experience a miserable own goal when Argentina lost both the war and its championship.

When the war began in earnest, the junta let it be known that the Argentine national squad might consider pulling out of the World Cup out of respect for the nation's soldiers. It was an empty gesture to which the régime knew it would not be held – FIFA, under the presidency of João Havelange, had endeavoured to keep politics out of its competitions. Later, while Argentine conscripts fell hungry or were blown to bits in the hills around Port Stanley, Maradona agreed to a deal with Barcelona, which made him potentially a millionaire five times over in addition to paying him $70,000 a month. It was a payment nicknamed the Maradollar. One of the largest sums in transfer history, the deal set a new benchmark for the commercialization of international football. It also set aside the old controversy about whether or not Maradona should be allowed out of the country. The reality was, as Nuñez had rightly calculated, that no Argentine club could now afford him, and the régime's control on football, like so much else, was beginning to slip through its fingers. For his part Menotti had the assurance he wanted that Maradona would play in the national squad, as well as the prospect of being manager of Barcelona one day.

Four days before the start of the World Cup competition, Maradona pulled a hamstring during a training session. 'I feel as down as I did in 1978 when I was left out of the national squad. I just can't find a way of getting out of this mood,' he confided to Horacio Pagani of *Clarín*, who enjoyed a long-running friendship with the player. The thought that Maradona might not be fit and that Argentina would start the championship without their star player threw Menotti and his squad into a state of crisis. Menotti turned to his old friend, the team doctor Ruben Oliva, to see what he could do.

Menotti and Oliva shared the view that Maradona needed to be indulged. They believed that the only place he could realize himself as a personality was on the football pitch, and that everything was permitted as long as it ensured that end. As Menotti put it to me, 'Maradona has one place where he feels strong enough to confront the world, and that is when he is on top of the ball. Take a ball away from Maradona and it's like taking a Colt .45 away from a cowboy. He feels naked.'

Oliva had made a name for himself in Argentina as a result of his outspoken attacks on what, he alleged, was the widespread misuse of drugs and unnecessary surgery in the Argentine football league. He had set up a practice in Milan and had been awarded the Italian Order of Merit for services to the national Olympic team – an equivocal distinction given the reputation Italian athletic competitions had for widespread evasion of doping controls. Oliva was a controversial figure in more ways than one. Left wing politically, he had nevertheless, like Menotti, participated fully in the 1978 World Cup, writing a regular newspaper column extolling the physical virtues of Argentine footballers.

Oliva proclaimed that most injuries were less physical than symptomatic of a state of mind, and that his own powers of persuasion were sufficient to put a player back on his feet and on to the pitch again. Oliva was mistrusted by fellow doctors, but held in awe by some of his patients, who looked upon him less as a scientist than as a healer with magical powers. By the time of the World Cup in Spain he had begun to exert an unrivalled influence over Maradona. The player mistrusted orthodox doctors but in Oliva he saw reflected a medicine man – not unlike the witch doctors his parents had known in Corrientes – with mystical powers to heal the footballer sent by God.

On the eve of Argentina's opening World Cup tie with Belgium, Maradona was declared fit to play. Whether he would have been by any other doctor but Oliva is open to question. As subsequent events proved, will power is not in itself sufficient to win a match. On paper, Argentina looked the better side. Maradona still seemed to the outside world to have his reputation intact. In the words of one of international football's most experienced commentators, the British journalist Brian Glanville, Maradona was a host in himself, 'twenty-one years old, thick-thighed, enormously quick in thought and movement, a superb finisher and a fine tactician'. Behind him were lined up other stars including his former team mate from the youth championship, Ramón Díaz, his English 'adviser' Ossie Ardiles and the star of the 1978 championship, Mario Kempes.

The Argentines played wearily, however. Maradona himself showed little inspiration, only once seriously threatening the Belgian defence with a free kick that hit the crossbar. Belgium won 1–0. Argentina showed spark in a subsequent 4–1 win over Hungary, with Maradona demonstrating his own wide range of talents in a variety of moves, including two successful strikes at goal. After beating El Salvador, Argentina went into the next round. But the defending champions now lost against Italy and were finally eclipsed by Brazil in a bruising and humiliating encounter which ended with Maradona being sent off five minutes from the end for a blatant foul on the Brazilian half-back Batista. Argentina lost 3–1 and were eliminated.

The fading fortunes of Maradona in the World Cup in Spain coincided with the last days of the Falklands War and the collapse of the military régime in the aftermath of Argentina's surrender. With the possible exception of Ardiles – still a Tottenham player having to come to terms with the reality of Englishmen killing his own countrymen – no one in the Argentine squad was as traumatized by the effects of the war as Maradona. Before flying out to the World Cup, to the extent that he thought about the war at all, he had been content to believe the régime's propaganda that Argentina was winning it. When he arrived in Spain and saw the uncensored local coverage he was brought face to face with the reality on which he had turned his back. Maradona would later recall, 'We were convinced we were winning the war, and like any patriot my allegiance was to the national flag. But then we got to Spain and discovered the truth. It was a huge blow to everyone on the team.'

The links between politics and football had become so close under the military régime that it was perhaps inevitable that the Falklands defeat would also shatter the illusion of invincibility that had been built up around the figure of Maradona. In Spain, the player, like his team, was unable to count on the support which the régime had manipulated in Argentina's favour during the 1978 World Cup. On the contrary, the sense of national pride with which Maradona had been so identified lay in ruins on the Falklands battlefields. In Spain, Argentine journalists no longer felt, as they had been ordered to do in 1978, that they had to defend the honour of the national squad in all circumstances. The government had lost its power to intimidate, and Spain was well beyond its reach. Media coverage of the 1982 World Cup thus had a different focus. The Argentine squad was depicted as poorly motivated, lacking discipline and leisurely to the point of hedonism. And it was no exaggeration. In the luxurious seaside near hotel Alicante where the players stayed,

Menotti was repeatedly photographed emerging from his sleeping quarters with his arm around a German model. He was in fact being no more of a womanizer than he always had been, but he now stood accused of spending more time in bed than training his players. Among the more turbulent episodes, again witnessed by several journalists, one in particular seemed to sum up the mood of the Argentine squad: Tarantini's wife throwing a tantrum on the beach and threatening her husband that she would go to bed with another man.

It was in such an atmosphere that Maradona found himself subjected to the kind of public scrutiny he found so difficult to deal with. As far as local journalists were concerned, Maradona was no longer a symbol of Argentina's success, but just another example of its excesses. To the hotel he brought with him what the Spanish media now disparagingly referred to as the Maradona 'clan' – parents, brothers, sisters, cousins, friends and Claudia Villafane. Claudia's idea of public relations was to kiss Maradona in front of journalists and declare as loudly as possible, 'Dearest, you are a genius.' Domingo Trujillo, a reporter with the Spanish daily *MARCA*, noted in one dispatch how much the Maradona clan, and Diego in particular, ate and slept and generally seemed to do everything but train.

It is scarcely surprising, therefore, that Maradona began to develop a paranoid view of journalists and the public at large: they were either with him, or out to crucify him unfairly. But the comments of one person in particular seem to have overshadowed all the others: those of Pele, the former Brazil international, whose title as King of Football Maradona was supposed to inherit. Writing a guest column for *Clarín*, Pele suggested that Maradona's talents as a footballer were being undermined by his failings as a human being. 'My main doubt is whether he has the sufficient greatness as a person to justify being honoured by a worldwide audience,' Pele wrote.

Three years earlier, Maradona had made a pilgrimage to Rio de Janeiro to fulfil one of his childhood dreams: that of sitting and talking to Pele, a shanty-town kid like himself who had entered the hall of fame. In 1958, two years before Maradona was born, the seventeen-year-old Pele was already being described as the finest player ever to come out of Brazil. In 1970, when Maradona was ten, Pele took Brazil to World Cup victory in Mexico. In Spain, in 1982, Maradona felt betrayed by his idol, a resentment that was to fester for many years afterwards.

Pele's comments only helped to fuel another source of pressure on Maradona: a public debate in the Spanish press over whether Barcelona had paid too much for him. Not surprisingly the charge of extravagant spending was made by Madrid-based newspapers. By contrast Nuñez and other Barcelona directors used the local Catalán press to make the acquisition of Maradona a symbol of the club's power and ambition.

On balance, Maradona's experience of the 1982 World Cup was a bad one. His state of mind, which Menotti and Oliva had thought they were capable of influencing, was in the end undermined by the crude tactics of his opponents. It was the coach of the El Salvador team who bluntly identified Maradona as a prime target and Claudio Gentile, the Italian defender, who effectively neutralized him. Brian Glanville described Gentile's repeated fouling of Maradona – ignored by the referee – as a 'blemish on the match, the tournament and Italy's eventual success'. Maradona was clobbered, held and hacked to the point of being denied any room whatsoever to show off his talents.

Menotti may have been partly to blame for making Maradona play too far upfield and therefore more vulnerable to Gentile's tackling, although Maradona himself blamed the referee for not offering him sufficient protection, and the Italians for converting the magic that can be football into the crude punch-up of a street brawl.

For Maradona, the World Cup ended as it had begun – waiting for a plane to take him across the Atlantic. Only this time there were no crowds at the airport to give him a celebrated send-off, no media pack jostling for a quote, not even a single autograph hunter. He sat seemingly unnoticed and uncared for, just one more passenger waiting to board. In an immediate sense the public pressure that so worried him was off. But Maradona knew that he was facing an even tougher challenge now – the prospect of having to return to Spain and prove to the world that Barcelona had got their money's worth.

11

BREAKDOWN IN BARCELONA

Not since Eva Perón's visit to Franco's Spain in 1947 had the arrival of an Argentine generated such expectation among Cataláns. On Friday 4 June 1982, Diego Maradona, not yet twenty-two years old, accompanied by Jorge Cyterszpiler, flew into Barcelona to sign one of the biggest transfer deals yet seen in football. Surrounded by adoring fans and flashing cameras, he was hustled into a waiting limousine and driven the ten miles that separates the international Prat Airport from the enormous premises of Barcelona Football Club.

The signing ceremony took place in the club's main boardroom. It had all the pomp and circumstance of a peace treaty after a long war. Those present included the presidents of the two Argentine clubs involved, Boca Juniors and Argentinos Juniors. Across the table were the bankers, lawyers, middlemen and businessmen who made up the powerful body of Barcelona FC, one of the world's richest football clubs. Flanked by Juán Gaspart and José María Minguella, vice-president and middleman respectively, two of the sharpest brains in European football, sat club president José Luís Nuñez, a short, stocky megalomaniac who was now out to prove to the sceptics in Madrid that his club had the power and the money to deal with one of the most controversial football stars in the world.

Overlooking the whole scene was Jorge Cyterszpiler. He had no doubt that he had pulled off the biggest coup of his career as an agent. For over three years, he had played off one group of negotiators against another, so as continually to raise the value of his childhood friend turned international superstar. The precise details of the contract remained carefully guarded to protect the cast of characters who took a cut of it. But according to the club's official records, Barcelona formally agreed to pay a total of $7.3

million in six instalments, with Argentinos Juniors getting $5.1 million and Boca Juniors the remaining $2.2 million. Maradona himself would be paid a minimum of $50,000 per season, excluding perks and bonuses. In an annexe to the contract signed between Barcelona and Maradona's own company, the latter was described as having the only 'legitimate and exclusive rights to all advertising rights and merchandising of the name Maradona'. It envisaged additional income from sponsorship over a six-year period of $3 million.

The speeches had been perfectly scripted to match the occasion. The Boca president, Noel, spoke with the emotion of a father parting from his favourite son. He said he regretted Maradona's departure but reassured his new owners that the player would be worth every cent they'd paid for him. 'I congratulate Barcelona for signing the best player in the world. I have no doubt that Maradona is going to ensure success and provide wonderful entertainment,' Noel said. The president of Argentinos Juniors, Tessone, was not short of superlatives either, declaring that the day was a historic one for football: 'We now have the best player in the world playing for one of the biggest and greatest clubs in the world.'

Next spoke Maradona himself. There was those inside and outside that room who had long formed the opinion of him as a naive, rather unintelligent young footballer, open to manipulation by his agent. And yet once again Maradona, with a keen eye for the journalists listening in, played his cards exactly right, avoiding any comment about money and instead laying the emphasis where few had shown the guts to challenge him: his determination simply to play football to the best of his ability. 'A footballer's career is very short, so it's only logical that one should try and insure oneself against the future. I don't know if I'm expensive or cheap. What I can say and assure you is that I shall play with my whole heart so that Barcelona achieves all the success it deserves.'

Finally Nuñez spoke – half businessman, half chief celebrant – welcoming Maradona's sentiments and adding some advice of his own: 'Our economic success depends on our footballing success . . . the only thing I ask of Maradona is that he looks after his image on the field and shows himself humble with his colleagues.'

And yet for all the fine words and mutual backslapping that day, there was one image more than any other that should have conveyed a sense of impending disaster – the contrast between the long-haired, T-shirted Maradona, looking like a young colt squeezed into a horse-box, and the grave, sombre-suited Barca officials, self-assured in that panelled boardroom filled with trophies and portraits and thick leather furniture where football was summed up in two words: power and money.

Barcelona FC made Boca and Argentinos Juniors seem like amateur clubs by comparison. Its motto, 'More than a club', said it all. It was the biggest sports club in the world, with over 110,000 paid-up members and nearly 1,000 fan clubs from Peking to Ohio. Its premises in a modern suburb of Barcelona reduced La Bombonera, the Boca stadium where Maradona had won the Argentine league championship a year previously, to the memory of a rather squalid backyard. They consisted of an impressive complex of sporting and administrative facilities and museums – a mini city with the gigantic Nou Camp standing in the midst of it all as one of the great cathedrals of football.

Barcelona FC had got where it was thanks to politics. Founded in 1899 by a group of Swiss businessmen working in Barcelona, the club developed into a symbol of Catalán nationalism, taking its strength from the siege mentality imposed on it during the repressive Franco years. Cataláns had their political freedoms severely curbed by the régime, but they expressed their cultural identity in Nou Camp, turning each match against Real Madrid into a virtual declaration of independence, and the presidency of the club into the most important civilian post in Catalonia.

When Maradona signed his contract in 1982, Franco had been dead for seven years and Spain had a democratically elected government. Yet Barca remained unchanged in its attitude towards outsiders. It had retained its symbols of political freedom – Catalán flags and language – but also its essentially corporate structure: officials, managers, players and fans were supposed to be united behind the Barca ideal, with no room for deviation or indiscipline. At board level, vice-president Nicolau Casaus, who had been instrumental in awakening Barcelona's interest in Maradona, remained as the oldest club official. The club's president, José Luis Nuñez, was of a different ilk from the elderly diplomatist. Nuñez was a tough Basque-born businessman from the construction industry who ran the club like a personal fiefdom. You were either with him or out. He was looking forward to an extended term in office after shaking up the club's financial structure. Following his election in 1978 he had persuaded the club membership – effectively its shareholders – to advance and increase payment of their annual fees. With the additional revenue he increased the size of the Nou Camp and branched out into a range of new investments, including expanded seating arrangements and the purchase of Maradona.

In buying Maradona, Nuñez was aware of the risks he was taking. While a national hero in Argentina, Maradona was still untested professionally in any club outside his own country. His less than impressive performance in the World Cup – his first real international challenge – had revived scepticism in Spain about his true worth – most of all in Madrid.

Nuñez was determined to prove the sceptics wrong. He planned to exploit Maradona's talents to the full so as to maintain his renovated stadium at full capacity and keep new members flocking in. To do this, Nuñez knew he had to set his sights high. Barcelona had gone through a series of peaks and troughs over the previous decade, never quite recovering the greatness of the period of the management of Helenio Herrera or of its subsequent star foreign player, Johan Cruyff. It had just struggled to victory in the European Cup Winners' Cup, but to most Barca fans this seemed scant compensation for a poor performance in the previous league season, compared to arch-rival Real Madrid. Nuñez had his eyes firmly on the league championship and the European Cup, with the plethora of sponsorship and TV contractual rights these would entail. For his club to succeed he would need two things from Maradona, and two things only: discipline and success.

What soon became clear was that in Barcelona people were not prepared to indulge Maradona. They expected results and quickly, and had no time for the player's idiosyncrasies. On 28 July 1982, three weeks after Argentina were knocked out of the World Cup, Maradona took the field at the Nou Camp with the rest of the Barcelona team for the traditional start-of-the-season presentation ceremony. There were 50,000 fans there that day – a record for such an occasion – but Maradona's popularity was temporarily eclipsed by that of Bernd Schuster, the star of West Germany's triumph in the 1980 Nations Cup, who had subsequently been signed by Barcelona. It was cries not of 'Maradooooona' but of 'Schuuuster' that reverberated round the Nou Camp. The German midfielder was on his way to recovery from a knee injury which had kept him out of the World Cup.

The third foreign 'star' in the Barcelona line-up was the Danish international Allan Simonsen. Because of rules restricting the number of foreigners playing in a Spanish club side to two in any match, it was widely expected that the Dane would become the fall guy, leaving Schuster and Maradona as the main driving forces behind the remodelled team, managed by the German Udo Lattek. Maradona himself seemed to have no doubt that he had reached an important crossroads in his career. 'The moment of truth has arrived for me,' he declared. 'I haven't come here to convert myself into the star of the team, but into one more of the team, because Maradona alone cannot win matches. That's why I hope that I and my team mates can help each other to ensure that Barcelona becomes champion.'

From the outset Maradona went out of his way to win the confidence of his Barcelona team mates. He struck up an early friendship with one of the team's most popular players, 'Lobo' Carrasco, who had been headhunted from the club's youth team. Carrasco, two years older than Maradona, was a good communicator, prepared both to offer advice and to listen. For his part, Maradona was still shell-shocked from his encounters with Barcelona's officials and warmed to Carrasco's lack of arrogance. They shared a room at the club's pre-training camp in Andorra. In conversations lasting sometimes late into the night, Maradona poured out his feelings about his new contract. Off the field and out of the media glare, Carrasco found an honesty and straightforwardness in the Argentine which belied his star status.

'I was very impressed by his humility, and how essentially human he was. In Argentina he had become a demi-god, but with me he seemed only too conscious of his roots. He made me realize how much he had struggled to get to where he was and how much he still felt he had to achieve to secure the future of his family. He came across as a kid full of dreams. He seemed to be still terribly innocent and hungry. His eyes were like two big plates. He wanted to eat the world, and that scared me. The more friendly I became with him, the more I worried about him, the more I feared it would all end in tears,' recalled Carrasco.

Whatever insecurity showed itself in the privacy of their shared room instantly dissipated when a football came into the equation. 'He was like a chameleon. On the football pitch he'd be transformed. He was so sure of himself. He seemed to have total control of the ball. When Maradona ran with the ball and dribbled his way through the defence, it seemed he had it tied to his boots. I remember our early training sessions. The rest of the team would just stop and watch him. No one seemed to generate such interest. We all felt it was a real pleasure just to be able to witness what he could do.'

Maradona was only too conscious of the awe in which he was held by some of his colleagues. Talking about his time at Barcelona over ten years later, he described Carrasco as his 'accomplice', although there was no doubt in his mind who had learned more from the other: 'Carrasco tried to imitate everything I did. He understood everything very quickly and made enormous progress alongside me.' During much of his career, Maradona's very presence in a team tended to overshadow and diminish the less experienced players. But in Barcelona, local players like Carrasco drew inspiration from him. The respect of his team mates in turn helped boost Maradona's self-confidence in the early games he played for Barcelona, during which he demonstrated some of his magic.

While clearly unused to Udo Lattek's hard training methods, Maradona started the season, as had been widely predicted, forming the team's foreign tandem alongside Schuster. Simonsen was left on the bench. Lattek declared that the German and the Argentine complemented each other perfectly. And they did, initiating and combining brilliant moves from their midfield positions and driving home goals reminiscent of the golden days of Cruyff. In one of the early matches, against Barcelona's local rival Español, Maradona also showed that he was capable of drawing on some extraordinary hidden resources. Still only half recovered from a leg injury, he persuaded Lattek to bring him on at half-time when Español was holding Barcelona to a goalless draw. Within minutes he had contributed to the game's one and only goal. Eleven days later, the Barcelona team left the stadium in Belgrade to a prolonged standing ovation after a stunning European Cup Winners' victory against Red Star. Maradona and Schuster scored two goals each, ensuring a 4–2 win over the Yugoslav champions.

Had it been any other team than Barcelona, this auspicious beginning would simply have turned into the first stage of a successful team benefiting from a six-year contract with a talented player. But the combined characters of Nuñez, Lattek, Schuster and Maradona, in the stifling atmosphere that was Barcelona FC, proved an explosive and destructive mix.

Maradona never really lost the respect of his colleagues for his sense of camaraderie. He is still remembered for the way he used to pick up the balls after the training sessions, a gesture usually left to the water boys. But what from early on filled players like Carrasco with apprehension was the thought of whether he would cope with the pressures of not being able to lead the life he had grown used to leading in Argentina. The history of Barcelona FC showed how easily foreigners divided between success stories and disasters, sometimes provoked by an underlying racism. During the 1970s the fortunes of Johan Cruyff had contrasted with those of the coloured Peruvian Hugo Sotil. While Cruyff learned Catalán and settled down with his family, the poorly educated Sotil earned the nickname the King of Mambo for his nightlife exploits. Cruyff used his skills to establish himself as an unrivalled star European player, while Sotil was condemned both on and off the field, and left Barcelona in disgrace.

Carrasco had a simple message for the new boy Maradona: buckle down or else the club will destroy you. 'I recalled the experiences of other foreigners and told him: be careful when you go out at night. Monday or Tuesdays are OK but if you go out on a Friday before a match, be much more careful, and don't let the local media catch you.' It was advice that Maradona found it difficult to follow – to his enormous cost.

However great the solidarity he established between himself and his team mates, it proved insufficient to offset the feeling of alienation that began to undermine Maradona in Barcelona almost from the outset. Less than a month into the start of his first season, he withdrew temporarily from the team with a pulled muscle. He refused to be treated by Barcelona's medical team, regarding them as little better than stooges of the club's money-obsessed officials. Instead he insisted on having his old friend Dr Oliva flown over from Milan. He also took on as his personal trainer Fernando Signorini, one of the local Argentine residents who had recently joined the Maradona clan. Signorini's energy, ease of manner, and youthful good looks belied the fact that he was ten years older than Maradona and seemingly a little overaged for the job of bringing one of the world's most famous footballers to peak fitness. He had recently arrived in Barcelona, newly married and looking for better opportunities than those on offer in his native Argentina.

He took a job as a night watchman in the Paseo de Gracia, where some of Barcelona's most expensive apartments are to be found.

On his days off he began to frequent Barcelona's training sessions near the Nou Camp. Thanks to his wife, he managed to penetrate Maradona's inner circle. She worked as a tennis instructress at a private club frequented by Maradona's girlfriend Claudia and one of his younger brothers, Lalo. Lalo was as mediocre at tennis as he was at football but he enjoyed a successful series of matches in a local championship after the club teamed him up with one of the top-seeded players. Signorini subsequently found himself invited for the first time to the Maradona home and offered the job of personal trainer by Maradona on Claudia's recommendation.

It was an offer Signorini knew he couldn't refuse. 'I told Diego that having someone as unknown as me as a personal trainer could lay him open to criticism. He told me, "To hell with what people may think. I need you." I felt gobsmacked. He'd offered me a job people would die for.'

Such was the world Maradona was creating around himself – a world of personal alliances based on unwritten codes of loyalty and protection not unlike those Maradona's parents had known in Esquina, and the family had developed in Villa Fiorito. It was a world in which Maradona could move as lord and master, indulging himself and being indulged, to the detriment of his relations with the club that had bought him.

Both Oliva and Signorini shared the view that Maradona was a special player with special needs and that only they knew what these were. But Barcelona doctors regarded themselves as the best in Spain and did not like being lectured to by a South American medicine man. For his part, the orthodox and authoritarian Lattek, the German manager, had banned Cyterszpiler from his training sessions, having taken the view that Maradona's friend and agent was a bad influence. He equally looked upon the appearance of the amateurish Signorini as an insult to his profession.

From then on there was a growing lack of communication between Maradona and Barcelona's hierarchy. Maradona may have shown humility in the changing rooms, but in other aspects of his personal life he seemed determined to pursue his own agenda on his own terms. Barcelona is a city of grandiose buildings and elaborate design, but the palatial home Maradona chose for himself in the rich neighbourhood of Pedralbes would not have been out of place in Hollywood. Maradona had it redesigned to include indoor fountains, a swimming pool painted in the colours of Barcelona and enough floor space to accommodate his extended family and friends. 'It was the kind of house that knocked you back. It was so over the top. It was so big that it was asking to be filled up,' Juan Carlos Laburu, Maradona's personal cameraman and one of his early guests, recalled. Maradona remembers his stay in Barcelona as the 'unhappiest period of my career', with particular misery setting in the first Christmas he found himself away from Argentina, and with only his mother to comfort him. 'I felt separated from the rest of my family and from Claudia,' he said.

But it was not long before Maradona and Tota were joined in the villa at Pedrales by Claudia, his sister Maria, and her husband Gabriel. Chitoro came and went, preferring to look after the family affairs in Argentina. Other residents included a group of friends and hangers-on who had grown up with Maradona from his early days and now counted on his protection. One of them was Oswaldo Buona, a former Argentinos Juniors player who had never made the grade in his home country but whom Maradona had managed to get into a second-division Catalán team during his final negotiations with Barcelona. Another was Ricardo Ayala, 'El Soldadito' – 'Little Soldier'. Ayala had been abandoned as a young child in Esquina and he had spent the early years of his life as an urchin, begging or stealing, before being taken into care by a middle-aged couple and forced to go to school. Maradona had met him on one of his first visits to his father's homeland when Ayala was working as a houseboy for a local businessman. The two boys had gone fishing together. Maradona liked Ayala's ability to crack a good joke, his adventurous spirit and seeming irreverence towards anyone in authority. He subsequently offered Ayala a job as his chauffeur and general bodyguard. In his new employment, El Soldadito was encouraged to make a virtue out of remaining both tough and streetwise. Both Buona and El Soldadito reminded Maradona of some of the friends he had as a young boy in Villa Fiorito and whom he had had to leave behind on the road to success. Faced with the cold sophistication and social snobbery of Barcelona, Maradona needed them as much as he needed his family. He trusted in their loyalty, but above all he could afford to be himself in their presence.

They in turn discovered that while they enjoyed Maradona's patronage, the world could be transformed. Buona has spoken of the great 'adventure' of following Maradona to Barcelona. He has said of his time there, 'I discovered a very beautiful city where it was possible to lead a life similar to that in Buenos Aires. On

Sundays and Mondays we would do just as we did in BA, go clubbing. The nightlife really buzzed along the Ramblas.' The Ramblas, Barcelona's famed boulevard stretching from the centre down to the waterside, could deliver all things to all men: flower shops and coffee shops, restaurants and sex shows.

The Maradona tribe grew to include fellow team players and an assortment of Argentines resident in Barcelona who provided a range of personal services. Maradona discovered that there was a fellow countryman willing to cater for his every need: the pizzaman who produced a Calabresi just like in the old quarter of Buenos Aires near to the Boca stadium; the barman who cut thin white sandwiches just like the ones Maradona had enjoyed at his teenage birthday parties. There was a friend to provide the best Argentine meat for barbecues, and a friend to hire out videos and provide tapes of Julio Iglesias, Maradona's favourite singer. In Pedrales, Maradona created a world within a world, a sort of Buenos Aires in microcosm, with its Villa Fiorito-style tribal unit to provide comfort.

The main point of contact for the Pedrales castle was not with Barcelona FC but with Maradona Productions. The company's European headquarters were installed by Cyterszpiler in one of Barcelona's most luxurious office blocks and renamed First Champion Productions. Cyterszpiler had an immediate row with the landlords when without their permission he turned part of the office into a kitchen in order to have one of his favourite foods – a bowl of pasta – near at hand at all times. The landlord complained that the smell pervaded the whole block and accused Cyterszpiler of living like a gypsy. He was told to get rid of his kitchen or get out. The kitchen was made inoperable. Thus did Cyterszpiler begin to find out that he could not take life for granted in Barcelona.

And yet he did not allow himself to be demoralized. He stayed on in the office and brought in accountants and secretaries for the purpose of keeping the tax authorities and other potentially embarrassing intruders at bay. He also installed a film crew he had hired in Buenos Aires and set about pursuing one of his more ambitious projects. Using archive material smuggled out of Argentina and additional exclusive footage shot by his own crew, Cyterszpiler began preparing material for 'A Life of Maradona' in twelve languages to be commercialized worldwide. A seventy-minute video with accompanying soundtrack was subsequently prepared using state-of-the-art techniques in separate studios in

Los Angeles and New York, bringing the total cost of production to over $1 million.

Cyterszpiler then began to pursue an advertising deal with McDonald's, the US hamburger chain, and the photographic company AGFA, similar to the ones he had struck with Puma and Coca-Cola prior to the World Cup. In a sense First Champion Productions, with its crude appeal to commercialization, seemed a world removed from the uncomplicated life which Maradona sought with his family and friends. And yet the one world depended on the other. The successful marketing of Maradona projected the player as a simple family man who had become an international star thanks to his genius on the football pitch. This was the Maradona that was supposed to get Spanish parents and children away from the tapas and the wine, and lining up for the Big Macs and cans of Coke. We could all be Maradonas if we wanted to, the admen were saying.

And yet in the real world of Barcelona, some men proved more equal than others. However sympathetically Maradona wished to be judged, the world he created for himself was viewed with increasing disdain by senior officials of Barcelona FC. They were rarely invited to Maradona's home, but the reports they heard from other players and their allies in the local press were sufficient to confirm them in their view that the player was behaving like a degenerate adolescent. They were told that the Maradona mansion contained enough pornographic videos to make Copenhagen seem saintly by comparison; that alongside the occasionally civilized barbecues there were also outrageous parties lasting into the early hours of the morning with prostitutes in attendance, and guests inevitably ending up in the swimming pool. As Ramón Miravitillas, the deputy editor of the mass-circulation magazine *Interviú*, recalled at the time, 'My relationship with Maradona during the time he was in Barcelona consisted of me having to listen to, and seemingly discredit, a stream of approaches from young women with old, tired and sad eyes who in exchange for some money were happy to tell me how much and by whom they'd been fucked during the intimate parties organized by the clan.'

About the only member of the Barcelona board who had shown himself consistently sympathetic towards Maradona was Nicolau Casaus. But even he grew increasingly despondent, blaming not so much Maradona himself as the world which surrounded him for the player's unhappiness: 'Maradona arrived in Barcelona saying he was prepared to give the club his all. I believed him. It seemed very typical of him – all heart, the head doesn't come into it. But then as the days went by I realized that he had no control over his own life. It was Cyterszpiler who did. I realized that the first time I went to visit Maradona at his new home. He was surrounded by seven to eight people, including Claudia. It was a human wall and I couldn't get through it,' Casaus lamented when I interviewed him in 1995.

Barcelona FC officials disliked having to spend an increasing amount of management time sifting through the rumours only to discover that the facts were the kind they would prefer not to have to live with. The dubious activities of the 'Clan Maradona' were spreading beyond the walls of the Pedrales castle to the closely monitored jet-set scene of the city. Here the tension between the local monied classes and the 'Sudacas', as South American residents were disrespectfully called, surfaced in the gossip columns of the local press, with one incident in particular avidly picked up by the paparazzi. One evening Maradona and a group of friends and relatives decided to end a night out on the town with a visit to one of Barcelona's most exclusive nightclubs, downstairs at the 'Up & Down'. The 'clan' arrived laughing and talking loudly after a series of celebrations elsewhere. Soon, however, Maradona felt that his group were not being given the VIP service he felt they deserved but instead were being treated with coldness and animosity. Members present – mostly Cataláns – certainly made little effort to hide their disapproval of a group of people they saw as lacking any class or education. The precise sequence of events that evening was never fully clarified, but it would appear that at some stage Maradona and one or two of his friends made a rather unsophisticated attempt to pick up some of the women present, not all of whom were unaccompanied. A brawl developed, and Maradona was asked to leave the club.

Of the many rumours that reached officials of Barcelona FC, only one seems to have been consciously suppressed. This was that at some of the parties held at Pedrales, and during some of his nights out on the town, Maradona took drugs. According to some reports, at certain nightclubs he had a habit of disappearing into the bathroom with friends and emerging several minutes later with glazed eyes. The suspicion was that he had been snorting cocaine. Maradona waited sixteen years before confessing publicly that a life-long drug habit had had its tentative beginnings in Barcelona.

While he lived there he dismissed half the stories written about him as lies, and threatened journalists he didn't like with charges of libel.

'The first time that I tried cocaine was in Barcelona in 1982, when I was only twenty-two years old. I did it because I wanted to feel alive. In football, as in other walks of life, drug-taking has always existed. It's not just a present-day problem. I want to make one thing very clear. I was not the only one who began taking drugs. Lots of others were at it as well,' Maradona said in January 1996.

When he was in Barcelona, Maradona's occasional coke-taking remained a secret known only to a close circle of loyal friends and suspected by others outside the clan who lacked the sort of proof that could stand up in the courts. So successfully did Maradona lie about his habit that he was paid by the Barcelona mayor's office to co-operate in an anti-drugs campaign. An advertisement showing a clean and healthy Maradona on a Catalán beach surrounded by equally clean and healthy young kids and the slogan 'Enjoy life. Drugs kill' was regularly shown on prime-time TV, with the sponsors apparently unaware that the player had either already snorted or was soon to snort his first line of cocaine.

There is no evidence to suggest that while he was at Barcelona Maradona ever took cocaine or any other illegal substance prior to a match or that he was ever dope-tested positively by his doctors. Officials had their suspicions, but kept the issue under wraps, judging it not serious enough to make a public fuss about. It was a position to which the club adhered rigorously for years after Maradona had left. When I interviewed senior officials of Barcelona in 1995, they insisted that Maradona's dope problems had began only after he had been transferred to Italy.

There were other issues on which senior officials of Barcelona FC were unable to turn a convenient blind eye. In early November 1982, scarcely two months after the start of the season, Maradona asked Lattek to give him a rest from the relentless programme of friendlies, league and international matches he had been forced to play since arriving in Barcelona. The request was rejected. Maradona travelled to France for another friendly, with the French champions Paris Saint-Germain. He went reluctantly but having kept his reputation among his fellow players intact. In an angry exchange with Barcelona officials he had insisted that all the players should receive the same large bonuses he was being offered. The Barcelona team, seemingly inspired by such solidarity, won 4–1, with Maradona recovering from his tiredness and contributing positively to the outcome.

That evening Maradona gathered his friends round him and persuaded half the Barcelona team to celebrate the victory by spending all night and most of the next morning in Parisian nightclubs. The 'celebrations' were followed by Catalán and French journalists and word got back to Nuñez that Maradona had taken the entire team out on the town. The club president was furious and in a statement issued in Barcelona while the team was still in Paris publicly rebuked Maradona. 'I never go out at night ... I'm going to have a word with Diego Maradona because all our fans want to see him play with efficiency on the pitch and with unimpeachable behaviour off it.'

Maradona replied defiantly that the way he conducted his life was 'my concern only' and added, 'I'll go out wherever I want. The life I lead outside the club shouldn't be of concern to anyone as long as it doesn't damage my capacity as an athlete and a player.'

According to Cyterszpiler, the public slanging match was a pale reflection of the dialogue he personally had with Nuñez. After reading Nuñez's statements in the press, Cyterszpiler, with Maradona's blessing, rang Barcelona from his Paris hotel. 'When I asked Nuñez for an explanation of why he had said what he had said, he told me that it was to show who was the boss. I said, "You're a son of a bitch."'

What became known as the 'the night in Paris row' brought to the surface a fundamental clash of personalities between Maradona and Nuñez. By instinct and upbringing, Maradona considered himself beyond good or evil, answerable only to himself because he had been chosen for greatness by God. Nuñez was, like Maradona, a small man who thought big, only his priorities were different. He had seen great players come and go at Barcelona, but none of them had succeeded through insubordination. Nuñez could not conceive of running the club with one of its star players turning revolutionary.

The tensions between the two men continued throughout Maradona's stay at Barcelona, always simmering and on occasion reaching a very public boiling point. Another memorable clash occurred in May 1983 when Nuñez refused to let Maradona travel with Schuster to Munich to play in a testimonial match for the German international Paul Breitner. The two Barcelona players shared a professional respect for Breitner. Nuñez argued that the testimonial was too close to the key King's Cup final, which Barcelona had reached. The two matches were separated by four days. What particularly angered Maradona was the fact that Nuñez had declared his position, as he had during the Paris controversy, in a statement to the media, while refusing to talk to the player directly. 'I rang Nuñez and he put the phone down on me after just two minutes. He said he was in a hurry to go and watch a youth match. When the match was over I went up to him, and said, "Well, now can we talk?" and he just walked away.'

The row, of course, had very little to do with football. It hinged on a point of principle, with Maradona seeing the withdrawal of his passport by Nuñez as an intolerable affront to his personal freedom. The incapacity and unwillingness of a club like Barcelona to accept such a libertarian notion was underlined the next day when a group of Barca fans physically assaulted Maradona as he drove away from a Nou Camp training session. Maradona played down the incident, claiming that the hooligans were not representative of the club as a whole. Privately, however, he harboured a less generous attitude towards Nuñez. In his view, Nuñez epitomized the worst aspects of football officialdom, treating uneducated footballers with the disdain of a feudal lord towards his serfs. Since childhood, Maradona had been pampered by benevolent father figures. He would always find it difficult to come to terms with the cold realities of commercial football to which a part of himself was inexorably linked.

Barcelona FC had had, for much of its history, a reputation in the world of football as a club of constant and often acrimonious internal feuds, in which the burden both of its political history and its financial requirements had fuelled periodic disputes between players, and between players and management. Yet even by Barcelona standards, the Maradona era was traumatic. To his open conflict with Nuñez Maradona added a series of no less public battles. His relationship with fellow striker Schuster was an ambiguous one. Maradona was conscious that Schuster regarded the sum Barcelona had paid for him as excessive and that he feared being upstaged by the Argentine's arrival. Creative tension sometimes works wonders, however. Maradona made an effort to develop a partnership with the German which in some matches at least worked very much to the club's advantage. Over the Munich incident, the two players had shown remarkable solidarity in standing up together against what they regarded as Nuñez's bullying tactics. But Maradona never fully relinquished his ambition to be regarded as the best in any team he played for, and he deliberately allowed Schuster's bad relationship with Udo Lattek to fester. In one celebrated interview, the German midfielder called the manager a drunkard. Maradona's own relationship with Lattek was a tempestuous one, and he never convincingly denied that he and Cyterszpiler were behind the eventual sacking of Lattek and his replacement by César Menotti in March 1983.

Menotti had resigned as Argentine national coach after his country's failure to retain its world championship in Spain in 1982, but his reputation was still sufficiently weighty for him to be headhunted by Barcelona. Lattek had lasted just over one season before Barcelona officials convinced themselves that this was one season too many. Still struggling to regain the glory of the Cruyff years, Barcelona had in 1982–83 failed for the tenth consecutive year to win the league championship, and had been equally frustrated internationally. In a SuperCup encounter in January 1983, Barcelona had lost 3–1 on aggregate against Aston Villa. But the real humiliation, and the death knell for Lattek, came two months later with Barcelona's premature exit from the more prestigious European Cup Winners' Cup. Boca was beaten by Memphis, a little-known Austrian club who fielded a side of eleven players which, as one football commentator remarked at the time, 'together would probably fetch less on the market than Maradona alone'.

The question was once again being asked: was Maradona *really* worth all that money? In his first six months at Barcelona, he had managed just six goals in league matches, then fallen ill with viral hepatitis. Coinciding as it did with his first Christmas without his extended family, the illness sank Maradona into one of his periodical depressions. Only a few weeks earlier, he had provided a rare insight into the insecurity which he kept hidden from the public when he told Domingo Trujillo of *MARCA*, 'Loneliness scares the shit out of me. I need to be surrounded by people that I know love me. They are my underlying support from which I can draw strength to play. I play much better when my family is around.'

Maradona's unhappiness deepened as the media laid siege to his home, where he holed himself up during the twelve weeks his illness lasted. He had long since formed the view that the majority of local journalists were mere lackeys of Barcelona's senior management, acting either as informants or purveyors of misinformation. Cyterszpiler considered Maradona's enemies analagous to 'members of the Gestapo or CIA agents'. Certainly when it came to reporting on the Argentine player, whether on or off the pitch, the Maradona rat pack found nothing too trivial to mention. Thus among the snippets of information that the Catalán media found it relevant to convey to the outside world was the fact that Maradona owned 250 videos and that his favourite was E.T. Maradona let that pass. Only when one report suggested that his illness was not really hepatitis but gonorrhoea did he threaten libel.

Maradona's recovery and reappearance with Barcelona followed within days of Menotti's arrival as the new manager. Menotti had always claimed that he was one of the few managers in the world who could both understand Maradona's idiosyncrasies and transform them into something positive. By hiring him, club officials hoped that he would prove as good as his word.

Initially Maradona warmed to Menotti like a lost son who had found his father again. He particularly welcomed a change in the training régime which Lattek had imposed so vigorously. While the German had insisted on morning sessions, Menotti opted for a three o'clock start, an hour he argued was more compatible with a football player's natural biorhythms. It was certainly more compatible with Maradona's and Menotti's lifestyle off the pitch. Both enjoyed Barcelona's nightlife – Maradona dealt with his insomnia either by going out dancing or by watching videos till the early hours – and found the concept of an early start the next morning difficult to cope with. 'I found Maradona an easy footballer to deal with, a boy capable of taking orders. I never had any disciplinary problems with him either during the World Cup or during our time in Barcelona,' Menotti told me. Certainly for a while he brought a new sense of inner harmony to the team, re-establishing a close bonding between Maradona and the other players, including Schuster.

Maradona recovered his enthusiasm for the game, overcoming his instinctive reluctance to train regularly. While the league championship remained elusive, the new Argentine partnership delivered the goods in the 1983 final of the King's Cup between Barcelona and Real Madrid on 4 June. A beautifully timed and accurate pass by Maradona in the thirty-second minute of the first half had Victor driving in Barcelona's and the match's first goal. Real Madrid equalized soon after half-time, but it was Barcelona, thanks to further acts of magic by Maradona and Schuster, who dominated the game. Nine minutes into injury time, Julio Alberto dribbled down the left wing, centred and the unmarked Marcos delivered a volley of such precision that Real's goalkeeper, Miguel Angel, stood wondering how it had ever happened. Barcelona had won the cup.

Nuñez looked like a man who has grown in his shoes as his captain, Sánchez, led Maradona and the rest of the team to pick up the trophy from King Juan Carlos. All seemed forgiven. For the next twenty-four hours, Barcelona celebrated in characteristic style, with Maradona and Menotti high up on the list of heroes. The city's socialist mayor, Pasqual Maragall, with one eye on the nationalist vote, hosted a reception and declared: 'This triumph satisfies the wishes of an entire people.' Only the local newspaper *La Vanguardia* dared utter a note of caution: 'We mustn't forget that the season has not been as good as we'd hoped. Till when must we wait before winning the league and the most prestigious of the competitions, the European Cup?'

Menotti failed to win either. Instead he opened up a new potential minefield for Maradona, by drawing him into a bitterly fought public controversy over how football should be played. Menotti had lost none of his pride in his philosophy on football, however much it may have been contradicted by his own players during the two World Cups for which he had been responsible. He had written an erudite thesis called *Football Without Tricks* which had sold well in post-Falklands Argentina. In it he contrasted his admiration for a free and creative style of football with the 'tyranny' of the defensive, destructive play favoured by authoritarian managers.

Such tyranny, in Menotti's view at the time, had its most brutal exponent in Xavier Clemente, then manager of Atlético de Bilbao, who would go on to become manager of Spain. Within days of his arrival, Menotti had embarked on a widely publicized verbal debate with Clemente, declaring cheekily that 'the day Spain [i.e. Clemente] decides to be a bullfighter rather than a bull on the pitch it will play better football'. Clemente made it clear that he would take no lessons from a flippant Argentine who seemed to spend more time pursuing women than teaching football skills. So acrimonious did the clash become that it seemed only a matter of time before the troops followed their respective generals into bloody battle. For Maradona, Clemente's attitude towards Menotti was a painful reminder of what he believed was the racist attitude underlying his own conflicts in Spain. He had also become increasingly convinced that Spanish referees made it easier for Clemente's style of football to succeed by adopting a far too lenient attitude to fouling. He blamed the poor quality of Spanish TV coverage for encouraging players to foul 'off screen'. Maradona already seemed unwilling to accept his own personal responsibility for discrediting the game by often throwing himself to the ground when he was tackled in an effort to attract attention.

It was against this background that Menotti's Barcelona found themselves facing Clemente's Atlético de Bilbao in a crucial league match at the Nou Camp on 24 September 1983. Barcelona had started off the new season badly, beaten in two out of three games, and now faced Bilbao, the defending league champions. Barcelona began well, easily dominating the first half, and suffering little of the physical abuse they feared from the tough, uncompromising Basque players. The home side had established a commanding 2–0 lead by half-time. It was in the second half that disaster struck. Twelve minutes in, Maradona had begun a skilful run down the centre and seemed on his way to goal, when he was caught from behind by the Bilbao defender Goikoetxea and hacked to the ground. Even by Bilbao standards, it was one of the most brutal fouls ever delivered in the history of Spanish football. Edward Owen, a British freelance journalist who watched the game, coined the memorable phrase the 'Butcher of Bilbao'. It was the ultimate insult to a people like the Basques who had used such words to describe the repression against them by successive Spanish officials. In a post-match press conference Menotti referred to Bilbao's long history of employing players for the sole purpose of crippling opponents. He accused Goikoetxea of belonging to a 'race of anti-footballers' and demanded that he be banned for life. Goikoetxea, having escaped from the match with a yellow card, was subsequently sanctioned with a ten-match ban by the Spanish footballing authorities.

All this, however, was no consolation for Maradona. He suffered such a severe injury to his left ankle tendons that it was three months before he could play another match. During this recovery period, the neurosis that had plagued him during his bout of hepatitis returned to haunt him. The injury fuelled a sense of persecution and injustice. He blamed Goikoetxea as much as Nuñez for the trauma of his time in Barcelona.

Following the injury, Maradona once again turned to his inner circle for comfort. The division separating the Maradona clan from Barcelona FC deepened. Barcelona's own surgeons initially operated on Maradona while he was under a haze of anaesthetic, implanting three pins which they thought would aid his recovery. But Maradona soon displayed his life-long distrust for orthodox medicine, sending once again for his old friend Oliva. The doctor flew in weekly from Milan to attend to his patient, often contradicting what the Barcelona medical team had prescribed. Early in November Oliva persuaded Maradona to throw away his crutches and show his strength of will by walking on his injured foot. The Barcelona doctors were outraged. Oliva insisted that they didn't understand Maradona's psychology. That Christmas, Maradona flew to Buenos Aires and was joined by Oliva. There the player submitted himself to Oliva's personalized programme of recovery. Cyterszpiler, never one to miss a business opportunity, had his camera crew film the event. The film showing Maradona working out to the title music of *Flash Dance* and *Rocky* was subsequently sold to a Catalán TV station.

Maradona was declared fit to play again for Barcelona in the New Year of 1984. In his first match, against Sevilla, he played like a man reborn, scoring two goals and leading his team to an impressive 3–1 victory which had the entire Nou Camp celebrating his return. Three matches later, for the first time since his injury, he faced the Basques again in Bilbao's San Mames stadium. The Argentine played like a man obsessed, fearless in the face of the opponent who had nearly wrecked his career, and leading his colleagues through one of the dirtiest games ever played in the stadium. The two teams committed a record of more than fifty fouls between them. Maradona managed to score two goals, sufficient to give his team a 2–1 victory.

Perhaps had Maradona been playing for any other team, these two performances alone would have been sufficient to earn him praise and honour. Not for the first nor the last time in his footballing career, he had hit the lowest point only to pick himself up again and prove he could still be among the best. But Barcelona was Barcelona, and no amount of personal heroism could make up for the club's failure to win the league and the European Cup. In the league, Maradona's successful revenge against Bilbao was judged ephemeral. Barcelona ended up in third place, with the double humiliation of Real Madrid in second, and Bilbao in first.

A month before Barcelona realized it had failed yet again to win the league championship, the team was eliminated from the European Cup Winners' Cup by Manchester United. United won the first leg at Old Trafford 3–0. Hours before the start of the second leg at Nou Camp, Maradona developed one of his recurrent back pains. It was one of many physical complaints he suffered which divided the opinion of Oliva and his Catalán counterparts. While the doctors argued over causes, Maradona insisted he wanted to play. When his colleagues began to change for the match, he was taken to the infirmary and given a series of pain-killing injections. He was then declared fit to play. The jabs quickly anaesthetized the pain. But minutes into the game, Maradona began to suffer secondary effects. Both his concentration and his reflexes seemed to abandon him. None of this, of course, was known to the more than 80,000 Barcelona fans who were in the Nou Camp that night. What they saw was a team trailing dangerously behind the English champions on home ground, and in the middle of it all Maradona seemingly unable to kick a ball straight.

Watching with increasing concern from the bench was Menotti, aware that his own survival as team manager was linked to the outcome of this game. He felt he had no choice but to substitute Maradona before half-time. As the player walked off he was accompanied by loud whistles and boos from the Barcelona fans. Maradona did not join the bench, but instead kept on walking until he had reached the dressing room. There, in the presence of Cyterszpiler, he became hysterical, sobbing uncontrollably and raging against the world he felt had betrayed him yet again. At one point Maradona screamed, 'Why, why do I sacrifice myself if when I struggle to play I'm treated like this?'

That evening all the bitterness and frustration that had been simmering below the surface from his early days at Barcelona boiled over. Whatever doubts he might once have had about not sticking to his contract, he decided there and then that he wanted to quit. In his agent and friend, Cyterszpiler, he found a sympathetic ear, for by then Maradona was also in deep financial trouble.

12

TERRY AND DIEGO

M aradona Productions had been conceived on an extraordinary flight of fancy: that Jorge Cyterszpiler could make himself and his client a fortune just as Mark McCormack had done for many of the world's other great sports personalities. From the first tentative beginnings in 1979, negotiating sponsorship and merchandising agreements in Argentina, Cyterszpiler had set his eyes on the wider world, setting up deals in Germany and Spain. It was then that he began to get out of his depth. The bigger Maradona became, the harder it was to control him. The player was unpredictable, his personal life a helter-skelter. For his part Cyterszpiler's talents were not limitless. He knew how to drive a hard bargain on a transfer, but he was less adept at dealing with the more complex world of international marketing. And while he had the instincts of an entrepreneur, constantly dreaming up new ideas with which to make money, these ideas were sometimes badly judged and badly implemented.

Towards the end of Maradona's time in Barcelona, the business to which the player had lent his name was generating insufficient revenue to meet its debt. Maradona's periodical bouts of injuries, coupled with Barcelona's failure to win a national or European championship, had led to a drastic reduction in the forecast revenue from advertising and sponsorship. The crisis had its farcical side. Thus McDonald's found itself having to shoot a film of the player waist upwards and immobile, not in full flight of play, because his foot was in plaster. Soon afterwards McDonald's abandoned Maradona's image altogether, substituting him with pictures of an anonymous boy.

There were problems too with the sale of a video film on the life on Maradona on which Cyterszpiler spent over $1 million. He had used his own production team and studios in New York and Los Angeles to dub the video in twelve languages. Cyterszpiler attracted early interest from Saudi Arabia, but this fell well short of the worldwide sales on which he had been counting. Copies of the video were put in cold storage and years later disappeared without Cyterszpiler knowing their whereabouts.

What gave Cyterszpiler his worst headache, however, was the way that Maradona Productions' account had to be plundered in order to finance Maradona's own extravagant lifestyle. Cyterszpiler admitted that the main failure of his professional life was his inability to control Maradona's spending on clothes, cars, women, travel and generally having a good time whenever he was not playing football. There was also the added problem of the 'clan' – that extended kinship of relatives, friends and hangers-on who lived off the player's patronage. Cyterszpiler told me, 'You have to remember that I was both manager and friend. As manager perhaps I should have imposed greater diligence. But as a friend I felt there was a limit to how far I could go in controlling his money. The money was after all his. He would tell me, buy that house or that car and I had no choice but to buy it . . . High spending was part of Diego's life.'

For much of the time he was in Barcelona, Maradona's financial problems were a well-kept secret, and to this day Maradona Productions' accounts have never been properly audited, let alone published. It is not inconceivable – for we only have their words to go by – that the financial problems may have been exaggerated by Maradona and Cyterszpiler, as they were later by the manager's successor Coppola, as a form of tax avoidance, although again there is no evidence of this. The fact remains that Maradona's financial crisis was taken seriously enough by officials of Barcelona FC to create a new source of friction between them and the player. Early in 1984, a cheque from Maradona Productions in payment for the ongoing services and expenses of Maradona's personal doctor, Oliva, bounced. Cyterszpiler passed the bill on to Nuñez who refused to pay, arguing that Oliva was not registered as an official member of the club's medical staff.

Maradona's financial problems were identified by Terry Venables soon after he arrived in Barcelona to take over the management of the club in May 1984. Venables would later recall that he resigned himself to losing Maradona within days of his appointment. While there had been speculation that Maradona hated the English because of the Falklands War, and that the new manager simply didn't fancy handling a player of such a stature, this was invention, according to Venables. The main reason was that Maradona, one of the highest-paid players in the world, was in financial difficulties, largely because, as Venables put it, 'people were sponging off him'.

'Like most people, I'd heard the rumours about his big entourage. But until I got to Barcelona and made my own enquiries, I didn't realise the hopelessness of the position. There were hundreds of bills all over town all signed in the name of Maradona. Most, of course, had been signed not by him but by his "family", friends and assorted hangers-on . . . He'd been practically bled dry and the only solution was for him to secure the kind of money that a transfer would bring. Giving him a £1,000 a week pay rise wouldn't have begun to solve the problem,' Venables later recalled.

The three months between the humiliation of the Manchester United match and Venables' arrival saw Maradona and Cyterszpiler putting in place a carefully worked-out strategy for staying afloat. This was aimed once again at maximizing the player's transfer value, having first left Barcelona directors with no option but to let him go. 'Our strategy was a simple one,' Cyterszpiler told me with characteristic bluntness, 'get Nuñez really pissed off so that it would become impossible for him not to let Maradona go.' He recalled with relish how he had suggested as an opening gambit that Maradona should call Cataláns sons of bitches, dropping the phrase into an interview with a friendly journalist. Maradona did just that while on a visit to New York. When he returned to Barcelona he denied having ever said it, but by then he knew the damage had been done.

In his manipulation of the sports press, Cyterszpiler showed himself more than a match for the Barcelona directors. By the middle of 1985, he had let it be known among news editors that he had a story to tell which was guaranteed to sell more copies than endless accounts of Maradona's injuries. He arranged for a series of leaks of his transfer negotiations with Juventus and Napoli, provoking a split in the Barcelona board of directors. Nuñez was reluctant to let Maradona go, not because he had become reconciled to the player's insubordination, but because he thought a break in the massive contract he had signed with him would play into the hands of those critics who had urged against signing the player in the first place. As a gesture of goodwill, his vice-president Juan Gaspart told Cyterszpiler that Barcelona was prepared to assume the debts of Maradona Productions and guarantee its future financial viability. Other directors, including Casaus and the club treasurer Tusquets, believed that Maradona should be allowed to transfer if he wanted to, as to force him to stay against his will would undermine his playing capability with a detrimental knock-on effect on the club's revenue, particularly that generated by ticket sales.

The moment of definition appears to have come as a result of another bruising encounter between Barcelona and Atlético de Bilbao. On 30 April 1984, Bilbao won the league again. One week later the two sides met in the final of the King's Cup in Madrid in the presence of the Spanish Royal Family, and a crowd of 100,000 packed into Real's Bernabeu stadium. At least half of Spain had their eyes set on the TV screens that evening for the coverage of the match.

The war between the two sides which had been declared by Menotti and Clemente had by now touched the excitable Maradona and presented him with a further opportunity for controversy. On the eve of the match he declared, 'Clemente hasn't got the balls to look me in the eye and call me stupid.' Clemente replied, 'Maradona is both stupid and castrated. It's a shame that a player like him who earns so much money has no human qualities whatsoever.'

The scene was thus set not so much for a football match as for a violent scrum. It came at the end of the match. Bilbao had won by a single goal scored in the thirteenth minute by Endika. While the team celebrated its victory around the pitch, Barcelona players began to make their way off it, clearly angry at having had their efforts at goal repeatedly blocked by consistently rough and solid defensive work. Maradona, never a good loser, seemed particularly angry. He exploded when one of the Bilbao players, Sola, provocatively bid him farewell with the Spanish equivalent of a 'fuck off' sign. Maradona punched Sola to the ground, and was promptly attacked by a group of Bilbao players. Among them was the 'butcher' himself, Goikoetxea. Having broken Maradona's ankle in that earlier brutal encounter, he now delivered a kick which miraculously failed to cripple the Argentine player again. Few members of either side kept themselves out of the general brawl that followed. The punches and the kicks worthy of an encounter between street gangs in the Bronx were watched by a horrified King Juan Carlos and millions of Spaniards. It left the directors of Barcelona FC seething, convinced that the reputation of one of the world's best-loved clubs had been tarnished by the irresponsible thuggery of an uneducated Argentine. One director recalled, 'When I saw those scenes of Maradona fighting and the chaos that followed I realized that we couldn't go any further with him.' From then on Nuñez was prepared to hold out just long enough to secure the best possible financial deal.

Maradona and Cyterszpiler for their part were determined to bring their time at Barcelona to an end, and accelerated their transfer negotiations with Naples. It had been agreed by both men that Naples offered a better professional challenge than Juventus. Naples was in the process of a major revamp of players – a lot were being sold off simply with the aim of accommodating Maradona – both to avoid relegation and in a bid to get to the top of the Italian league within the next two to three years. By contrast, Juventus was already established at the top of Italian football with international superstars like the Frenchman Platini well incorporated into the team. After his experience at Barcelona, Maradona had had enough for a while of clubs that thought themselves superior, and where stars on a team competed among themselves.

When Menotti resigned as manager of Barcelona FC soon after the débâcle of the King's Cup, Maradona lost both a counsellor and a friend. That he didn't take that opportunity literally to walk out of Nuñez's office slamming the door behind him there and then was due in part to the fact that the transfer deal with Naples had yet to be signed and sealed. It also had something to do with the character of Terry Venables, the man Nuñez had picked as Menotti's replacement.

As has often been remarked, Venables' reputation has always exceeded his achievements. In 1984 he was little known outside his own country, let alone to Maradona. Within the UK he had won no trophies either as a player – Chelsea and Spurs – or as a manager – Crystal Palace and QPR – and his record hardly compared with that of Alex Ferguson, George Graham or Howard Kendall. As a young Chelsea player, he had played at the Nou Camp, but his return to Barcelona as manager was based more on recommendation than on memory.

Menotti told me that 'Terry got to Barcelona thanks to me. Most people hadn't heard of him.' And Menotti had heard of Venables thanks to a British journalist he had befriended during the World Cup, Jeff Powell of the *Daily Mail*. 'I talked to Powell and asked him which English manager is competent. This is a team of important players. He mustn't be a dictator. They've already had a German.

He must be able to win over the players.' Powell recommended Venables. According to Venables, Bobby Robson and Doug Ellis also put in a good word on his behalf with Barcelona.

Venables was on a short list alongside Helmut Benthaus of Stuttgart, who had just won the German championship, and Michel Hidalgo, who was about to take the European Championship with France. Venables described the scene during an interview I had with him ten years later. 'So there I was with some pretty high flyers and I was just manager of QPR and I actually didn't know what I was doing in such company. And then I discovered they wanted an English guy. They thought the team wasn't fit and needed hammering and the English had a reputation for being quite tough. With Menotti they had had the experience of someone who had won the World Cup and was not so motivated. They wanted someone who had yet to become successful.' And was less expensive, Venables might have added.

The subject of Maradona figured prominently in Venables' first interview with the Barcelona directors. 'They wanted to know what I wanted to do with him, whether I wanted him to go or stay . . . I said I'd like to work with the best player in the world, although I understood they'd had problems with him. I was left with the feeling that the directors really wanted Maradona to go and were hoping that once I had heard the full story I would think the same.'

Venables took his time before delivering a formal verdict. He watched videos of the Barcelona team playing. His view was that it was not a cohesive unit, and seemed too dependent on Schuster and Maradona. He wanted to develop the Spanish players on the team. 'The team was made up of bit-part actors and a couple of stars.' With help from the club officials, he obtained information about Maradona's financial affairs, which he concluded were one of the main reasons why the player wanted to leave Barcelona.

He also talked to other players about Maradona. Here opinions were almost to a man positive. 'What I liked about Maradona,' recalled Venables, 'was that all the players spoke well of him. It's like Gazza. They all liked him and worried about him at the same time. Maradona was a giver. If he got some success he wanted it to be shared.'

Finally Venables talked to Cyterszpiler and Maradona himself. Maradona's instinctive reaction to Venables was a cautious one, verging on scepticism. Like many members of the Argentine working class he distrusted Englishmen, and could not imagine a decent replacement at Barcelona after Menotti. But in his first and only conversation with him, Maradona warmed to Venables, finding him accessible and unpompous, a welcome change from the Catalán directors.

Venables had taken the advice of his friend Bobby Robson and taken some language lessons so that he was able to communicate in Spanish, another point in his favour as far as Maradona was concerned. The only condition Venables stipulated was that Maradona should speak slowly and with the simplest use of words so he could understand him. That again was more a blessing that a curse for the player, who was not prone to academic discourse. Without the need to resort to interpreters, and with both men establishing a common ground around simplicity, Maradona opened his heart to Venables, summing up all the frustration and anger his experience of playing in Barcelona had brought to him. It was the final confirmation Venables was waiting for in order to make his own mind up. 'From what Maradona said to me I felt that the situation in Barcelona if he stayed would become very very difficult. The damage was perhaps irreparable.' And that seemed the end of it, as far as their future together was concerned.

Yet the relationship between the two men has its postscript. Early in 1987 Venables, in his second year as manager of Barcelona, was asked by the English Football Association to pick and manage for a day a World XI for a football league centenary match against an English team at Wembley. After his World Cup success, Maradona was an obvious candidate, a personal choice for Venables and for the organizers who judged his crowd-pulling powers to be far greater than those of any other player. 'If you are going to have a World XI you really have to have Maradona,' recalled Venables. 'At the time he was playing outstandingly well and the English organizers, felt that it was a coup to get him.'

Getting Maradona to England turned into a logistical nightmare, with the player holding out for increasing amounts of money. Matters were made worse by difficulties in communication. In the final days leading up to the fixture in August, Venables found himself with the Barcelona team in a remote training camp in Andorra staying in a hotel with a very small and inefficient switchboard. Now and then he would try and contact Maradona in Argentina either directly or through his then agent, Guillermo Coppola, only to be told that the player was fishing in the north of Argentina. In the end it took the personal persuasion of Ossie Ardiles, an inflated fee (reportedly upped from £50,000 to £90,000 for a single match) and a private plane laid on by the entrepreneur Terry Ramsden to get Maradona to play.

In publicity terms it was a disaster all round, but most of all for Maradona. The fact that he had put everyone to so much trouble and expense only to come on to the Wembley turf clearly unfit and uninterested in doing much fuelled his image as a prima donna who was a cheat to boot. After all, he had used the hand of God just a year earlier. Quite what Ramsden was really up to was never fully explained. But Maradona never did play for his Walsall club in aid of the Ramsden Foundation, as he had promised in return for the £10,000 cost of his flight. And Ramsden was prosecuted and convicted for a string of fraud offences, and never tried to organize a football match again.

13

KING AMONG GODFATHERS

Just after midday on 5 July 1984 a helicopter with Diego Maradona and his faithful friend and agent Jorge Cyterszpiler on board made its way to Naples' San Pablo stadium. Maradona had spent the previous twenty-four hours ducking and diving from the thousands of Neapolitans who had wanted simply to catch a glimpse of him. After Maradona's arrival at the city's international airport, his driver had taken a back route through secondary roads to avoid the fans who had clogged up the autostrada. Later a Maradona lookalike was hired to provide a further diversion on the island of Capri, briefly throwing the paparazzi off the scent of their real quarry, while the player and his agent escaped by fast launch back to the mainland. Now it was time to declare the chase formally over, with the presentation of the newly transferred Maradona to the *tifosi*. The local fans had been waiting for hours, working themselves into a collective frenzy which even by the standards of Italy's excitable football stadiums seemed to verge on mass hysteria.

Ever since news had first leaked out about the negotiations with Barcelona, the arrival of Maradona had been looked forward to with a reverence and sense of expectancy usually reserved for second comings. Naples has lived much of its history amidst subjugation and disaster, its rebellious leanings suppressed by a richer, more powerful North, and its closeness to death symbolized by the volcano of Vesuvius, and the remains of its last great earthquake. In the city no pastime was more passionately followed than football. And yet Naples' football club, Napoli, had constantly lost out to the big clubs of Seria A centred on central and northern Italy, never winning a league championship, let alone any major European title in its fifty-three-year history. The only trophy that sat in the Napoli boardroom was for an unprestigious tournament, since discontinued, called the Cup of the Alps.

The city of Naples was football and much else. It was Babylon-by-the-Bay, as much pagan as it was mystical, a huge melting pot of humanity where anything and everything was expected to happen. Maradona was flying into a city where people spent as much time working out the astrological meaning of numbers in dreams as they did on the pools, and where devils and harlequins stared from shop windows. But Naples was also the city of San Genaro, the martyred bishop whose freshly spilled blood, bottled by a devout spectator more than 1,700 years ago, still continued to liquefy and froth in its silver reliquary twice a year. Devotion to the local saint had until 1984 been equalled only by adoration of the local Madonna, whose small statue surrounded by candles reproduced itself across the poor quarters of the city.

But with the arrival of Maradona the Neapolitans acquired a third object of veneration. No matter that the footballer's career had so far been far from faultless, that he had yet to prove himself in a World Cup, or that he had left the majority of Cataláns disillusioned with the manner of his departure. Here was a player who believed in destiny and divine intervention and who when fate smiled in his favour could still play better football than anyone in the world. A player who was already up there among the international stars, and yet who came from a poor background and an Italian mother like so many Neapolitans. Maradona, Madonna, the words merged into each other, he was coming both as a saviour and as a mother, to take his rightful place in the Neapolitan pantheon.

When the helicopter began its descent, the *tifosi* looked up as if to heaven. Only when Maradona was subsequently blocked from their view by a posse of photographers did they realize momentarily that he was as human as they were. He could not walk over the heads of the assorted media as Jesus had once walked on water. The *tifosi* demanded that Maradona make his grand entrance again, entering the stadium through the passageway that leads from the showers to the turf, for only then would they have their true fill of him. So a second entrance was arranged by anxious officials.

Minutes later, Maradona duly emerged, walking out, it seemed, not so much from celestial heights as from deep within the volcano and above the fault line, a true messenger of the apocalypse. The stadium exploded with fireworks and streamers. So instant and huge was the roar that greeted him that Maradona felt it like the blast of a hurricane. Feeling its impact, he momentarily grimaced and stumbled, before running on. He was dressed in track-suit trousers, a white T-shirt and a Napoli scarf, consciously demonstrating that he was no old man, prematurely aged by the tension of living in Barcelona, but a youthful twenty-four-year-old, still full of vigour and love of life who at that moment felt he had come home. He smiled, waved and blew kisses, the *tifosi* chanted, 'Diego, Diego, Diego.' And then in the centre of the stadium, under the beaming eyes of Cyterszpiler, he took a ball and played with it, from one foot to the other and back again, up on his head and down again, spinning it out and in again, before stopping it dead.

Before completing his Olympian run round the stadium, Maradona picked up a bundle of blue balloons – the Naples colours again – and released them into the sky. He had brought his magic to the city of magic, and the stadium trembled and shook before its Messiah.

Among the 70,000 packed into the stadium that day were several individuals with a particular interest in seeing Maradona succeed. One of them was Antonio Juliano, or 'Totonno' as he was popularly known locally, the former Italian international who was then manager of Napoli. Juliano was something of a local hero with a background not dissimilar to Maradona's. Born into one of the city's poorest neighbourhoods, he had been discovered by a scout at an early age and signed up to play for Napoli's youth team. He had the record as the longest-serving and most successful of the home-bred players. As captain of the team he led Napoli to its one and only national trophy, and was one of the few players from the South picked to represent Italy in three World Cups. Since being appointed manager of Napoli in 1980, Juliano had set his sights on Maradona as the one footballer capable of at the very least taking the club to the heights it enjoyed in the mid-1960s, when it had ended runner-up in the league championship in two successive seasons thanks to another left-footed Argentine star of Italian football, Omar Sivori.

Also watching Maradona closely that day in the stadium was Corrado Ferlaino, the club president who had only belatedly come round to backing his manager's bid for the Argentine player. Ferlaino had succeeded to the presidency of Napoli, one of the city's major institutions, two years earlier, after cannily buying shares in the club and establishing a parallel power base as the head of one of the biggest local construction groups. He was a controversial character who initially seemed to spend rather less time and money furthering the interests of Napoli than in arranging dubious building projects which were given planning approval following the 1980 earthquake.

Only when serious difficulties emerged between Maradona and Barcelona, and word went out that the player had his sights on Italy, did Juliano manage to convince Ferlaino that here was an opportunity that couldn't be missed. The fact that Juventus had also expressed an interest in the player proved an added incentive. Ferlaino relished the idea of outbidding Gianni Agnelli, the Fiat magnate who owned the Turin-based Juventus, and turning the purchase of Maradona into a symbol of regional economic independence from the North and centralized political power.

Negotiations on Maradona's transfer had taken place in a series of secret meetings involving Juliano and Cyterszpiler, in Barcelona and on the island of Ischia near Naples in May and June 1984. Further meetings were leaked to the press by Maradona's people, attracting an invasion of Italian journalists into the Catalán capital for what turned into some dramatic last-minute brinkmanship involving Maradona, the Barcelona vice-president Gaspart and Ferlaino. The closing date for new transfers to be registered with the Italian league authorities in Milan was 29 June, a Friday. On that date Ferlaino flew into Barcelona convinced that he would conclude negotiations in time to have the transfer registered before the end-of-afternoon deadline. He was made to wait in a bar, awaiting the outcome of the latest meeting between Gaspard and Maradona in the neighbouring Hotel Reina Sofía. The meeting ended inconclusively late in the afternoon, with Maradona rejecting Gaspard's last-minute offer of an improved contract to stay on in Barcelona, but failing to achieve his formal release. 'If I stay on in Barcelona, I shall be injured one day, fail to turn up for training the next. I'm just not going to play here any more,' declared Maradona before the meeting broke up.

With the minutes ticking away to the deadline, Ferlaino instructed one of his officials to deliver a closed envelope to the offices of the Italian football authorities. The envelope contained the names of three foreign players with Inter Milan. By the time the authorities had met to consider the new list of transfers after the weekend, the only name which appeared registered by Napoli was that of Diego Maradona. By then a mysterious messenger, with the blessing of Ferlaino, had managed to penetrate the offices of the Italian football authorities and replace the contents of the original envelope. It was a typical gesture emanating from a city like Naples, where corruption at most levels of economic and political life was endemic.

In the forty-eight-hour interlude, Gaspard had given up his rearguard action to retain Maradona, and put his signature to another record transfer contract which netted Barcelona an estimated $13 million and the player an estimated $6.4 million. Barcelona officials and Maradona however were by no means the only ones who stood to gain financially from the deal. For stooping over the shoulders of Ferlaino and Juliano that day of celebration in San Pablo was a powerful and ruthless organization which weeks before had already set in train plans to exploit the presence of Maradona in their city: the Neapolitan Mafia known as the Camorra.

The organization had come a long way since its primitive beginnings as a rural counterweight to the power of the big landowners in nineteenth-century Italy and occupying forces from the North. It had developed its urban network in Naples during the Second World War, establishing a black-market economy first with the Germans and later with the occupying Allied forces. In the post-war years the Camorra, like the Mafia in Sicily, had increased their influence in society, thanks to building an intricate network of influence with key sectors of the Italian state like the Christian Democrat Party, and branching out into any area of the economy, black or otherwise, that stood to make a profit.

Its *modus operandi* was based on a mixture of patronage and intimidation. The Camorra maintained its grip on society through a structured human transmission belt along which power and influence travelled. At the top were the *capi*, the leaders of the families that ruled the poor neighbourhoods of Naples like feudal barons. Underneath them were the effective corporals and sergeants of the organization who maintained order and personal loyalties, co-ordinated the provision of services to clients and organized vendettas, carried out by any number of gangs or hit-men. The Camorra had easy access as much to men in high office as to numerous families who had been born and bred in a society where unemployment and misery were rife. It was also successful in intimidating the local media and judiciary.

Nowhere did the Camorra mix more openly with the people

of Naples than in the football matches played in the San Pablo stadium. There the *capis*, the sergeants and their rent-a-mob were indistinguishable from the thousands of other *tifosi* who lived out the collective obsession with football.

On the day of Maradona's presentation to the *tifosi*, one question in particular resonated around the accompanying press conference. It came from French journalist Alain Chaillou, who shared none of the gushing excitement of his Italian colleagues that day. Chaillou asked Maradona whether he was aware that the money that had been used to secure his transfer had been collected by the Camorra. Either Maradona hadn't heard or he didn't want to hear. The question was passed on to Ferlaino. This time the reaction was instantaneous. Ferlaino looked livid and pointed to the door, security men moving as he did so. 'Your question offends us. Naples is an honest city. As president of the football club, I ask you to leave.' Chaillou was surrounded by henchmen and bustled out.

Just like the Camorra, Ferlaino had made his money in construction. One of his uncles had been murdered by the Camorra. During the last football season before Maradona's arrival, a match had been temporarily halted when a light plane flew low over the San Pablo stadium and dropped pamphlets with the message 'Goodbye Ferlaino, come back Juliano.' In a subsequent public statement Ferlaino claimed that the stunt had been organized by enemies of his in the Camorra who wanted to bring down the price of his shares in the club. But it left unanswered the question of why he had been caught with the Camorra in the first place.

The bulk of the transfer money for Maradona was deposited in Barcelona Football Club's own bank, Banca Mas Sarda. It was underwritten by a group of Neapolitan banks, led by Banco di Napoli and Banca della Provincia di Napoli, through which some of the more dubious money in Naples was laundered. But before the negotiations of the transfer had got underway Barcelona officials had insisted at the last minute on a further deposit of $600,000. In the hours that followed, thousands of Neapolitans turned up with their savings books or pockets of cash and deposited an individual contribution at a major branch of a local building society, the Monte dei Paschi di Siena. It took little more than a day for the total amount required to be collected. The apparently spontaneous, Robin Hood-like gesture – the poor people of Naples giving to their poor football club – seemed to underline the extent to which the Camorra was not so much a group of people or any one individual but the expression of a social phenomenon.

The interest the Camorra had in Napoli had been fuelled considerably by the prospect of Maradona transferring from Barcelona. The club expected its ticket sales to triple, with an ensuing boom in resales, an activity at which the Camorra's touts excelled. There was also the prospect of an upsurge in the economic activity of other sectors in which the Camorra had interests.

The power of the Camorra was conveyed to Maradona from the early stages of his transfer negotiations. While still in Barcelona, he sent Cyterszpiler to Naples to establish contact with local football officials and also to get a sense of what it was like to live in the city. The concern Cyterszpiler felt for his client and friend's personal happiness was matched only by his determination to revive the fortunes of Maradona Productions. In Barcelona, Cyterszpiler had had to dig deep into the reserves of the company to finance the extravagant lifestyle of Maradona and his entourage. But he also blamed the company's bad performance on Maradona's repeated injuries and the lack of harmony between the player and the Barcelona officials. In Naples, he was confident that Maradona would feel much more at home and flourish as a footballer. In commercial terms Cyterszpiler believed that Maradona's high profile – there would be no other star players to cramp his style – would work to the benefit of Maradona Productions.

Cyterszpiler, however, was to discover that in Naples he could not take for granted the exclusive right to the Maradona business empire. He realized this soon after arriving on his first exploratory trip in the spring of 1984, when rumours of the local club's interest in buying Maradona were already rife in the Italian press. Cyterszpiler was just driving away from the airport and on to the motorway which leads into the city when he noticed a ragged street seller doing swift business by the side of the road. On sale was a bootleg cassette of a song that in time would reverberate round the stadium of San Pablo, but which was already a popular jingle in the Camorra-dominated poor neighbourhoods of Naples. Roughly translated its main verse went like this: 'Oh mum, mum, mum/Oh mum, mum, mum/do you know why my heart beats so?/I've seen Maradona, I've seen Maradona/and mum, I'm in love.'

Cyterszpiler was so taken aback by the sight of a Maradona

product being sold without his permission that he stopped the car. He recalled, 'I asked the guy how could he be selling cassettes of Maradona if he had't even been signed up yet by Naples. What if he never turns up? I asked. The guy just looked at me and shrugged. Why should I care, I've already sold 2,000 copies just in a day?'

In the negotiations Cyterszpiler subsequently had with Napoli officials, the issue of merchandising provoked argument and tension between the sides. Even after the transfer contract had been signed, Cyterszpiler resisted the idea of ceding control of what he had learned in Argentina and Spain was one of the more profitable outlets for the Maradona label. And yet the longer he stayed in Naples, the more he came to realize that the control over merchandising was no longer his. Paulo Pauletti, a TV journalist and Napoli official who came to form part of Maradona's close circle of friends in Italy, remembered one night when he and Cyterszpiler emerged from a pizzeria in the fashionable Mergallina district near the harbour and spotted another example of local enterprise. A boy at a traffic lights was selling boxes of Marlboro cigarettes, crying out as he did so, 'Cigarette Maradona, two for the price of one.' Pauletti remembered Cyterszpiler's look of amazement, tinged with chagrin. 'When Jorge asked him why he was selling Marlboro cigarettes as Maradona cigarettes, the boy simply answered that he sold much more that way. At that point, if he hadn't realized already, Jorge realized that he wasn't alone in believing the name Maradona meant big business.'

Cyterszpiler initially threatened to sue for breach of copyright anyone in Naples who sold Maradona-labelled products. But he was contacted by intermediaries of the Camorra and told that it would not be a good idea for him to operate in Naples without first reaching an understanding with the defenders of the poor, as the local Mafiosi liked to be considered. In Naples street-selling was a key activity of the local economy which was organized by the Camorra as a way of forging its network of influence among the poor and destitute. It also helped fund its operations from the cut it took on the sale of products.

The deal which the Camorra suggested was that the organization would retain control of local merchandising, leaving promotion and advertising deals in the hands of Maradona Productions. Cyterzspiler considered his own safety and that of Maradona, and reluctantly accepted it was an offer he couldn't refuse.

Maradona himself put his seal on the arrangement by declaring publicly soon after arriving in Naples, 'I am perfectly happy if businesses in Naples can survive because of my face.'

It was a comment that understated the relationship that was to develop between Maradona and the Camorra. The footballer was identified by the Camorra as a public figure who could and should be exploited. 'You have to imagine the Camorra at the time as a giant octopus with huge tentacles which reached out to take in most aspects of the city,' Rosario Pastore, a local correspondent of the prestigious Italian sports daily *Gazetta dello Sport*, told me. 'Maradona was an important figure who could not be ignored. The Camorristas wanted to be identified with him. They saw him as symbol of power.'

In the months following his arrival, Maradona's popularity in Naples seemed to have no boundaries. The *tifosi* of San Pablo – some 70 per cent of whom were thought to have some connection with the Camorra, according to judicial estimates – revelled in and applauded Maradona's football. In his first season at Naples, Maradona played with all the freshness and inspiration which had characterized his pre-Barcelona days. He looked trim and energetic, visibly enjoying the opera of Italian football with its diving and gesticulation and the frenzied adulation of the fans. After the disciplined corporatism of the Nou Camp, he was back among a primitive tribe, a San Genaro with boots on, making miracles out of the mundane.

Much of Italian football at the time was still dominated by the defensive style known as the *catenaccio* or padlock. The *catenaccio* entails both the unyielding man-to-man marking throughout a match, and the placing of the sweeper behind a solid line of defence, which is expected to draw out the opposition. In the 1982 World Cup in Spain, a disorientated and badly motivated Maradona had been neutralized by the *catenaccio* as practised by the Italian national team, in particular Gentile. Now in Naples Maradona seemed to cover the pitch in stardust, managing to weave around defenders and, when not driving the ball through himself, inspiring fellow team players like Careca, De Napoli, Francini and Crippa to break towards goal with a newly discovered sense of precision. Once again the ball seemed to be tied to Maradona's boots or else guided through the air with the deadly curve of an exocet. The *tifosi* loved their *Rei* or King, and he in turn payed them homage long after he'd scored his goal, turning cartwheels, kissing the heavens, or just running to where the crowd was thickest and frothiest and saluting with his fists.

The love affair with Maradona extended beyond the San Pablo stadium to embrace a whole city. The closely knit circle of Argentine friends and relatives who had felt so alienated in Barcelona now joined Maradona in Naples, basking in the collective celebration. Here the term clan was not used in any derogatory sense. It expressed a social reality based round informal relationships of kinship and favours. With their garish Versace shirts and leather, the Maradona clan were indistinguishable from the other clans that existed in the Camorra-dominated neighbourhoods of the Quartieri Espognoli and the Forcella and hung out in the cafés and nightclubs of downtown Naples. In the six years he lived in Naples, Maradona was less predator than quarry of the Camorra. The criminal organization drew Maradona into the so-called *seconda societa* or underground society and for a while saw its grip on the city of Naples strengthened.

The Camorra made its first direct bid for Maradona one day in January 1986 when two emissaries from one of the most powerful Camorrista clans – the Giulianos – arrived at the Napoli training ground. 'The Giulianos want to get to know you better,' was the basic message conveyed to the player. They spoke not as the hit-men of criminals but as *tifosi* conveying respect for the great star. They looked and spoke the same as Maradona, and neither the player nor his agent seems to have objected to the idea of replying positively to the written invitation that followed the visit. A few weeks later Maradona was one of the main guests of a party given by Carmine Giuliano, one of the bosses of the Giuliano clan whose interests spanned football, drugs and tobacco smuggling, and prostitution. It was a typical clan party with champagne flowing, and an assortment of pastas and cakes distributed with similar generosity. It was attended by Al Pacino and Sophia Loren lookalikes. At one level it seemed a joyous occasion. There was laughter and a lot of backslapping. But beneath the apparent familiarity was the tension of those who knew they were there because they owed a favour or two, and others who still had debts to draw on. Reverence was paid whenever Carmine passed. With his mop-like hair, thick-set dark eyes, and short, compact build, Carmine looked like just one more among the thousands of Neapolitans who straddle the globe from the cafés of Naples to the pasta bars of New York. He could have been an off-duty waiter, or even one of Maradona's team colleagues. Yet the man was more feared than anyone in that house. He only had to give an order and it would be carried out.

The Giulianos were masters of the art of patronage. They knew instinctively who needed reassuring, or simply reminding. This was not the occasion to discuss business in any detail, but simply to reassert the dynasty publicly. Their judgements of guests could be measured by the manner of their greeting. Maradona, like Carmine, looked no outsider in that party, but he was a focus of special attention. From the moment he arrived, a house photographer was on hand to record his principal encounters. The photographer's main assignment was to snap as many pictures as he could of Maradona in the presence of one or other member of the Giuliano family. The Giulianos, led by Carmine, embraced him, kissed him, raised their glasses to him. They brought along their most trusted henchmen and most beautiful women. In their company Maradona felt relaxed, unthreatened. Here were people with money and influence, who had come up from the back streets just as he had. They spoke his kind of language, shared his world view. In Barcelona, he had always been made to feel an outsider by the Cataláns, an upstart South American, a Sudaca. But here he felt as Neapolitan as the rest. This was to be one of several parties organized by Camorristas which Maradona attended while he was in Naples. They included a very public Giuliano wedding, which was not unlike the opening sequence of *The Godfather*. There too Maradona was snapped, a kind of Camorra mascot, lending legitimacy to the occasion. For a while these photographs were kept by the Giulianos, but like the others taken in 1986 would return one day to haunt Maradona.

Maradona's initial contact with the Camorra raised few local eyebrows. The player himself appears to have attached little importance to the fact that he attended their parties. He regarded it as only natural that an organization that for better or for worse had such intimate links with the local football scene would want to identify itself publicly with the star player. He was there as a football player, not as a partner in crime. The first invitation to a Giuliano party had seemingly come to him via Cyterszpiler, who in turn had been approached by a senior organizer of the Napoli fan club. 'I had no idea what the Giulianos did. Somebody else asked me to go to their house and, as I often did, I accepted,' Maradona later recalled when first confronted about his connections with the Camorra. He was being somewhat economical with the truth, as Maradona's Italian lawyer Vincenzo Sinischalsci conceded when I interviewed him in Naples in November 1995: 'He knew in general they were members of the Camorra, but this doesn't mean he became part of their organization.'

It was only with the benefit of hindsight that Maradona would reflect less flippantly on why he had allowed himself to be drawn, however superficially, into such a criminal fraternity. 'I became a favourite of the Camorra not because I was pretty or good, but because I made the people happy, the same people that maybe they exploited,' he said in an interview in January 1996. 'The relationship came down to a question of power and money, in other words.'

The ease with which the relationship between Maradona and the Camorra was accepted socially at the time, at least in Naples, can only be understood in the context in which it developed. Maradona's establishment as football king in Naples came at a time when the Camorra still enjoyed considerable freedom of movement. The anti-corruption campaign spearheaded by the judges had yet to get underway, and the old power brokers in Naples, be they Christian Democrat politicians, Camorra clan leaders or the network of individuals engaged in the local economy who were linked to one group or the other, still operated with immunity. As for the media, few journalists regarded it as in their interest to upset the apple cart. One who thought differently was a young freelance reporter, Giancarlo Siani. In 1985, he set out to investigate the links between local politicians and the Camorra in a small town near Naples, with the intention of selling the story to one of Italy's national newspapers. Siani was shot dead before he had even had time to assemble his notes. Another local journalist decided that silence was less risky than knowledge and survived. He told me, 'You have to understand what it was like in Naples then. We had a phrase that we would quite commonly use as an excuse for our professional shortcomings. It simply said, "I have a family." What it meant was, look, I can't write about the Camorra because I might lose one of my relatives if I don't get killed myself.'

It was not just the Camorra who could strut in public, seemingly beyond the power of good or evil. For a while Maradona became as untouchable as any clan leader. He was protected by virtue of his success on the football field, and the tribal loyalty which that generated, while all around him was constructed a veneer of moral respectability worthy of Mother Teresa. Maradona was granted an audience with the Pope, and appointed an ambassador for UNICEF. To the Vatican went the Maradona of divine intervention, conceived in a slum, born under an angelic star; the natural talent who gave public thanks to his maker by making the sign of the cross before each match and a sign to heaven with each goal. To UNICEF went Maradona, the slum kid who could never quite turn his back on his roots, and who when he first arrived in Naples had not yet lost his capacity for generosity. This was the Maradona who on a day of freezing rain in the winter of 1985 interrupted his intense schedule of public functions and club commitments, to join his two brothers Hugo and Lalo in a charity football match. In another charity match he risked serious injury playing on a poorly turfed village football pitch in one of the more backward areas of southern Italy. Months later he flew 10,000 kilometres to Pasadena to play in another fund-raising match for poor children organized by UNICEF. Unlike other international stars who said they would be there, Maradona kept to his promise. 'The generosity that Maradona was capable of then is unimaginable in the cold unscrupulous world of money that football subsequently became,' recalled Bruno Pasarella, an Italian-based Argentine journalist who closely monitored Maradona.

While Maradona's good deeds were publicized, other aspects of his life became less subject to scrutiny. This was not because Naples is a private city. Far from it – as the most densely populated metropolis in Italy, Naples, while seemingly impenetrable, has few hiding places. This strange dichotomy is nowhere more striking than in the city's poor neighbourhoods which Maradona made his own. The streets twist and curl in shadows, a complex warren, weathered by time, of alleyways and dead ends, crumbling churchyards and improvised sleeping quarters. And yet many of the front doors are open, and the people gossiping within seem quite used to being looked in on. Out in the streets, it is rare not to come across a group of locals wildly gesticulating as they engage in passionate debate about some personal or political issue. Naples teems with life, and, at a superficial level, it is possible for everyone to see everything.

And yet such transparency has not translated itself into account-ability in a city that has successfully thwarted outside authority for several thousand years. Neapolitans feel answerable to themselves, not to the rest of Italy, still less the world beyond, and within their city it is the family first, then the clan, and then Naples. Such a society made it possible for Maradona to carry on his life not unnoticed but, for a while at least, uncensured.

In the early months, Maradona and his 'family' established themselves in the Hotel Royale, one of the city's more expensive hotels near the waterfront – at one point the party consisted of more than twenty people. At first Maradona insisted that he would only move if his new club found him a residence of similar size and scale to the palatial villa he had inhabited in Barcelona. What he was offered was a modern two-floor apartment block in the Via Scipione Capece. The address was in Posillipo, a rather cramped if well-heeled residential zone perched on a hill overlooking the Bay of Naples. Napoli officials told him it was the best they could do for him, given the city's scarcity of large private residences and the chaotic distribution of real estate following the earthquake.

Maradona judged it a gesture of unnecessary meanness. The residence would in time become a point of contention between him and the club. But initially he did not allow it to cramp his style. In Naples, he continued to spend lavishly on himself and on his family. He acquired a yacht and built up a fleet of cars, some of which he bought himself, while others were arranged for him as part of a sponsorship deal. The cars included a Rolls-Royce, registered in Monte Carlo, and a black special-issue Ferrari Testarossa, similar to the one owned by his movie idol Sylvester Stallone. The Ferrari was in normal circumstances difficult to obtain. However, it was supplied at short notice to Maradona after Cyterszpiler had talked personally to Gianni Agnelli and convinced him that the sight of Maradona driving the car would prove a good publicity boost for Ferrari and a reminder to the upstart South of where the real power of Italian business lay.

Unlike his experience in Barcelona, where he had felt himself rejected by the upper classes, Maradona found during his early period in Naples that no part of the city was barred to him. He moved about it, like a king in his dominions, unchallenged by the media or the authorities and surrounded only by people willing to satisfy his every need. Women became as available as boats and cars. They sought out Maradona in droves, hoping to get their photograph into the newspapers as a way of furthering their careers. Among those who succeeded in their mission was Heather

Parisi, a leggy twenty-one-year-old blonde model from California who had endeared herself to Italian male viewers by showing off her attributes on a Saturday night TV cabaret show. In January 1985 she had a brief relationship with Maradona while Claudia was away in Argentina. The encounter was given wide publicity by the Italian kiss-and-tell magazine *Oggi*. That January was one of the coldest winters ever recorded in Naples' history, and yet the couple, halfway through their week-long sojourn, dutifully gave the magazine what it wanted by appearing together smiling and relaxed on the balcony of Maradona's apartment. The 'exclusive' pictures snapped with a long lens by a paparazzo were subsequently sold worldwide at a reported figure of $8,000 a piece.

Such escapades might have temporarily satisfied Maradona's libido and boosted his finances, but they contributed little to family harmony. Tensions in his relationship with Claudia set in soon after he moved to his Naples residence. They were witnessed by an Argentine, Juana Bergara, who was taken on as a housemaid in 1985. Although her contract, signed with Maradona Productions, stipulated that she would work during the day for Claudia, it soon became obvious to Juana that Claudia's regular absences from the flat had an underlying cause which might affect her employment. When Juana asked the secretary at Maradona Productions when she might expect to see Claudia again, she was told not to expect a firm date. 'It's a real crisis . . . Diego said he didn't want to see her any more, and I think this time he really means it.'

From Maradona's sister Maria, who was then living in the ground-floor flat with her husband, Juana got the following additional information: 'I was told by Maria that Claudia and Diego were like two strangers, they no longer cuddled each other or exchanged sweet phrases, just insults and swear words, which would climax in really violent exchanges.'

According to Maria, the tension was fuelled by the fact that Claudia was getting on badly with Tota, the person who from an early age had established such a dominant influence on Maradona. And yet she is thought to have been told by her son before his departure to Barcelona that if he was going to marry any woman one day it would be Claudia. Her potential daughter-in-law is also thought to have assured herself of a binding financial relationship with the footballer as soon as he began to earn big money. This included shared rights to property and responsibility over any children they might have. These were practical considerations that neither Tota nor anybody else in the Maradona family could easily ignore. From way back, Tota, a practical and sharp-witted woman, had known that tolerating Claudia was probably in her son's better interests.

'During the first months that I worked in the Maradona household, I never saw Claudia; it was as if the earth had swallowed her up,' recalled the housemaid Juana. The temporary annihilation of the relationship extended to photographs of Claudia that were spread out around the apartment. In a fit of pique, Maradona stripped the apartment bare of them, according to Juana.

Next, Maradona turned on Jorge Cyterszpiler, his childhood friend and agent. In September 1985, Cyterszpiler was in Mexico negotiating a television rights deal for Maradona, when the earthquake struck, destroying hundreds of buildings and claiming large numbers of victims. Cyterszpiler survived unscathed, only to be told a piece of news that really did pull the ground from beneath his feet. As soon as Mexico City's communications with the outside world had been restored, a friend rang him from Naples to tell him that Maradona had sacked him. A few hours earlier, Guillermo Blanco and Juan Carlos Laburu, the two Argentines who had been employed by Maradona Productions as public relations officer and cameraman respectively, had personally been called in by Maradona and summarily dismissed. With the air of a cold businessman who has lost sight of his shop-floor workers amid the noise and mechanical contortions of the assembly line, Maradona said simply that Maradona Productions was in financial difficulties, that Cyterszpiler was no longer his manager, and that they were surplus to requirements. He told them that they should work out any outstanding payments they thought was due to them with Guillermo Coppola, the man he had appointed to take over from Cyterszpiler.

It was a terrible shock to those in the firing line. Each of the three considered themselves not just employees of Maradona, but loyal friends. Blanco had spent most of his journalistic career conveying Maradona to the outside world both as a footballing genius and as a sympathetic human being. As Maradona's personal public relations officer first in Barcelona and then in Naples, he had been the ever-present shield protecting his master from the onslaught of more aggressive colleagues. Laburu had abandoned his stable if somewhat unexciting job with Argentine TV, to devote himself full time to recording on film every aspect of Maradona's private and professional life that might prove helpful in promoting the footballer's image as an unrivalled genius. In the early days in Naples, when Maradona was staying in the Hotel Royale, it was to the modest home of Laburu and his wife that Maradona escaped for a night of pizza and cards, safe from the glare of publicity.

But perhaps no one had more reason to feel betrayed than Cyterszpiler, the man who from his teens had devoted all his energies to Maradona. When the news of his dismissal was conveyed to him that day in Mexico, the past came back to Cyterszpiler in a series of quick snapshots. It reminded him of his unswerving friendship: Cyterszpiler buying Maradona a can of Coke and some biscuits, and inviting him to the boxing ring, well away from the shanty town; Cyterszpiler negotiating a contract with Boca Juniors; Cyterszpiler negotiating a contract with Barcelona; Cyterszpiler negotiating a contract with Napoli. If there was a kingmaker it was Cyterszpiler. Yet all this appears to have counted for very little when one day Maradona got a call from Buenos Aires, to be told that Maradona Productions was once again on the verge of bankruptcy, and that one of its recent financial transactions had been a bad loan approved by Cyterszpiler. There was no evidence to support an allegation that Cyterszpiler had indirectly embroiled himself in an operation that effectively defrauded the very company he had helped set up, yet it is this allegation that appears to have stuck in Maradona's mind. He suspected that Cyterszpiler may have been taking advantage of him. For he was beginning to find it difficult to distinguish accurately between those who were his friends and those who were milking him. There was no such doubt in his actions, however. Maradona demanded loyalty and was ruthless whenever he suspected betrayal.

What is certainly true is that Maradona Productions had not recovered from the financial problems into which it had got itself in Barcelona. The pattern of conspicuous overspending and irregular revenue had continued in Naples, with Maradona investing in his personal leisure as if there were no tomorrow, and the Camorra cutting into the financial gains made from the promotion of Maradona's image. 'Maradona began to spend more and more money and Jorge [Cyterszpiler] just didn't know how to say no. Maradona would say buy me this, and he would,' recalled one member of the Maradona staff in Naples.

And yet the financial problems of Maradona Productions were no worse in Naples than they had been in Barcelona, and do not in themselves explain the manner in which Cyterszpiler and the others were treated. It is curiously apposite that Maradona should have chosen the feast day of Naples' patron saint San Genaro to make known his drastic decision, as if once again he felt called to act by some divine intervention. Cyterszpiler, Blanco and Laburu, however, would spend the following years grappling with more mundane explanations for their betrayal. The more they looked back on those days in Naples, the more they came to believe that it was there that Maradona's process of decline and fall had begun. Pressurized by the expectations of a whole community, not to mention his own parents, undermined by the inherent difficulties of combining his professionalism with an increasingly unstable domestic life, Maradona had began to lose sight not just of who his real friends were, but also of who exactly he was.

14

STARDUST

It was in December 1985 that Maradona met someone who for a short time was to help him get in touch with himself: a twenty-year-old Neapolitan woman called Cristiana Sinagra. She belonged to the coterie that had formed round Maradona's sister Maria, her husband Gabriel Esposito, and Maradona's two younger brothers, Hugo and Lalo. Cristiana's best friend was going out with Hugo, while her younger sister had set her eyes on Lalo. It was Maria's idea to expand the near-incestuous ménage by introducing Diego to Cristiana.

The opportunity came one evening when Claudia was away in Argentina. Maria organized a supper party for her friends in the ground-floor apartment below Diego's where she lived. Diego was invited and met Cristiana for the first time. The setting and the circumstances made a relationship virtually inevitable. Maradona found in Cristiana a person who had clearly been accepted as part of the tribe and yet who seemed to be different from the run of easy women he had had for most of his professional career. Small, modestly framed and with hooded eyes, Cristiana was no Heather Parisi. Nor was she Claudia. She had no reason to feel antagonistic towards Maradona. Her values were traditional rather than feminist, which made her initially cautious yet ultimately vulnerable to Maradona's seduction. Her account of how their relationship developed suggests that for a while true love rather than lust prevailed in the life of Diego Maradona.

The couple appear to have formed a genuine friendship before even contemplating having sex. 'We got to know each other only gradually. I found that there was a part of him that was very different to his public image. The Diego I knew was not the Diego that appears in newspapers. He seemed to me to be capable of real loyalty, and to care about what really matters in life. Not arrogant, not decadent. No overdrinking, no drugs. Just a very loving, caring, sensitive, sweet person who with me felt he was behaving true to his real self,' Cristiana told me. We had arranged to meet in a café on the outskirts on Naples in December 1995. She had picked a venue from where she knew she could observe newcomers, and was accompanied by two friends. Ten years on from that fateful first encounter with Maradona, her memory remained undiminished, as did her fear of a personal vendetta against her. Only later, when I had won her trust, did she offer to take me to see what for her was the undisputed evidence supporting her version of events.

Three days later, on a damp afternoon in the hills of Naples, where the smell of volcanic sulphur hung heavy in the air, she introduced me to her and Diego Maradona's son, Diegito. We sat watching him kicking a football around with ten other nine-year-olds who played in the local children's league. This was no dusty backyard in Villa Fiorito, but a large training ground belonging to a private fee-paying sports complex. The parents, like Cristiana, were all drawn from the middle class. And yet quite apart from the physical resemblance, there was no doubting from the gestures of the young player that there was a Maradona in our midst. Diegito's self-confidence and skill set him apart from the other kids. While most seemed to be struggling with the ball, Diegito took it as if he had never left it, dribbling it in and out of a line of plastic bollards before driving it home. After each goal, the boy would break away and run across the pitch to where his mother was, looking up at the sky and gripping his fists in a precise imitation of his father. Although he played with his right foot rather than his left, he seemed determined to go as far, if not further, than his dad. He had told his mother that his one ambition was to play for Argentina one day.

Ten years earlier, before Diegito was conceived, Maradona changed his lifestyle, cutting back on his nightlife and devoting his leisure time to intimate moments with Cristiana. The more time they spent together, the more Maradona found the approval he was always seeking from his family. His sister Maria was instrumental in helping fuel the relationship, taking Cristiana increasingly into her confidence. The two women would go on shopping sprees together, and often share in the nannying of Maria's young children. Most crucially, Cristiana seemed to win the seal of approval from Tota, the supreme queen of the Maradona tribe, forever watching over her genius eldest son. 'She's a great girl and deserves to be treated differently from Diego's other girls, there to be used one week and discarded the next,' Tota confided in a conversation with the housemaid at the time.

During Maradona's love sessions with Cristiana, he would whisper in her ear that he longed to have a child with her. They even discussed the possibility of marriage. Maradona would ring her every day from the training ground. 'A million kisses,' was his favourite sign-off. Cristiana, embroiled in the first love affair of her life, walked on cloud nine, and became less deliberately careless as oblivious to the consequences of unprotected sex.

The picture-book romance came down to earth with a bump in April 1986 when Cristiana was unable to conceal from the rest of the Maradona family that she was pregnant. She has always insisted that she had told Maradona at an early stage and that he was initially very supportive of her wish to have the baby. But when the news was shared with the rest of his family, pressure began to build up on her to have the child aborted. Maradona's change of attitude appears to have set in after he consulted some of his male friends. He was also deeply influenced by his family. Maria, claiming to know her brother rather better than Cristiana, told her that her best chance of saving her relationship would be to get rid of the child. As for Tota, she initially gave her blessing to the relationship, only subsequently to encourage her son to turn away from it. The loving, tender Diego evaporated overnight, and instead there re-emerged Maradona the King, the macho child of divine intervention, spoilt brat who could do no wrong, fated to pursue his ambition, untrammelled by worldly responsibilities. Maradona began to see Cristiana not as a deliverance but as a burden, dropping any romantic feelings and treating her instead to a spate of violent verbal abuse. At one point, Cristiana's father privately visited Maradona and begged him to show a sense of responsibility towards his daughter. 'Yes, that child is mine, but I don't want to see Cristiana give birth to it,' was the only reply he got. By then, the relationship was effectively dead, Claudia was on her way back to Italy, determined to reclaim her role as Maradona's girlfriend, and the man himself was busying himself with thoughts of his latest challenge: the World Cup in Mexico.

15

MEXICAN FIESTA

Whatever public doubts have surrounded the career of Diego Maradona, there has always been virtual unanimity surrounding his role in the 1986 World Cup in Mexico. Until then, seldom had a single player been the subject of such media focus or popular enthusiasm in the competition. To the hundreds of journalists and millions of spectators who watched the World Cup live and on TV, the event was virtually dominated from start to finish by Maradona's genius. It seemed to the great majority of those who witnessed his performance that, for all his troubles in Barcelona and in the World Cup in Spain in 1982, the boy from Villa Fiorito had at the age of twenty-five chosen the Aztec capital as the place to assert his status as the King of Football.

Yet behind the image of success lay a background of intense personal struggle, brutal rivalry and cynical management, which for the most part escaped public scrutiny at the time. Of all the burdens that Maradona carried with him to Mexico from Naples that summer none weighed so heavily on his mind as the imminent birth of an illegitimate child whom he had agreed to father only to reject subsequently. Before his departure he had given one of those periodic interviews with a journalist of his choice in order to bare his soul. 'Yeah, I feel really alone,' he told Ernesto Cherquis Bialo, then editor of the Argentine football magazine *Gráfico*, 'I've been feeling like packing the whole thing. Thank goodness my mum's been with me . . . although I can tell you there are some mornings when I see her and I say, "Mum, one of these days we're just going to get the hell out of here." Seriously. I'm in a bad way.'

By breaking off his relationship with Cristiana Sinagra, the child's mother and perhaps the only woman he had ever truly loved, Maradona had hoped that the problem would simply evaporate. The distance that separated Mexico from Italy had initially fuelled this self-delusion. And yet the problem returned to haunt him with a vengeance when, a few days before the start of the World Cup, a long-distance call from Naples was put through to his room in the Club America where the Argentine team were staying. The caller was his brother-in-law Gabriel Esposito, whose wife Maria had become one of Cristiana's best friends. Esposito volunteered the latest information on what in Naples would in time burst into the headlines as the 'Sinagra affair'. By then Cristiana was eight months pregnant. With the backing of her own family, and some of her friends, she had become even more entrenched in her position of wanting to have her child. She was also no longer prepared passively to accept Maradona's refusal to assume any parental responsibility. She told Maria that she had every intention of publicizing the birth, and letting the world at large know who the father was. Moreover, she was quite prepared to take Maradona to court if he persisted in denying his paternity. Maradona emerged from the conversation shell-shocked and wandered among his team mates for the next two days looking drawn and tense.

Maradona had flown to Mexico with an Argentine team which while not necessarily the favourite to win was generally regarded as one of the strongest contenders. At the time few observers appear to have noticed the tensions and divisions within the team and its inherent sense of insecurity as it prepared to do battle. Argentina had yet to recover from the humiliations of the previous World Cup. In its pre-Mexico warm-ups and qualifying matches, it had failed to gel as a unit. Instead the personality clashes between some of its key players had become more acute. Among them was that between Maradona and Daniel Passarella, the incoming and outgoing captains of the team. Passarella was one of the oldest and most experienced of the Argentine players and resented being replaced by someone as young and unpredictable as Maradona. Passarella had captained Argentina to World Cup victory in 1978, his autocratic style of leadership perfectly in tune with the military régime in power at the time. He had raised no objections to Menotti's decision to exclude Maradona from the team. Four years later, in Spain, Passarella had tried to keep up the morale of the team, only to see its discipline snap with Maradona as the worst offender. Ever since then the somewhat priggish Passarella had begrudged Maradona's success, believing him overvalued as a player and irresponsibly decadent in his private life. In one incident in the run-up to the Mexico World Cup, Passarella had stormed angrily into Maradona's hotel room and interrupted a party, shouting, 'If you are going to be captain, why don't you behave like one!'

There were also tensions, though between Maradona and Ricardo Bochini, the oldest member of the Argentine squad. As a young teenager, Maradona had put Bochini – 'El Bocha' – on his list of footballing heroes, along with Pele and Johan Cruyff, after watching him lead Independiente to victory in the South American Cup. El Bocha had been described by one of his colleagues as a 'Woody Allen of the football pitch', a small, seemingly hopeless body, a face destined for failure, and yet a talent with the ball that left taller, stronger and more handsome players as useless as broken statues in his wake. Now thirty-seven, El Bocha had passed his prime, and his status as Argentina's most popular player had long been overtaken by Maradona. But he felt loyal to Passarella's captaincy, and secretly envied the young prince Maradona who had risen to take over the kingdom.

As things turned out, the obsessively competitive Passarella didn't even get a place in the team, his position further undermined by an attack of Montezuma's revenge – the local colic – and a calf injury. El Bocha sat on the substitutes' bench for most of the competition. He was brought out for just six minutes at the end of the semi-final, to be greeted by Maradona with the words 'Well done, maestro!' Small wonder that when El Bocha returned to Argentina, he spoke of Mexico as the competition he personally would most prefer to forget. 'I didn't feel champion of the world,' he commented, barely hiding his sense of humiliation.

And yet Argentina did, of course, become World Champions once again. The success was down to the ability of Maradona to persevere through his own personal crisis for the duration of the competition. Such will power manifested itself almost from the moment the Argentine squad arrived at the Club America. It was witnessed at close quarters by Paulo Pauletti, the Italian journalist who had befriended the player. Youthful and outgoing, Pauletti had ingratiated himself with Maradona by helping to accelerate his departure from Barcelona and his transfer to Napoli with a very pro-Napoli TV interview. In Mexico, Pauletti was given exclusive access to the Club America, while the bulk of the world press had to content themselves with the impromptu press conferences Maradona gave from behind the barbed wire surrounding the squad's training camp. When Pauletti glimpsed Maradona for the first time sitting in the lobby of the Club America, he was taken back by the player's physical and mental transformation. 'He seemed full of strength, resolution and youthful energy,' Pauletti recalled. Other reporters who followed Maradona closely in that World Cup, like Ezequiel Moores, remembered how Maradona seemed to be unprecedentedly lucid. While in Mexico, he seemed to have resolved to have only one thing on his mind, to win.

In this, his principal inspiration appears to have been Carlos Bilardo, the new Argentine manager. Bilardo had no time for the café philosophies of his predecessor César Menotti, whom he blamed for the disorganization and ultimate defeat of the Argentine squad in 1982. Bilardo had none of Menotti's playboy good looks, nor did he share in his left-wing politics. Together with his assistant, Carlos Pachame, Bilardo came from the tough no-nonsense school of Argentine football, where anything was permissible as long as it secured victory. He and Pachame had learned their football playing for Estudiantes, the Argentine champions of the 1960s, who became notorious internationally for their dirty play. In one memorable clash between Estudiantes and Manchester United, Bilardo had head-butted Nobby Stiles, leaving it up to Pachame to kick open Bobby Charlton's shin.

But as a qualified doctor, Bilardo could also apply some science to the game, basing his strategy and training for each match on careful observation and analysis of each of his players and those of the opposition. Bilardo's football was eclectic. For him Maradona was a player who defied dogma and philosophy, a unique talent who required guidance and indulgence in carefully measured doses.

Bilardo had been a neighbour of Francis Cornejo, the Argentinos Juniors scout who had discovered Maradona as a boy. He had first watched Maradona kick a football during the interval of a first-division game, subsequently following his rise to star status as an official of the Argentine Football Association. When Bilardo was appointed to succeed Menotti in 1983, he consulted widely with Argentina's international players before flying into Barcelona and offering Maradona the captaincy of the team. The move was criticized by the Spanish press, which judged it an unnecessary distraction for a player whose relationship with Barcelona was already turning out to be conflictual. But Bilardo never had any regrets. 'I talked to him for five hours, until about three in the morning in his house. He was with his mum,' recalled Bilardo. 'I explained my plans for the team and I found him very happy, very enthusiastic ... I saw in front of me a great player, one that was potentially the best in the world ... I liked the idea of having him as my captain from the first day. In choosing him I put in all my experience as doctor, player and manager. I knew that the captaincy would in time become a major incentive for him. I also felt that he was going to be a popular choice with the players. Because he was the best, he would lead by example, and thus I could build my squad around him.'

Maradona's special status within the squad was accepted by Bilardo from the outset. While other players were subjected to a common and rigid training programme, together with rules about their sleeping and leisure habits, Maradona was allowed his own personal trainer, Fernando Signorini, and 'masseur' Victor Galindes, and permitted whatever flexibility was thought necessary to keep him in a positive frame of mind. 'I realized from an early stage that he had to have a different régime from the others,' Bilardo told me. 'I said to myself, there is Maradona and there is the rest of the team.'

In Signorini and Galindes there seemed to be reflected all the inherent contradictions of Maradona. Signorini was extrovert and good-humoured, while never losing his grip on reality. Having lived much of his professional life outside Argentina, he was not as susceptible to intrigue as many of the other members of the Maradona clan. He had lost none of the youthful ebullience that Maradona had first spotted playing tennis in Barcelona. Of all the members of the Argentine squad, he was the most thoughtful and self-disciplined, at all times trying against enormous odds to convince Maradona of the great benefits that could be gained from both a healthy mind and a healthy body.

Galindes, by contrast, inhabited the rougher edges of Maradona's existence. From a poor background like Maradona, he was one of several friends the player had taken with him to Barcelona who had immediately alienated the locals. Galindes' professional aptitude mattered rather less than his tribal loyalty and his representation of a world that Maradona could never quite put behind him. His qualifications for the job of 'masseur' were dubious. He spent rather more time carrying equipment and clothes for Maradona, and sharing his devotion to the Virgin of Luján, one of Argentina's most venerated religious icons, prior to matches. He was less religious than superstitious, believing that magic could be conjured up to ensure victory on the playing fields. When not praying or calculating lucky numbers, Galindes talked the tough, uncompromising language of the shanty town in a gravel voice. He had an aggressive personality which easily turned to violence. In Barcelona he had fuelled Maradona's sense of social alienation by accusing the Cataláns of deliberate racism towards Argentinians. Like his mentor, Galindes seems to have felt much more at home in Naples and in Mexico than in Spain.

As well as allowing Maradona a choice of who he wanted to be looked after by, Bilardo also showed some flexibility over the player's leisure time. He was allowed to see his family, and while other members of the squad were expected to be tucked up in bed by midnight at the latest, it was accepted that Maradona would always be the last to go to sleep. Bilardo, himself an insomniac as a result of studying at night as a medical student, would often stay up until two or three in the morning in conversation with Maradona.

Maradona's special régime extended itself to his treatment at the hands of other members of the medical profession. The injury problems which had dogged him from his early days as a professional footballer and had been aggravated in Barcelona had returned to haunt him in Naples. His body suffered the effects of a vicious circle of pain, recovery and more pain, brought on by the tendency of the doctors who treated him to rely on psychology and drugs rather than operations to keep up his performance. His squat, muscular frame was pumped full of cortisone and other painkillers, the ankle that had been so brutally broken by the 'butcher of Bilbao' still held together by a nail. In Naples, the ankle continued to bruise and inflame every time he played a match.

Before arriving in Mexico Maradona was sent to Rome to submit himself to a series of 'tests' with Dr Dalmonte of the Italian Olympic Committee, to ensure that his bloodstream did not contain any substances that might show up in a doping test during the World Cup. The move was somewhat ironic given the lack of official action against rampant doping in Italy. Similar tests were carried out by Argentine doctors on other members of the squad in the lead-up to Mexico and are thought to have shown up positive, although they were not reported to FIFA.

There is no evidence that Maradona took illegal substances to enhance his performance during the Mexico World Cup. According to one FIFA insider, the player was tested three times during the competition, but the results were all negative and therefore were never publicized. The world of drugs, however, continued to knock on the door of the Argentine squad. During the competition a member of the *barras bravas*, the notorious and fanatical organization of Argentine hooligans, was intercepted and arrested after offering members of the squad a regular supply of cocaine. Whether Maradona himself was caught up in the incident is unclear. What is certainly true is that doctors and officials once again conspired to ensure that Maradona played, whatever the longer-term effects on his physical well-being may have been. Maradona was no innocent victim in this. His own will power and determination to succeed caused him to accept treatment which most other players would have turned down.

Maradona's injuries were such that he was receiving a regular course of injections in the run-up to his first World Cup game in Mexico. Even then he was forced to play with one boot several measurements larger than his normal size, so inflamed did his ankle continue to become in the course of a game. The official Argentine doctor was Dr Madero. At one point his medical team included a doctor who is alleged to have been linked to a doping scandal involving a body-builder. As a medically qualified manager, Bilardo appears to have had few qualms of conscience about the harsh treatment through which Maradona was put. It was, like so many of his tactics on the field, a necessary means to an end. 'It was important that Maradona played, to have him on the pitch, whatever physical state he was really in,' Bilardo recalled. 'I felt that as long as he could walk, as long as he could bear the pain, he should be out there.'

It was the view of most football experts that Maradona's talent for the game had improved since the World Cup in Spain in 1982. His prolonged professional absence from his homeland had given him a better understanding of international football, particularly the skills and tactics of European teams. He had matured as a player. After his chequered time with Barcelona, he appeared to have recovered his enthusiasm and energy in his first two seasons with Naples. The prospect of leading the Argentine national team had given him the kind of self-confidence he needed to overcome his pressing personal problems. Since Bilardo had taken over the management in 1983, Argentina had chalked up a less than impressive record, winning only thirteen out of thirty-four internationals. But Maradona's particular genius had perhaps been no more clearly demonstrated than during a qualifying match against Colombia. As usual with encounters between the two teams, the match was played in a hostile atmosphere. Periodically, rival fans would shout abuse or throw some projectile on to the pitch. At one point a Colombian threw an orange at Maradona. Somehow the player saw it coming, caught it on his foot, tapped it gently to his other foot and continued to pass it from one leg to the other, before turning and kicking it with tremendous force back into the terraces. Maradona had played more elaborate moves with a football both with Barcelona and Naples, but the gesture alone suggested that he had not lost that magic and sense of enjoyment he had displayed as a young boy when he had first played with an orange before the cameras.

Bilardo arrived in Mexico conscious that his future and Argentina's fate were heavily dependent on Maradona. Other players, such as the Real Madrid winger Jorge Valdano and the former captain Daniel Passarella, privately conveyed to journalists their fears that one man's brilliance would be insufficient to outweigh the apparent weaknesses of the team. Valdano, a left-wing intellectual of the Menotti school of philosophical football, had adapted with difficulty to Bilardo's pragmatism, while Passarella's view appeared still to be tinged with jealousy. Valdano hugely admired Maradona, and was a personal friend. But he was equally aware just how potentially vulnerable Bilardo's Argentine squad was. With Maradona, Argentina might just reach the finals. Without him, the team's tactical game as devised by Bilardo, a 4–3–3 formation with Maradona as the offensive key, would collapse like a pack of cards.

As ever, it was left to the former Argentine international Ossie Ardiles to double up as diplomat and restore a sense of optimism around the figure of Maradona. 'If I had to put money on one man to run the show, it would be Diego Maradona,' Ardiles told British journalist John Motson on the eve of the competition.

And Ardiles was proved right. During the competition, players like Valdano and José Luis Brown, the central defender who replaced Passarella, helped to lift Argentina from its pre-competition doldrums. But it was Maradona who emerged as the undisputed star, not just of his own team but of the whole competition. His status was summed up by Hugh McIlvanney on the eve of Argentina's final against West Germany. 'Never before in more than half a century of World Cups has the talent of a single footballer loomed so pervasively over everybody's thinking about the final,' he wrote in the *Observer*. 'Maradona's impact goes far beyond the simple realization that he is indisputably the best and most exciting player now at work in the game. It is inseparable from the potent sense of declaration inherent in almost everything he has done in the field here in Mexico, from his vast public's conviction that he has chosen the Aztec stadium as the setting for the definitive statement of his genius.'

16

FALKLANDS ROUND TWO

For sheer drama and controversy Maradona's performance in Argentina's quarter-final clash with England was to hang in the memory of millions of fans long after Mexico '86 was over. With the exception of the infamous match between El Salvador and Honduras, which provoked armed conflict between two countries in 1969, no international encounter had been preceded by so much political mud-slinging. In Spain four years earlier Maradona's sending off had seemed to mirror Argentina's humiliation on the battlefields of the Falklands. Four years on, his encounter with the old enemy on the playing fields was preceded by a good dose of popular jingoism on both sides. While the British tabloids tried their best to portray the English squad as an updated version of the Task Force – 'Mexico alerts 5,000 troops,' warned one headline; 'Argies here we come!' screamed another – their Argentine equivalents did their bit. They put Maradona on a par with General José San Martín, Argentina's nineteenth-century revolutionary hero who helped liberate the country from its colonial shackles. 'We're coming to get you, pirates!' declared in bold headline the ever-populist *Crónica*. Thus prompted, groups of *barras bravas* boarded the planes from Buenos Aires to Mexico City, pledging revenge for their brothers who had died in the Malvinas and burning English flags as they went.

In conversations with Argentine journalists, Valdano seemed to view the game with England as part of a dialectical process in which colonialism would finally be overcome. The extrovert goalkeeper Nery Pumpido had less time for philosophy, declaring bluntly, 'To beat the English would represent a double satisfaction for everything that happened in the Malvinas.' Privately Maradona sympathized with the raw emotion of the *barras bravas*, and like a majority of his countrymen found it difficult to disengage his view of the English with the Argentine textbook portrayal of them as arrogant colonialist usurpers. These feelings undoubtedly fired his determination to beat England on the pitch. But in the run-up to the game, Maradona kept his feelings very much to himself, showing remarkable self-discipline in the midst of intense media pressure.

In England, it was Tottenham Hotspur fans who had had, a few weeks earlier, a privileged preview of the new Maradona. He had played at White Hart Lane, in a testimonial for Ossie Ardiles. Among those who played alongside the Argentinians against the guests, Inter-Milan, was future England coach Glenn Hoddle, who would later recall the game as one of the most enjoyable he had played in a long time. Maradona and Ardiles were greeted with thunderous applause by the Spurs supporters. Maradona did not extend himself to the full, but played with sufficient skill to confirm Hoddle and thousands of fans in their admiration for 'this stocky little genius'.

Maradona himself was struck by the particular skills of Hoddle, who as a child had learned his tricks from watching Brazilians on TV and who in adulthood showed the imagination and flair that seemed to many outsiders to be lacking in English football. From that time Maradona considered Hoddle among only a handful of English football personalities, including Platt, Keegan, Venables and Gascoigne, worthy of serious attention.

When Maradona and Hoddle next met, in Mexico, it was in very different circumstances: highly charged emotionally, with everything to win or lose. Hoddle was gratified that in spite of it all, Maradona had not forgotten him. As the two players stood together in the tunnel of the Azteca stadium minutes before the start of the World Cup quarter-final, Maradona caught Hoddle's eye, winked and gave him a thumbs up. Despite Maradona's habit of referring to himself in the third person, as is the wont of kings and gods, his humanity, his basic instinct also shone through. 'When we go on the field it is the game of football that matters and not who won the war,' he declared in one press conference, before his game against England. 'Look, mate, I play football. About politics I know nothing. Nothing, mate, nothing,' he insisted on another occasion when confronted by John Carlin, for the London *Times*.

What the media didn't know was the extent to which diplomacy and football had become interlocked in the run-up to the game. Behind-the-scenes talks between the British and Argentine ambassadors, and a phone call to Bilardo from the Argentine President

Raul Alfonsín resulted in the Argentine coach agreeing with his English counterpart Bobby Robson to depoliticize the game. From early on in the competition, when an encounter between Argentina and England had seemed inevitable, Bilardo had privately briefed Maradona as captain and the rest of the Argentine squad that on no account should they say anything in the comments to the press that might provoke the fans of either country. 'I told the players, "Señores, this is a World Cup, this is football, if anyone asks you about UK–Argentine relations, you just talk about football." I knew that the Malvinas war was still very fresh in people's minds, but I wasn't seeking revenge,' Bilardo recalled.

The English manager Bobby Robson adopted a similar strategy, as he later recorded in his diary: 'No matter how hard I tried to avoid the political undertones, I couldn't hide the fact that four years ago we had fought a war with Argentina. When I got the players together I told them not to become involved in the political aspects. The same went for me, too. We were here to play football and I am a manager, not a politician.' Robson was confident he would have no problem with his own players. His main anxiety was that the Argentine supporters might provoke the 'so far well-behaved' British, sparking off a riot in front of the world's TV cameras.

Maradona approached the English game with his performance in the World Cup already greatly assisted by some efficient refereeing. In Spain, both during the World Cup and in Barcelona, Maradona's game had often been so undermined by bad refereeing as to become almost unplayable. While deliberate fouls on him were often overlooked, his tendency to exaggerate his falls and show his frustration in operatic gestures was promptly dealt with. When his temperament boiled over when he found himself unable to protect his skills and play the game, far from winning sympathy he was simply punished all the more. By contrast, in Mexico Maradona found referees prepared to defend him, making it less necessary for him to retaliate and put on a show. He was also helped by Bilardo, who allowed him considerable flexibility on the field in order to counter the kind of tight marking that had neutralized him when Argentina played Italy in 1982. As the former England manager Ron Greenwood commented at the time, following Argentina's victory over Uruguay, 'He seemed to be in everything . . . He was hampered, he was pushed, but he didn't retaliate, he just got on with the job. I thought, "Full marks to you, old son."'

At no time did refereeing prove itself to be more critically on the side of Maradona than in the England game. Once the politics had been stripped away it was a match that seemed destined to become a titanic struggle not so much between two countries, or even two teams, as between two outstanding players – Maradona and the English goalkeeper Peter Shilton. The respective relationship of each to their teams seemed almost in direct parallel. While Argentina recognized its dependence on the offensive skills of Maradona, many English commentators believed that England's prospects had become inseparable from Shilton's capacity to block goals. Surveying his own team's prospects prior to the match, Robson was confident that Shilton would be backed up by a formation capable of controlling the one Argentine player all the English feared. In a pre-match briefing, Robson warned his players to be on their guard against Maradona, that he had the ability to change an entire game in five minutes, but not develop a phobia about him. As he later noted in his diary, 'We would crowd him, push him across the field. We would keep our back four in position, not lose our shape and not dive in.' While Bilardo was uncertain about his team's ability to support Maradona, Robson was quietly confident and sensed his players felt the same way. England had won its last two games by three goals, and in Robson's four years as manager had never lost by as much. 'This time one goal would be enough. I wasn't greedy,' he wrote.

The first half of the game proved an anti-climax, with Argentina's defence easily frustrating England's shameless use of the long-ball strategy. While Maradona saved his energies, Hoddle found himself and Peter Reid bypassed in the midfield, and strikers Gary Lineker and Peter Beardsley were up against an impenetrable Argentine wall. Ten minutes into the game, the first foul of the match brought an instant booking for Terry Fenwick from the Tunisian referee, Ali Bennaceur, which was to inhibit England's play from then on. Although the Tunisian had the reputation of being one of Africa's best referees, Robson detected he was nervous from the outset of the game, with a potential for pro-Argentine bias.

Five minutes into the second half, and with no goals scored, Robson's worst fears were confirmed. Maradona launched an attack on the English defence, beating a couple of players, before losing the move in a failed pass to Valdano. In the ensuing confusion near the English goal, Steve Hodge hooked the ball over his head, meaning it for Shilton. By then Maradona was set to recover what he had lost moments earlier, and rose to meet Shilton. The clash involved bodies and hands, some more legitimate than others. Into the net went the ball. Maradona was euphoric, racing, without waiting for a verdict, to celebrate with his team mates. Shilton and the rest of the English team appealed immediately for hand ball. The English goalkeeper was so sickened by the decision that he ran out of his area signalling the infringement. It was the first time the normally cool-headed Shilton had displayed such public emotion. The linesman and the referee agreed it was a goal. For Maradona that was all that mattered.

Four minutes later, Maradona scored again, this time with a goal that was to go down in the annals as one of the best in footballing history. In the words of Brian Glanville, it was a goal 'so unusual, almost romantic, that it might have been scored by some schoolboy hero, or some remote Corinthian, from the days when dribbling was the vogue. It hardly belonged to so apparently rational and rationalized an era as ours, to a period in football when the dribbler seemed almost as extinct as the pterodactyl.' Picking up the ball inside his own half and keeping it so close to his boots as to make it seemed glued to them, Maradona proceeded to carve his way through the English side, with the effortless movement of a racing skier in slalom. 'When I got the ball towards the right and saw that Peter Reid couldn't catch me,' Maradona later recalled, 'I felt a very big urge to go on running with the ball. I seemed to be able to leave everyone behind.'

A swerve to the left easily beat Gary Stevens. The next feint sent Terry Butcher running in the wrong direction, looking more like a startled sheep than an international defender. Fenwick tried to elbow Maradona, then hesitated. He had already been booked, and feared the consequences of bringing Maradona down. 'He couldn't slip me up. I had too much speed behind me,' recalled Maradona, who had no doubt that Fenwick wanted to up-end him. Having shrugged off Fenwick and without for an instant losing his control of the ball, Maradona found the time to assess Shilton's position. The English goalkeeper seemed desperate to second-guess the Argentine's next move, so Maradona kept going, leaving his strike to the last possible moment. The split-second delay prompted a final rearguard action by Butcher. He tried to break Maradona's momentum with an attempted tackle, again to no avail. The Argentine checked himself and effortlessly passed the ball from his right foot to his left before casually slipping it past Shilton.

This time the English squad could only hold their breath in sheer amazement. 'There was no lack of discipline on our part, no errors,' recalled Robson, 'just the genius of one player who went through half our team to score the best goal of the competition.' As for Maradona's colleagues, they saw the goal as a definitive statement of his very special status not just in the team but in the world of football generally. Of the Argentine players, it was perhaps the midfielder Valdano who had been best positioned to help Maradona turn his drive towards the English goal into a team effort. From the outset Valdano picked up speed from within his own half and tried to run with Maradona, only to realize that there was no part for him to play in the creation of a goal that could never have been rehearsed.

'At first I went along with him out of a sense of responsibility, but then I realized I was just one more spectator,' Valdano recalled. 'I didn't feel there was anything I could do. It was his goal and had nothing to do with the team. It was Diego's personal adventure, one that was totally spectacular.' England would later go on to score a goal, but Argentina won the match 2–1.

The post-mortem had English commentators in particular focusing on Maradona's first goal. There seemed absolutely no doubt in their minds that it was hand ball and should have been disallowed. The two players closest to the mêlée, Shilton and Hoddle, were utterly convinced it had been hand ball, and they made their feelings known to the referee. 'Some of the players confessed to me later that they had missed it and didn't really know what had happened until they had seen the action replay on television,' Hoddle later recalled in his autobiography *Spurred to Success*. 'But I actually saw Maradona's hand go up and punch the ball. I must admit he tried to disguise it very well, flicking his head at the same time as he handled. But it hadn't fooled me. I have seen that done in Sunday morning matches at the local park, and the players there have never got away with it.' Shilton similarly felt cheated, and had no doubt that the only way Maradona could have beaten him in that situation was by using his hand.

Terry Butcher was among the players who had to watch the action replay on TV to see Maradona quite clearly punch the ball in. On the field Butcher's view, like that of the referee, had been impeded by Maradona's head. But later in the game Butcher asked Maradona if he had handled the ball. 'He just smiled and pointed to his head,' Butcher later recalled.

None of the Argentine players had been near enough to the goal to see what had taken place. Nor did they, in their subsequent euphoria, think of questioning their captain. The Argentine manager, Bilardo, however, showed none of the certainty of his English counterpart. Robson protested and continued to protest for years afterwards that Maradona used his hand. No one in the English dug-out had any doubts at all. In 1995, Robson recalled in an English TV profile of Maradona, 'I was instantly aware that he'd handled it and for a couple of seconds didn't panic. Then I realized that everyone was rushing back to the halfway line, including the referee and the linesman, and my instant reaction was, Hell, they haven't seen it, and then suddenly it all dawned on me. This was a goal. We were one goal down. And they'd allowed it to stand.'

The moment the ball was in the net Bilardo had jumped to his feet and shouted, 'Goal.' According to him, both he and Robson were about 60 metres from the English goal and could only really be guided by the reaction of their players. Bilardo later heard from some of his own players that it might have been a hand ball, and asked to see a replay on video and was not so sure. 'When it happened I felt it wasn't hand ball. But then after watching the playback, I thought, well, there was some doubt. Put it that way. I'm not saying yes or no. I never question referees' decisions.'

There is a sense in which the goal was simply a product of commercial football, in which traditional attitudes of fair play have been replaced by the need to succeed by whatever means. In *Soccer Match Control*, a book published at around the time of the Mexico World Cup, the writer Stanley Lover noted that gamesmanship was the art of cheating while still believing that you are morally in the right. The referee is there to be outwitted and the only crime is to be found out. Cheating has become as much a part of football as sponsorship. Even Hoddle, who felt 'absolutely sick inside' as a result of the incident, blamed it less on Maradona than on the referee and the linesman (who was in a position to see) for not spotting the infringement. That Maradona's controversial goal, far from being condemned, was actually applauded by his fellow countrymen, was a reminder of how Argentines have traditionally always put their own interpretation on the notion of gamesmanship. The goal, particularly given that it was scored against the English, was viewed as a display of *viveza*, that quality of craftiness so admired in Argentina.

There is no doubt that, in football, cheating on the pitch is part of the game. Players try to score goals by hook or by crook. A good referee is one who knows how to distinguish between a peccadillo and a sin; a bad referee one who either punishes too much or misses too much. The first goal against England clearly fell into the latter category. As Hoddle put it later, 'All players, at some stage of their careers, have flicked a hand out or tried to punch the ball into the goal, more out of cheekiness than an urge to cheat. Few have ever got away with it.'

But what took Maradona's goal beyond these considerations was its symbolic nature. Had it been scored by any other player, it would probably have been forgotten by now. But in his case it became an expression of a flawed genius. Neither in the immediate aftermath of the game nor in the years that followed did Maradona ever admit to his folly. He called that goal the Hand of God. By that he meant not that he didn't use his hand, but that he did and got away with it, with God's blessing. His team mates, led by Valdano, turned themselves into disciples. They saw both goals against the English as emanating from a hugely individualistic talent that in style and vision was above and beyond them. Their perception fuelled Maradona's own claim of divine inspiration.

In the context of Maradona's life, one can see how both goals against England in Mexico that June belonged very much to the same man. The first showed Maradona the urchin child who had grown to be a star, still so unsure of his true self as to feel the need to cheat. The second showed Maradona the hugely gifted player of exceptional skill whose combination of acceleration, control, strength and accuracy translated into unrivalled greatness on the field. In Mexico, the small, stocky Maradona remained nimble enough and fast enough to evade his markers; his improvisation and vision were such as to allow him to get out of the toughest of holes when not creating extraordinary opportunities for his team mates, weighting balls perfectly. Lesser players might have had no option but to use their hands. Maradona's tragedy lay in believing he had to, and having to justify it afterwards, when his genius should have made it unnecessary.

Maradona emerged from the Mexico World Cup with his status as one of the greatest footballers of all time greatly strengthened, even though his image as a person was tarnished by dissension. Argentina's 3–2 victory over West Germany in the final proved something of an anticlimax after the controversy and brilliance of the match against England. But Maradona scored a personal triumph in his gladiatorial contest with West Germany's midfielder Lothar Matthäus, the sheer skill and self-discipline of the Argentine ultimately overcoming the tough and relentless marking of the German. And in the end it was Maradona who tipped the match in his team's favour: with a deft pass to midfielder Jorge Burruchaga, he set up Argentina's winning goal.

It was a fitting end to a competition that had confirmed the extent to which Maradona had matured as a player since transferring to European club football in 1982. He had arrived with his personal life in tatters, his team in disarray, yet conscious that his reputation as one of the best, if not the best, was to be put to the test in the most widely viewed World Cup ever. Such pressures would have cracked a weaker personality. Yet in Mexico, Maradona seemed to channel his inner tensions into a positive combativeness. Off the field, he took lessons in anti-capitalism from his socialist-leaning team mate, Jorge Valdano, then publicly attacked FIFA's president João Havelange. He criticized the football authorities for forcing football players to play their matches under a scorching midday sun simply to suit the coverage times judged most commercially viable for the worldwide TV rights. In so doing, Maradona clearly did not consider his own contribution to the commercialization of football. Nor did he have to. In Mexico, he had managed to touch an emotional nerve among the fans of the Third World who identified with him both racially and socially. If the Mexican wave was born in the Azteca stadium, bringing back joy in the aftermath of the earthquake, it was Maradona who had ridden on the crest of it, thanks to his magic on the field.

And whatever doubts there were about his politics, his quality as a player was now beyond dispute. In Mexico, the unpredictable, moody, egoistic Maradona of Spain '82 gave way to a player who not only seemed confident enough about how best to use his talents, but who had sufficient humility to respond to what others required of him. Despite the inspired individualism of such moves as his second goal against England, he demonstrated his co-operative efforts in other games, using the accuracy of his first-time touches and the weight of his passing to devastating effect. This flexibility extended itself to his movement around the pitch, and the way he repeatedly outpaced his opponents with lightning surges. In the way he played, Maradona raised himself above the commercialism and the appalling atmospheric conditions of the competition, and displayed more than any other player a total dedication to the game.

In weighing up Maradona's performance, Havelange and his lieutenant Joseph Blatter, the autocratic bosses of FIFA, were left in a quandary. Three separate reports on the England–Argentina match carried out on behalf of FIFA and subsequently filed in the organization's classified archive contain no criticism whatsoever either of Maradona or of the referee for the Hand of God goal. It was perhaps in FIFA's nature to turn a blind eye to a controversy which in the end in no way affected the commercial success of the World Cup. If anything, the way Maradona's overall performance had caught the popular imagination confirmed that here was a player who stood to be a huge financial asset in future competitions. The money men of football could not ignore that fact.

What complicated their calculations was the growing realization in Mexico that Maradona was not only a player who could not easily be controlled or subjected to rules and regulations, but one who seemed bent on challenging the very authority of FIFA. Years before, such insubordination would have been quelled or brushed aside. But the power of TV and the fascination that the media generally were beginning to show with the Maradona phenomenon warned the men of Zurich that here was a player who would not easily be neutralized.

Maradona returned triumphant to Italy via Buenos Aires. In the Argentine capital he was taken in a euphoric cavalcade from the airport to the Casa Rosada, the presidential palace, and invited by the civilian President Raul Alfonsín to show the World Cup to thousands of fans from the main balcony. Having been elected with a convincing popular mandate following the collapse of the military régime in 1983, Alfonsín had lost much of his support because of his failure to tackle hyperinflation. Once again Maradona allowed himself to be exploited politically, gracing with his presence the besieged seat of government, and imbuing Alfonsín, however fleetingly, with an aura of success. Not since General Galtieri had appeared on the balcony to announce the 'historic' recovery of Las Malvinas in April 1982 had so many joyous Argentines turned their eyes on the Casa Rosada.

Even this popular fervour proved relatively tame stuff compared to the expression of collective ecstasy that surrounded Maradona when he led Naples to their first-ever Italian league championship win in the spring of 1987. In the hundred years of its existence,

Napoli had, like the city it represented, played a subservient role in the country's league. Italian football, like the Italian economy and Italian politics, had for years been dominated by the North, the two Milans and Juventus, with occasional inroads by Roma. Thanks to Maradona, Naples was able to throw off its inferiority complex and cock a snook at the rest of Italy, at least in football, the one subject that engulfed the majority of Italian families in a high dose of passion. In the city's calendar, 24 May 1987 would go down among a handful of dates that Neapolitans would never forget. The day Napoli FC secured its *scudetto* or league championship cup, the city's administrative life was abruptly halted and replaced with a wild carnival atmosphere that would carry on for nearly a week. Neapolitans took to the streets in a way they had not done since their liberation by the Allies in the Second World War. As one of the many present recalled, 'The night we won the *scudetto*, Naples went mad. The celebrations took hold of everyone regardless of age or social standing, as if everyone was sharing a dream.'

Mock, light-hearted 'funerals' of the Milan clubs were staged. For years Napoli FC had been derided as a donkey; now Neapolitans dressed up as donkeys were to be seen pulling the tail of the devil, their symbol of the North. As for Maradona, his status as king and saint was confirmed. Streets and babies were renamed in his honour, whole families offered up to his collective blessing and godfathership. He was more Neapolitan than the Neapolitans themselves, born in the back streets and crowned with success. The stars were clearly in his favour.

17

UNDER THE VOLCANO

E ven at the moment of his maximum achievement, Maradona's world became inexorably intermingled with more sinister interests. During the celebration of Napoli's championship victory in 1987, the Giuliano clan took to organizing many of the street celebrations and distributing free champagne and food. The Camorra had been preparing for such a day ever since Maradona's transfer from Barcelona, just as their forefathers had done for the Allied victory. In 1987, the clan leaders still had sufficient control over the city's political and economic life to turn the *scudetto* victory into an opportunity to reassert their power and influence.

That Maradona's own relationship with the people of Naples was no longer as straightforward as it seemed was brought home to a select group of trusted journalists on the evening of that day in May. After covering the decisive match of the championship – a 1–1 draw with Fiorentina on Napoli's home ground – the journalists were invited by a club official to a private party being given for Maradona. They were given instructions on how to get there, but told that details of the evening should go unreported, for their own sake. Of the journalists invited, only Bruno Passarella, the Rome-based correspondent of *El Gráfico*, subsequently came anywhere near to describing the true nature of the world into which Maradona was slipping. Passarella gave this account of the evening, but refused to elaborate any further:

> That night, Maradona took refuge in a house in Nola, one of the many satellite villages that are spread out like mushrooms around Naples. When we asked who the owner of the house was, the name and surname were kept from us. The mansion, for that is what it was, was built like a bunker, with gates that opened by remote control, closed-circuit TV all over

the place, and an enormous mastiff dog chained near the main entrance. It was an extravagant and lavish evening, with Moët et Chandon champagne flowing like water and served in silver-lined goblets, a huge video screen that kept playing back Maradona's goals, and a whole lot of guests with enormous rings on their fingers. It was an atmosphere with the unmistakable stamp of new money, laundered quickly and easily, the kind of money that in Naples has ensured unexpected riches for certain people. That dawn we returned to Naples, with none of the journalists any the wiser as to who had been our host.

Earlier Maradona had celebrated his World Cup triumph in Buenos Aires, with his childhood sweetheart Claudia Villafane back at his side. This was a very different Claudia from the girl who had sheepishly avoided the cameras in the early days of Maradona's footballing career. Different too from the Claudia who, humiliated by Maradona's promiscuity, had fled Naples. This Claudia was clearly prepared to do everything possible to win back her place in the world of fame that had mushroomed around Maradona. She had bleached her hair blonde and submitted herself to plastic surgery on her nose. Her wardrobe was no longer that of a simple girl from a Buenos Aires suburb, but of an aspiring star. Outwardly Claudia had metamorphosed into the plastic sex symbol which Maradona seemed to find so tempting.

Four weeks after the World Cup, Claudia joined Maradona for a much publicized 'romantic' holiday on a Polynesian island. Maradona declared that he had promised Claudia the holiday years before, but had only just got round to it. The Argentine media celebrated the 'honeymoon' as the player's reward for his alleged sexual abstinence during the competition.

Only later, when he returned to Italy at the start of the new football season, did the past Maradona had temporarily escaped catch up with him with a vengeance. On 20 September 1986, his former lover Cristiana Sinagra gave birth to a son, who was promptly given the name Diego Armando. In an interview with Italian State TV, Cristiana announced that the baby had been conceived during her four-month relationship with Maradona, from December 1985 to April 1986. The news provoked after-shocks worthy of a Neapolitan earthquake. Cristiana and the baby were besieged by dozens of journalists eager for more details. From the outset, Cristiana gave the impression of being not so much a woman scorned, as one with nothing to hide. The baby was for her the most natural thing in the world. By contrast, Maradona reacted like a thief in the night. Journalists caught up with him after a match between Napoli and Udinese in which he gave one of the worst performances of his footballing career, passing badly and seemingly uninterested in scoring any goals. 'About this I know nothing, absolutely nothing,' was his only comment on the woman he had once loved. In fact Maradona was deeply concerned that he was losing control over his own life. From the maternity clinic, Cristiana pressed on relentlessly, sensing that public sympathy was on her side. Her lawyer, Enrico Tuccillo, well known for taking on high-profile cases on behalf of the underdog, issued a statement warning that a paternity suit would be filed against Maradona unless he publicly accepted that the child was his. Maradona refused to do anything of the kind. Thus did 'Diegito' become the focus of an acrimonious legal battle which was to last for nearly five years. Long before the suit ended in Cristiana's favour, Maradona had suffered its consequences.

Maradona lost some of his quintessential Neapolitanism over the 'Sinagra affair'. In a city where extended family ties formed part of the social fabric – where, as a local popular phrase put it, '*I figli so' figli*', 'children are children' – Maradona tried to abdicate his responsibility as a father. The crime seemed all the more abhorrent given the status of king/saint he had been granted. The collective passion and veneration that had built up around Maradona made any son of his the equivalent of a dynastic heir, although the reluctant father did not perceive this at the time. The widespread public sympathy for Cristiana, and the way that the media bulldozed into Maradona's personal life, should have sent a warning signal. Maradona would be King of Naples only as long as he ruled his kingdom the way his subjects wanted.

Quite apart from creating the first rift between Maradona and the people of Naples, the Sinagra affair was to have a profound effect on Maradona's emotional life. Claudia, pregnant at the time that Cristiana gave birth to her baby, would in the following two years give Maradona two daughters. But the thought that he had rejected the son he had always longed for, and his inability to control events, forced him to seek solace in his new family unit. Close friends began to see a significant change taking hold in the aftermath of the Mexico World Cup and the Sinagra affair. Maradona seemed to be gripped once again by the moodiness that had plagued him in the past, only this time it was more deeply entrenched, leading to extended bouts of depression and swift eruptions of anger. He became less approachable, more arrogant, increasingly careless about the image he gave to the outside world.

By now Maradona had a new manager, Guillermo Coppola. 'I've come to do a job that is both very simple and very complicated at the same time: put Diego's accounts in order and allow him to handle his money without problems,' Coppola declared soon after arriving in Naples in January 1986 to replace Jorge Cyterszpiler. A few months earlier Maradona had confided in his fellow Argentine and former Real Madrid star Alfredo di Stefano that Cyterszpiler's mismanagement of his estate had brought him to the verge of bankruptcy.

With none of Cyterszpiler's physical disabilities or nostalgia for a shared childhood, Coppola brought a harder, more sinister edge to Maradona's existence. He was a youthful thirty-eight-year-old divorcé with a weak spot for well-endowed women, Versace clothes and nightclubs. He was also a graduate in business studies and a former banker who had built up a powerful network of influence in the Argentine football industry as a financial adviser to several top players. Coppola had made his reputation in 1975 when he successfully speculated on the local financial markets on behalf of two football players who had nothing better to do with their earnings. He tripled their investments on the bond market, gambling during a particularly volatile week of coup rumours, devaluation of the local currency and spiralling inflation. From then on he gradually built up his client portfolio, so that by 1985 he had over 180 players on his books. They included Oscar Ruggeri and Ricardo Gareca, two star Argentine footballers for whom he arranged a controversial joint transfer from Boca Juniors to River Plate.

Coppola had always claimed that it was a source of personal pride that most of his early dealings with players were based on personal favours rather than formal payments. 'I'd arrange contracts for them and in return I got a Rolex, airline tickets, a motorbike and clothes. When I did the Ruggeri/Gareca deal I was given the keys to a new Mercedes Benz.' He was introduced to Maradona by one of his more controversial clients, a young Boca Juniors player called Carlos Damian Randazzo. A few months earlier Randazzo had been suspended by his club after being charged with drugs possession and trafficking.

The introduction was sufficient to forge a friendship between Maradona and Coppola that was to survive many additional scandals. Maradona entrusted Coppola with some financial transactions in Esquina, including a dubious purchase of some prime land overlooking the River Corrientes where the Maradonas planned to build a mansion. For Coppola, becoming Maradona's manager was the high point of a life dedicated to the pursuit of power, leisure and money. In Naples he became the player's alter ego, less guardian angel than trusted friend who ensured there was enough money around for Maradona to indulge his fantasies. The new manager moved quickly to build on several promotional contracts set up by his predecessor, revaluing his client as the 'best footballer in the world' following Mexico. Of Italian descent himself, he found he could drive a hard bargain with the Neapolitans. From early on he enjoyed Maradona's full confidence.

There was a part of Maradona that held Coppola in awe. Coppola came from a lower middle-class background – a self-made man who had turned his life into a success story, without making excuses for getting there. The player looked up to the jet-set financier, who despite being ten years older seemed to know how to live life to the full rather better than the average twenty-year-old.

On arrival in Naples, Coppola moved into the Hotel Paradiso. The Paradiso, with its commanding views of the Bay of Naples, good-humoured staff and easy access, was a favourite haunt for illicit couples and honeymooners. Just a few hundred yards down the road from the Maradona household, it became a convenient destination for some of Maradona's escapes. The player and his manager would often end up there after a night out together in one of Naples' many nightclubs or restaurants, often accompanied by women they had picked up on the way. Apart from stimulating Maradona's nightlife, Coppola devoted the rest of his time to using his financial talents to boost the player's assets.

For the sake of efficiency he formed a business triumvirate consisting of himself, an accountant, Juan Marcos Franchi, and a lawyer, Daniel Bolotnicof, both fluent English speakers and experts in international commercial law. They began by reregistering Maradona Productions, whose reputation had become increasingly tarnished since the player's days in Barcelona, under a new name, DIARMA (DI for Diego, AR for Armando and MA for

Maradona). Following the practised art of tax avoiders and others wishing to shun outside scrutiny, Coppola kept the new company registered in Liechtenstein. He then proceeded to try and exploit Maradona as a TV star, securing him a weekly sports programme on the local channel with a contract worth close to $500,000.

But Coppola's greatest financial coup came halfway through 1987. He showed himself as tough and astute a negotiator as his predecessor by securing a large financial commitment from Ferlaino, the Napoli president, in return for Maradona extending his contract for a further five years. The deal was worth over $7 million. Coppola would say of the contract, 'It ensures that Maradona's children will eat caviar for the rest of their lives.'

Bolotnicof arrived in Naples under strict orders to sort out the administrative chaos which Maradona blamed on Cyterszpiler and his team. But what most affected him initially was the state of mind in which he found the player: 'What really shocked me was that he seemed to be doing nothing else between training sessions but sitting in his room with the blinds down, watching TV all day and night. He seemed to be acting like a prisoner in his own house. I asked him what was wrong. He told me he wasn't being allowed to lead a normal life by the public. People were even climbing on to the trees in the street outside his house in order to get a better look at him through the windows. Napoli promised him a house with a park and high walls to give him greater privacy, but the club never delivered.'

On 1 May 1988, in its penultimate game of the season, Napoli saw its hopes of a second successive championship evaporate when it was beaten 3–2 by AC Milan, managed by the determined Arrigo Sacchi. Maradona's occasional magical touches failed to inspire his team, and his performance was overshadowed by the strategic brilliance of the two Dutchmen, Marco Van Basten and Ruud Gullit. The loss of the *scudetto* saw Napoli once again relegated to the position of poor rival of the powerful North, a humiliation reversed on only one more occasion – the following year, when Maradona's team won the UEFA Cup. No one felt the reversal more personally than Conrado Ferlaino, the club president. The construction giant was livid at the thought of AC Milan's success enhancing the power of another businessman, its president Silvio Berlusconi, the wealthy owner of Italy's Channel 5 TV.

Maradona's own growing tensions with Ferlaino were initially channelled through a dispute between the player and Napoli's manager, Ottavio Bianchi. It had always taken a peculiar mixture of diplomacy and pragmatism to deal with Maradona, and Bianchi lacked both at a time when his star player was beginning to show some of the pathological symptoms which had so undermined him in Barcelona. Bianchi had earned the nickname 'the iron sergeant' and his reputation for dealing ruthlessly with any problem that confronted him surfaced with a vengeance soon after the Milan match. He sacked six of his players who had threatened to strike because they objected to his methods. Maradona, who had issued a statement in support of the players in a gesture of solidarity, was furious. He declared publicly that Ferlaino would have to choose between Bianchi or him. Ferlaino initially gave his full backing to his manager and reminded Maradona of the contract he had just renewed. It was the opening exchange of what was to become an increasingly acrimonious public conflict, of far greater consequence for the player than his earlier 'war' with Barcelona.

From an early stage, Maradona's decision to confront Ferlaino shattered the collective support he had enjoyed on his arrival in the city and which had reached its zenith with the conquest of Napoli's first *scudetto*. One of Napoli's longest-serving club officials, its head of information Carlo Juliano, was among those whose personal and professional affection for Maradona was dented by the attitude that the player adopted. 'I think Maradona wasted the opportunity that was offered to him at the outset really to build up a strong relationship with Ferlaino. The president had been his greatest fan. He would have remained so if only Maradona had acted differently.'

The point, of course, was that in personality and professional terms Maradona had no precedent. His aides would argue that it was not so much Maradona mishandling Napoli, as Napoli misunderstanding Maradona. Few of his inner circle followed the final years in Naples as closely as Marcos Franchi, the man Coppola brought in as his accountant and who would eventually replace Coppola as Maradona's manager. 'The problem was that Ferlaino acted not much differently from any other president of a football club. For him, football players were mere employees. Maradona simply didn't want to be treated as an employee. No genius has ever had a boss. That's what made Maradona uncontrollable. In Napoli, there had come a point when, notwithstanding all this, Maradona had become more powerful than the president. Ferlaino couldn't cope with that. He wanted to tie Maradona down, and tried all the means at his disposal to do so. Inevitably a power struggle developed that was fought at every conceivable level.'

Once again Maradona's injuries became both a symptom and a cause of conflict. Dr Ruben Oliva flew in regularly from Milan to attend him personally. As he had done in Barcelona, the player insisted he wanted nothing to do with surgeons or the club's doctors, and would only be treated by Oliva. In this, Maradona had the full support of his mother. Soon after Maradona's transfer to Italy, Oliva had received a phone call from Tota: 'The best thing about Diego going to Italy is that you are going to be near him. I hope we can count on you.'

Oliva believed that there were few aches or strains in a football player that some elementary psychology could not put right. He was a tough if convincing exponent of his ideas, with a quick eye for his client's potential weaknesses, which he was usually adept at exploiting. Oliva thought he could deal with Maradona's neurosis simply by empowering his strength of will. The doctor was once witnessed in action by one of Maradona's closest friends in Naples, Paolo Pauletti: 'I was at home with Diego when Oliva turned up. I remember it was Friday, and there was a match due that Sunday which Diego wanted to play in but felt that because of his injury he couldn't. Diego put a magazine between his teeth and bit on it when he felt the pain of a huge syringe with which Oliva injected him. When it was over Oliva said to Diego, "Without any doubt you are going to play on Sunday." Later when I took Oliva to the airport, the doctor turned to me. "Boy, I'm going to let you into a little secret. I did give Diego an injection, but do you know what I put in it?" "No," I said. "Water," he said.'

Maradona played that Sunday. However, with increasing frequency from 1988 onwards, he began to absent himself from Napoli's training sessions. In May 1989, he declared himself unfit to play on the eve of a crucial away tie against Bologna, claiming that he was suffering from a recurrent back injury. A month later he absented himself again, this time from a match against Ascoli, maintaining that he had a stomach disorder. Within a week he was playing again, at home in the San Pablo stadium against Pisa, only to demand his own substitution for the first time since he had arrived in Naples, with an apparent muscle strain in his right leg. As Maradona limped off the pitch, just seventeen minutes after the start of the game, the *tifosi* broke out whistling, turning their anger with gesticulations and insults at the presidential box, where sat Coppola and Claudia, holding the first-born Maradona daughter, Dalma, in her arms. Maradona emerged from the match furious, and with a characteristically emotional knee-jerk reaction was prepared to leave Naples there and then. He felt that his family honour had been insulted, and he personally had been betrayed. But rather than quit, he added it to his list of growing grievances against the club and the city, with the conviction of a long-term prisoner who knows that his sanity depends on escape one day.

Few episodes sharpened this determination more than Ferlaino's decision to reject, unilaterally and without negotiation, an offer to buy Maradona from Bernard Tapie, the owner and president of Olympique Marseille. After Napoli won the UEFA Cup Maradona had told Ferlaino that he felt he had done everything he could for the club, and that he would like to be transferred to a European country where football was less demanding than in Italy. And yet the player only found out about the Olympique Marseille offer when he read in the papers that Tapie had been to Naples and left empty-handed. Tapie would eventually be arrested and jailed in France for his involvement in a financial scandal. As with so many crossroads in Maradona's professional life, one is inevitably drawn to the question: what if? Perhaps Maradona would have been drawn into the corruption of French football, bringing his career to a premature halt. Or he might have emerged unscathed and avoided the decline and fall that brought him down in his last months in Naples and on his return to Buenos Aires.

What is certainly true is that Tapie's frustrated transfer attempt had a hugely negative impact on Maradona's relationship with Ferlaino, fuelling the player's sense of being trapped against his will. It was the point of irrevocable breakage; from then on Maradona scattered his emotional firepower in all directions, fuelling the impression that the King of Naples was losing control of himself.

When Napoli qualified for the UEFA Cup final, Maradona went for a celebratory dinner with Coppola and other friends to La Stangata, one of the city's most popular restaurants. The group emerged at five in the morning and Maradona began singing and dancing in the middle of the street. His celebration was interrupted by an old woman, a neighbour of the restaurant, who looked out of her window and shouted to him to shut up. 'That's enough!' she screamed. 'Who the hell do you think you are, the owner of Naples?'

Maradona looked up, and with a huge smile, called out at the top of his voice his name as it had been collectively expressed by football fans worldwide for years: 'I'm Maradooooona.' Recognizing him, the old woman broke out in spontaneous applause and blew him a long, heart-felt kiss.

Such gestures of popular adulation were increasingly hard to come by after the Olympique Marseille débâcle. Instead Maradona found himself the focus of growing rumours that linked his poor performance on the pitch and his absenteeism to his seemingly reckless nightlife. For his part, the footballer came to believe that there was a campaign being orchestrated against him. He began to vent his anger on the media, at one point trying without success to have certain journalists banned from training sessions and some matches. His weekly TV programme, which had begun as lucrative PR exercise, was transformed into a platform from which he could launch personal attacks against his alleged detractors.

Journalists shrugged off Maradona's conspiracy theories, considering his allegations the symptoms of a paranoiac. Doubts about his mental stability increased on the days when he chose to pay personal visits to newspaper offices to harangue the staff. On one occasion, he took a piece of newspaper and stuffed it into the mouth of a journalist who had written a critical piece about him.

In the summer of 1989, Maradona left Naples for Argentina, threatening never to come back. He flew on to Esquina, hoping once again that by returning to his roots he could rediscover a sense of self. It was pure escapism, which did little to alleviate the growing tension he had left behind in Naples. There the *tifosi*, the media and club officials were nurturing a deep sense of betrayal. A series of interviews conducted in the poor quarter of Forcella – one of the strongholds of the Giuliano clan and the hundreds of *tifosi* who paid allegiance to them – showed to what extent popular feeling had turned against Maradona. A survey by *Il Mattino* had some of the inhabitants of Forcella threatening to carry out personal vendettas against the player, while others volunteered to fly to Buenos Aires to beg him to return.

Maradona was by now caught in a vicious circle of claim and counter-claim. The more he was criticized, the more paranoiac he became, fuelling the ire of his critics by hitting back at them with increasing venom. While he was in Argentina Coppola issued a statement on his behalf in which Maradona alleged that he and his family were the victims of a concerted campaign of intimidation and harassment. The statement made a special reference to the match between Napoli and Pisa which he had abandoned after seventeen minutes and which had seen fans vent their anger by throwing bottles at Coppola and Claudia. It mentioned too some unexplained incidents such as a mysterious break-in at his sister Maria's apartment in Naples – below his own – and damage done to one of his cars by an unknown hand. 'All this convinces me that there is a concerted campaign against me, which has as its targets my partner, my children, my brothers and sisters, and my parents, with the aim of putting them in a situation of real danger.'

There was at this stage very little if any evidence to back up any of Maradona's allegations. The incident in the stadium seemed the spontaneous reaction of disillusioned fans rather than a premeditated attack. The alleged persecution of Maradona and his family had gone no further than the usual crowd pressures and individual stalkings that accompany any celebrity the world over. The damage to the car had been reported to the police two years earlier, and had involved a fan throwing a stone through the windscreen. The culprit had never been found and no one had claimed responsibility for the incident. But it was the reference to what had happened to Maradona's sister's flat that had potentially the most serious implications. By referring to a break-in in which furniture and papers had been tampered with but nothing apparently stolen, Maradona was pointing the finger at the Camorra, for this kind of action was one of several that the Mafia clans used to warn their victims.

Maradona later denied responsibility for the statement, leaving it up to Coppola to weather the storm, although such a damage-limitation exercise convinced no one. The statement was the product of a joint miscalculation. Maradona and Coppola seem to have had no more complicated motive than that of making an excuse behind which Maradona could justify his continued absence from Naples. They also hoped that the statement would win the sympathy of the *tifosi*, and persuade Ferlaino to adopt a more conciliatory line towards his star player, or, if not, to concede that he should be allowed to be transferred on his own terms. What neither Maradona nor Coppola seem to have realized is the growing sense of betrayal that was taking hold in Naples, and the extent to which Maradona's special status had slipped from his fingers.

During the early Napoli period, no conspiracy had been

denounced, because Maradona was a dutiful protagonist of the conspiracy that was Naples. No need to account for his nightlife, or the strange friends he made. He played good football and won Napoli championship cups and prestige. That was all that mattered. If there had been a conspiracy, it was the conspiracy of silence, in which club officials and journalists thought it best to overlook the darker sides of Maradona's life: his attendance at parties organized by the Camorra, and the suspicion that he might occasionally take drugs. Now, in the eyes of the *tifosi* and some members of the underworld, he was behaving little better than a grass, breaking his side of the conspiracy and trying to seek pardon through betrayal. As far as the world that had protected him was concerned, it was gloves-off time. Maradona could no longer count on the people of Naples for immunity from public scrutiny and exposure. This was no longer a conspiracy, it was all-out war.

Within days of his statement, *Il Mattino* published a four-column photograph of Maradona toasting champagne alongside the two leaders of the Giuliano clan, Raffaele and Carmine. It was one of the set of photographs taken at a party Maradona had attended three years earlier but which had been kept discreetly out of the public eye. The caption to the photograph read, 'It is absurd to think that anyone would want to challenge the Camorra by threatening its idol.' The argument was clear, although not entirely convincing. How could the Camorra possibly be behind a campaign to discredit a player they had once stood to make so much money on, and through whom they had asserted their power over the *tifosi*?

Conspiracies are by their very nature hard to prove. But there is at least circumstantial evidence to suggest that during that summer the Camorra both orchestrated and manipulated the public revulsion against Maradona's alleged betrayal, with the aim not of destroying him but of bringing him back into line. The godfathers were not in the business of allowing favoured sons to defy them publicly, and they were not prepared to make an exception for Maradona.

18

AMBASSADOR FOR SPORT

M aradona's public shooting match with the people of Naples lasted most of the summer of 1989. By the end of it, a temporary ceasefire was declared. If there was one factor that always allowed Maradona to break free from a crisis, it was the thought of a fresh professional challenge, and by then the prospect of another World Cup – Italy 1990 – was looming over the horizon. Once again sheer will power helped Maradona pull himself out of the depression into which he had sunk during his absence from Naples. As had happened and would continue to happen on and off throughout his career, Maradona's temporary abandonment of training and match playing had been followed by a rapid increase in weight and a softening of his muscle tissues. The transformation was the result of the abuse to which his body had been submitted at the hands of doctors from an early age. The body-building injections of his teenage years had been followed by cortisone jabs to alleviate his injuries. The TV image of Maradona as a small, compact dynamo belied the innate vulnerability of his physique. Only his will power and hidden reserves of strength saved his body from being as useless as that of a retired weight-lifter. At the end of that summer he submitted himself to an intensive diet-controlled personal training programme, which trimmed off the excessive fat and hardened his muscles, allowing him to rejoin his club, albeit somewhat belatedly.

If there was a moment when Maradona could have let bygones be bygones and buckled down to a period of simple commitment to the game, it would have been then. The volatility of Neapolitan emotions was such that they could return to loving him just as easily as they had turned to hating him. Unfortunately Maradona carried his enemies within as well as without. While claiming to want to be left in peace, he could not live for long without the adrenalin of the limelight. So it was that within weeks of his return to Italy, the world was invited to witness one of the most extravagant public acts ever put on by a sportsman: Maradona's marriage to Claudia.

Ever since he had become a player of world fame, Maradona had resisted pressure to submit his relationship with his teenage sweetheart to the requirements of convention. His widely reported 'honeymoon' with Claudia after the Mexican World Cup had taken place while both were unmarried, as had the birth of their two children, Dalma and Yanina. Illegitimacy had been hidden by Maradona's parents when he was young, but fame and riches allowed him to flaunt the formal rules of the Catholic Church. Maradona believed that he had as much right to do this as the hundreds of couples from Argentina's ruling classes who had traditionally filled the gossip columns of the country's magazines with tales of their infidelities. To conduct his personal life exactly how he wanted gave him a sense of liberation from his poor background, a feeling that money and success brought social acceptance.

The organization of the Maradona wedding was the most blatant expression of social *arrivisme* in Argentina since Eva Perón lavished millions of dollars on her wardrobe. Like the other totems of which Maradona had assured himself at key moments in his emerging career – his first big family house in Buenos Aires, his Barcelona castle, his yacht and fleet of cars in Naples – the scope and scale of the wedding was his way of telling the world that he was up there among the powerful and the great, that he owed no one any favours. It was also Maradona's way of telling his fans, just as Evita had told the 'shirtless ones', that anyone can make it as long as God is on the side of your talent and ambition.

As an act of conspicuous indulgence the wedding was pure Hollywood. Claudia wore a dress that had been specially made for her by the country's top fashion designer. It was reported down to its minutest detail: weighing 15 kilos, studded with pearls, decorated with gold, and with lace imported from Switzerland and Lyon, at an estimated cost of $30,000. In a further defiant gesture towards the upper classes of Buenos Aires society who looked on the new rich as social upstarts, the Maradonas managed to get the formal endorsement of the local Catholic Church to stage a full religious ceremony in Buenos Aires Cathedral. Flanked by their two daughters as bridesmaids, and observed by a packed congregation, the Maradonas walked up the aisle to be blessed amidst a showy display of music, incense and vestments.

Later that day, the Maradonas laid on a party for nearly 1,500 guests at the Luna Park, the boxing arena Maradona had frequented as a young spectator. A jumbo jet was chartered to bring in foreign guests. Coppola was Maradona's right-hand man and the effective master of ceremonies, organizing media and TV coverage, the attendance of his jet set and an evening of wild entertainment. Maradona's team colleagues and several Napoli club officials were among the guests, flown all the way to Argentina and put up in a five-star hotel at no expense. 'It was a perfectly organized occasion and we all felt genuinely touched at being invited,' recalled Napoli's chief of information, Carlo Juliano.

And yet the wedding, far from restoring Maradona's image as the people's champion, ended up further denting his reputation, reinforcing an image of a star player who could no longer control the effect he had on the outside world. On the day both Maradona and Claudia struggled to keep up the pretence of a fairy-tale romance. Maradona in particular looked tense. On his way into the civil register, he hit out at a photographer who had tried to get near him, and was later observed pacing alone up and down a room of the building like a caged lion. The cavalcade which later made its way through the streets of Buenos Aires, with Maradona and Claudia sitting and waving to the crowds from an open limousine, had a surrealistic edge to it. The groom looked like a stuffed peacock in his morning coat, with the irony of his gestures not lost on the many journalists who were covering the occasion. The wedding was taking place notwithstanding a national strike by public transport workers, who claimed that their salaries were insufficient to feed their families.

Italian journalists who infiltrated the carefully screened guest list focused on further alleged scandals. It was claimed that prostitutes had been flown in from all over the world to attend to guests, and that cocaine was one of the most widely available stimulants in the Luna Park. This was subsequently strongly denied by Marcos Franchi, Maradona's accountant and one of those who had helped Coppola organize the wedding. Franchi insisted that the alleged prostitutes were in fact interpreters, and that the cocaine was sugar laid out in bowls on guests' tables. But the latest damage-limitation exercise failed to stop the rot that had set in during Maradona's time in Naples, and which deteriorated further in the run-up to the World Cup in 1990.

Early in May 1990 a curious meeting took place in the downstairs bar of a hotel in Vienna between Maradona and the Argentine journalist Fernando Niembro. Maradona was in the Austrian capital with the Argentine team for a pre-World Cup friendly. The event was the kind that Niembro, as one of Argentina's leading TV and radio sports commentators, would have normally put on his working schedule. But he had flown to Vienna via Italy on a strictly political assignment – to put a special request to Maradona on behalf of Argentina's President Carlos Menem, for whom Niembro now worked as official spokesman. Menem wanted to appoint Maradona an 'ambassador for sport', representing Argentina before the world as one of the greatest figures in the history of international football. Menem planned to confirm the appointment by personally giving Maradona his diplomatic passport at the beginning of the World Cup. Exactly what Maradona was supposed to do thereafter was left deliberately vague, but the President had secured the backing of several top companies in Argentina to help finance an eventual international promotion tour by the player. Those prepared to put up money for Menem's great diplomatic offensive included Amalita Fortabat, the president of Argentina's biggest construction company and one of the richest businesswomen in the world.

The decision to offer Maradona such an ambassadorship may have seemed eccentric but it was the product of political calculation. One year earlier Menem had been swept to power on a pro-Peronist ticket. The short man who wore his sideburns long and bushy as a tribute to the nineteenth-century gaucho leader Facundo Quiroga had stirred some of the primitive emotions of the Perón era. His campaign organizer had been none other than Jorge Cyterszpiler, the football agent who had transformed Maradona from backstreet boy to international star. In spite of his sacking, Cyterszpiler still considered himself a loyal friend of Maradona, and looked back on his days with the player as the most rewarding of his life. But an increasingly active network was to revolve around the figure of Ramón Hernández, the presidential private secretary and one of Menem's most trusted aides. Hernández and Menem's son Carlos were friends of Coppola's, part of the Buenos Aires jet set that embroiled itself in a world of political intrigue, social frivolity and questionable business practices.

It was against this background that the natural affinities linking Menem to Maradona were deliberately encouraged behind the scenes. Menem was no aristocrat. The snobs of Buenos Aires initially turned their noses up at 'El Turco', the nickname of this son of a first-generation immigrant from Syria. Menem had never lived in a shanty town, but his father had struggled to make a decent living peddling goods round the villages of northern Argentina on the back of his mule. Menem's rise to power, like Evita's and Maradona's, was in a sense typical of an emerging nation with a large immigrant population. It showed that society, for all its innate bigotry and xenophobia, was permeable enough to allow the descendants of poor immigrants to be part of a New Argentina. This was a country that sought a sense of identity in old myths – making heroes of gauchos and liberators – and extravagant consumerism. Menem and Maradona intermingled their devotion to Perón and the Virgin Mary with their love for football, fast cars and women.

By May 1990 Menem was struggling both to retain his popular appeal at home, and to win new friends abroad. It was a mirror image of Maradona's situation, although the repercussions of the player's falling out with Naples had yet to be fully assimilated by the Argentine media. In Buenos Aires, Diego Maradona remained a hero, the most important Argentine in the world. By contrast the new President was trying to impose a semblance of economic order on a country ravaged by hyperinflation and periodically diverted by the scandals emanating from the presidential household. The tantrums of Menem's highly strung wife Zulema, and the extravagance of his two children, Carlitos and Zulemita, were Argentina's worst-kept secrets. Abroad, foreign investors and commentators of the developed world were still finding it hard to take seriously a President with a reputation for home-spun demagoguery.

Enter Fernando Niembro, a journalist who had devoted much of his professional life to ensuring that football flowed through the veins of his fellow countrymen. He had witnessed at first hand the extraordinary influence that the sport had on society and politics. In 1978, he had watched how Argentina's victory in the World Cup had transformed the black days of the military junta into a triumphant celebration. In 1986, when Argentina, thanks to Maradona, won the cup a second time, the country recovered a sense of national pride that had been badly dented as a result of the Falklands War. Now another World Cup was looming, and Argentina was once again one of the favourites. Extending the presidential patronage to Argentine football's highest-profile player would at worst provide Menem's countrymen and the world with a useful distraction, at best identify the régime once again with the potential for success.

Niembro recalled, 'I'd followed Maradona closely since 1976, and I'd never doubted his genius. He lived for football, breathed it. He was also better known worldwide than Pele or the Pope. The very word Maradona signifies an idol who is respected internationally. When I came up with the idea, Menem was very worried about his image. He wanted to attract investment and create confidence. I reminded him of the sportsmen who had brought us international respect, people like the racing champion Fangio. I said I was sure that Maradona would open doors for his presidency all over the world, and that the World Cup in Italy was a window of opportunity that he shouldn't miss.'

Niembro had little difficulty in convincing his President that he should bring Maradona into his court. Menem's ultimate fantasy was to be Maradona. 'Football is the thing that formed me physically and it has given me a great deal of spirituality,' he had said. His childhood dream had been to play for Argentina. Only as President had he realized it, putting on the national colours and joining the Argentine team in a training session. He later formed his own eleven in a charity match against a team led by Bobby Charlton. 'He doesn't move at all. He just stands in the centre of the field and his team mates bring him the ball and he gives these really easy safe passes to the guys standing next to him,' Charlton would later remark on Menem's talents.

To Marcos Franchi, one of the few members of Maradona's inner circle who treated the player with real understanding rather than self-interest, Niembro's passport idea defied reason. 'When it comes to understanding Maradona one has to make a distinction between a public person and a popular person. Diego, a popular person, was given a football shirt because he played well: he went on to the pitch and was the best, that's it . . . One day they went and offered him an official diplomatic passport, without him knowing what the hell it meant. They offered him an ambassadorship. But did anyone involved in that decision bother to ask themselves whether Diego was prepared mentally, psychologically or intellectually to take on that responsibility? No, they didn't, because they didn't care. All that mattered was that he had to be an ambassador and so they went and gave him a passport,' Franchi said.

On 7 June 1990, at 6.35 p.m., President Menem arrived for a packed press conference next to Milan's San Siro stadium, formally to give Maradona his passport and announce to the world that Argentina had a new sporting ambassador. The English novelist Peter Davies was among hundreds of journalists present, watching with a keen eye some of the more memorable eccentricities of Italia '90. 'Maradona kept Menem waiting fifteen minutes. But when you're running a mess like Argentina, let's face it, you need Maradona plenty more than he needs you,' Davies wrote later in his book *All Played Out*. 'Menem looked, in the famous phrase about former US presidential candidate Michael Dukakis, like a baby shark that just burbed. Or, with his weird hair and his nervy, wall-to-wall grin, like a chipmunk that got dipped in an oilspill.'

Most of the journalists present were Argentine, led by the TV cameras which unquestioningly beamed back reports of Menem's diplomatic triumph to Buenos Aires. The Argentine manager Carlos Bilardo was there, as was Maradona's manager Guillermo Coppola. Menem looked on, flanked by equally beaming officials. Maradona himself, confronted by such a complicity of mutual adoration, temporarily forgot who he was and where he was and for a moment genuinely believed it all. No one had been keener on him accepting the diplomatic status than his mother, Doña Tota, forever driving her son down the road marked out to him by God. Maradona offered up the occasion to her, and Chitoro. 'My parents will most certainly be proud of their son today. We shall now start defending Argentina,' he told his audience.

Menem milked the occasion for all it was worth, leaving no superlative unturned. 'We here inaugurate a new form of accreditation, a new type of diplomatic image ... Plato said sport makes wise and careful men – the type of men the world needs now.'

Peter Davies was among those less than impressed. 'The world needs wise and careful men like Diego?' was Gary Lineker's rhetorical question when Davies asked him for his reaction to the diplomatic appointment. Someone else next to Davies muttered, 'Does this mean he'll stop cheating?'

The World Cup of Italia '90 will be remembered as the competition of tears. They were shed before millions of TV viewers by two of football's most idiosyncratic personalities, Paul Gascoigne of England and Diego Maradona of Argentina, although the reasons for each man's crying were very different.

Public displays of emotion do not come easily to the English character. Crying is better done discreetly or not at all. And yet as Ian Hamilton, one of Gascoigne's biographers, noted, Gazza's tears in England's semi-final tie against West Germany transformed him from soccer's bad boy to a national celebrity. Those tears were first of all for himself – he had been shown the yellow card, a second tournament booking, which would have excluded him from the final if England reached it. But in the end, when the final whistle blew, Gazza's tears managed to fuel a collective show of heartfelt emotion, a feeling of sympathy and genuine disappointment that England had lost after a game played with grit and heroism. Gascoigne's Turin tears achieved symbolic resonance, 'the stuff of posters, T-shirts, scarves and mugs'.

Maradona's tears came at the end of the final England had missed out on, against West Germany. No heroism here, still less magic. It was a brutal, graceless affair, arguably the worst, most ill-tempered final in the history of the competition. Two Argentine players were sent off, adding to the four who had been suspended in the course of a competition that Argentina stamped with foul play. Maradona was jeered and whistled throughout the match by the largely Italian crowd.

The growing unpopularity of the Argentines in Italia '90 had encouraged the team coach Carlos Bilardo to consider an innovative idea for damage limitation. Bilardo thought the Argentine national anthem overlong and unsuitable for football matches. He felt that it distracted players and gave unsympathetic fans much too much time in which to vent their anger before the match had even started. At the very least he wanted the anthem shortened, cutting out the lengthy operatic finale in which Argentines boldly swear their willingness to die for the flag. Sensing that such a scheme might provoke a nationalist uproar in Argentina, Bilardo decided not to pursue it too vigorously in Italy. But he lived to regret it.

It was as the Argentine team stood stiffly to attention while their anthem was played in the final game that the venom of Italian fans first expressed itself collectively. Their boos and whistles drowned the music and made a mockery of the pomp and ceremony. Maradona reacted by swearing openly in front of the cameras:

'Sons of bitches,' he mumbled. His words were inaudible but there was no need to be a trained lip reader to understand them. They were picked up by the TV commentator and by millions of viewers. When it came to his tears, they fell like drops of rain on a gutter, uncared for and unwelcomed. Maradona had shed tears once too often. Like his periodical protests to the referee and his communications with heaven, his emotional outbursts suffered from overuse. This time the tears seemed to belong to no one else but Maradona. To the millions who saw them, they were at best an overreaction born of arrogance, at worst the latest evidence of Maradona's mental instability. In Italy it was not Gazza but Diego Maradona who seemed to have cracked.

Maradona's latest emotional breakdown had been building up in the months leading up to the competition. The previous November he had been suspended by the new Napoli manager, Arrigo Sacchi, an hour before the club's second-round UEFA cup tie against Wettingen, having been declared unfit to play. He had missed several training sessions and was thought to have spent the night prior to the crucial match on one of his hedonistic escapades. Just as he had in the Camorra incident three months earlier, Maradona once again spoke of a plot against him. The following month his paranoia reached new levels when he declared that the draw for the World Cup had been fixed.

The statement, based on no evidence whatsoever, was the latest in a series of personal tirades against the world's major football organization, which FIFA officially dismissed as a symptom of Maradona's immaturity as a person. FIFA's general secretary Joseph Blatter said at the time, 'Either he is stupid, or bad.' It was a sentiment that was beginning to spread among Italians who resented the way that Maradona seemed bent on rubbishing anything that was not inspired by him. And some of that inspiration seemed lacking.

By Christmas Napoli was once again near the top of the Italian league, but Maradona had scored only six goals from sixteen games, three of them penalties. The prospect of playing in another World Cup and captaining the Argentine side temporarily restored his motivation. He began to train harder and submitted himself to a health cure to reduce his weight further and strengthen his muscles. He also cut down on the cortisone injections. For a few weeks, he seemed to recover some of his genius, as he led Napoli to its second league championship. But the achievement turned into a pyrrhic victory. The Neapolitans' celebrations showed rather less of the collective enthusiasm that had surrounded Maradona when the team won its first *scudetto* in 1987. And what jubilation there was was soon overshadowed by the reactions elsewhere in Italy.

Italians north of Naples had never shown much love lost for Maradona. Now their resentment was fuelled by the controversial circumstances in which Napoli overtook Milan in the closing stages of the season. Maradona's club was awarded two points by an Italian football tribunal after the Napoli goalkeeper Alemao was hit by a coin thrown by an opposing fan during a match against Atalanta. Milan's president Silvio Berlusconi insisted publicly that the incident had been exaggerated out of all proportion, and that Alemao was pretending to suffer from a non-existent injury. His objection was overruled, but it was sufficient to spread the popular impression that the North of Italy had been cheated by those upstarts in the South, led by the biggest upstart of them all, Diego Maradona.

After winning Napoli's second *scudetto*, Maradona made the following statement: 'I want to say something to my fellow Argentines. I dedicate this cup title, this new joy, to my old man. No sooner had the match finished than I talked to him on the phone and we cried together . . . He told me that he was happy for me and those close to me, but for no one else. He doesn't forget that people have called me irresponsible when everyone knows that I really fought to get to where we've got, from the bottom upwards . . . I cried, we cried together. I dedicate this to him, because he suffered for me.'

God the Father, God the Son, nothing less. And yet the image others had of Maradona seemed to fall well short of divinity. By the time Italia '90 got underway, a video had begun to circulate in the country. It featured Ilona Staller, 'La Cicciolina', the Italian porno star and Member of Parliament. The film showed a voluptuous fairy queen, La Cicciolina herself, doing her patriotic duty by physically exhausting the Italian team's opponents before matches. The villain of the piece, and her prime target, was Maradona, played by an overweight actor, a man so in love with himself that he preferred to masturbate than to cede to the advances of the delectable Cicciolina. The film ends climactically, with Maradona in complete self-absorption, yelling, 'Bravo, bravo.' By the beginning of the World Cup, Maradona had convinced himself that even if the Italians in the North had turned against him, his popularity in the South was sufficient to carry the fans with him throughout the competition. On more than one occasion he made statements indicating that he expected the *tifosi* of Naples to back the player who had almost single-handedly brought their club successive triumphs, rather than their national team. In so doing he came close to undermining the spirit of a competition that FIFA had struggled for years to keep free from political intrigue and personal vendettas.

Maradona might have escaped some of the opprobium which followed him had he dispensed with these public utterances and concentrated instead on his football. But the magic that seemed to accompany Maradona in Mexico was rarely seen in Italia '90. He played like an obsessive, with little joy. Those close to him partly blamed the lack of direction given by Carlos Bilardo, and the pressures which had been building up on Maradona ever since his relations with Napoli had started to turn sour. Maradona had little impact on Argentina's opening match against Cameroon. The cup-holders lost 1–0, and Milan's San Siro stadium erupted into a roar of approval. Maradona initially found greater warmth when Argentina went down to Naples to play against the Soviet Union. For a while the old cries of 'Diego, Diego' once again resonated round the San Pablo stadium as Argentine and Napoli fans joined forces behind their common hero. And yet although Argentina won the match, it was partly overshadowed by a poor referee's decision which once again involved Maradona in cheating. The Swedish referee Fredriksson did not see Maradona's right hand go up inside his own penalty box and divert a header from Oleg Kuznetsov which would have otherwise gone straight into the net.

Only against Brazil in a match played in Turin did Maradona seem to recover his will and strength sufficiently to show off his talent, cleanly and with flair and vision. The teams were evenly matched, 0–0 until eight minutes from the end. Then Maradona drew his rabbit out of the hat, effortlessly manoeuvring through Brazil's sweeper system, before setting up the winning goal for his friend Claudio Caniggia, the long-haired blond striker who had recently been transferred from River Plate to Verona. When Argentina returned to Naples to play Italy in the semi-final, Maradona once again became his own worst enemy, letting his arrogance get the better of him and reigniting a national controversy which jarred with the sheer sense of fun with which most fans had been following the competition.

Maradona tried to turn the game into a political and social confrontation, declaring, 'The Italians are asking Neapolitans to be Italian for a day, yet for the other 364 days in the year they forget all about Naples. The people do not forget this.' His open appeal for division was judged a master stroke of psychological warfare by some Argentine commentators, but it succeeded only in dulling the enthusiasm for what in different circumstances would have been a fascinating encounter between two ancient rivals. Journalists covering the match detected an unnatural restraint among the *tifosi*, with the public support for Italy nowhere near as vociferous as in Rome or Milan. In the end only the Argentine fans came away genuinely satisfied with a game that had to be resolved by a penalty shoot-out, with Maradona scoring the winning goal.

Maradona ended Italia '90 as he had begun it, being jeered and whistled. It was hard to think that this was the same Maradona who had emerged so triumphantly in Mexico, still less the Maradona who had brought such joy to so many Italian fans when Napoli embarked on its first successful assault on the *scudetto*. It was a sign that something had irrevocably cracked in Maradona's Italian experience. And there was much worse to come.

19

AN ITALIAN VENDETTA

The process through which an inner circle based on trust and tribal loyalty gave way to an insidious network of underworld characters had been developing ever since Maradona first came into contact with the Camorra in 1985. 'As soon as he arrived,' Maruja Torres, a journalist with Spain's *El País* newspaper, was told by Francesco Maglione, a lawyer for the Camorra, 'Maradona asked for the person who had the greatest power in Italy. He didn't want to get to know the mayor or a leading intellectual, but one of the Camorra bosses.' It turned into a two-way process with the gang chiefs similarly anxious to be identified with the star.

By the end of 1990, however, the sinister network into which Maradona had allowed himself to be dragged was no longer immune from outside scrutiny. Magistrates and police up and down the country had begun a drive against organized crime, and the complicity of silence that had protected Maradona since he arrived in Naples could no longer be assured. Indicative of this sea change were the thinly veiled hints in the Italian press that began to appear about Maradona's drug problem. On 22 November 1990, the day after Maradona had excluded himself from another match with Napoli, this time against Fiorentina, the prestigious *Gazetta dello Sport* published a signed article by one of its leading locally based journalists, Franco Esposito. 'It would seem as if Maradona is not well, that physically he's become a rag,' wrote Esposito. 'A dark evil appears to have taken hold of the greatest footballer in the world . . . What obscure, mysterious illness is Maradona suffering from?' Like a growing number of his colleagues, Esposito had no doubt that Maradona was fast developing a drugs problem which was affecting his football. For their part, Napoli officials, increasingly angry with Maradona's outbursts of insubordination, for the first time failed to contradict the rumours outright. As for the twilight zone, this no longer assured Maradona of protection. Far from it. With the police progressively moving in on them, the prostitutes and the drug dealers saw no reason why Maradona should not be betrayed.

Thus the evidence which Maradona's critics had long been seeking to back up their speculations presented itself early in 1991. Just after midnight on 7 January, the day after Napoli, with Maradona playing, had lost 1–0 to Juventus in Turin, the phone rang in the house of one Carmela Cinguerama. A prematurely aged forty-six-year-old with rugged peasant looks, Cinguerama was one of Naples' most notorious madams. She helped run a prostitution ring in some of the dingier quarters of the city on behalf of another Camorra gang leader, Mario Lo Russo.

Cinguerama was half asleep when the phone rang, but the caller, a man with a gruff Neapolitan accent, got straight to the point: 'Diego gave me this number . . . for two women,' he said. 'Yes,' said Cinguerama, responding with time-tested professionalism to the request. 'Good women, mind you,' the man went on. 'We want to meet in the Via Manzone, by the Airone.' The Airone was a piano bar near to the Maradona residence and the Hotel Paradiso. 'Is Diego there?' asked Cinguerama. 'I want to speak to him.' She was told he was not. But later that night the phone rang again. It was 3.38 a.m. This time the voice on the other end of the line seemed to be Maradona's. It asked for more details about the girls Cinguerama had promised to provide. The arrangement was confirmed.

Just over two weeks later, Cinguarama's husband, another creature of the Neapolitan night, by the name of Mario Falcone, conducted a telephone conversation with a friend: 'They didn't come tonight, but he did,' Falcone said. 'He wanted some "gear" [local slang for coke] . . . Maradona came here, he wanted the women and the "gear".'

The conversations were taped by the Nulceo Napoli 1 police, the local equivalent of the flying squad, as part of their investigation into a suspected cocaine and call-girl ring straddling South America, Italy and France. The investigation, codenamed 'Operation China' and led by Major Vittorio Tomasone, initially focused on Lo Russo, Cinguerama and her husband, and Italo Jovine, the owner of a leisure complex called the Chalet Park. But it soon expanded to include the Maradona household. According to testimony handled by the police, it was Maradona's brother-in-law Gabriel Esposito who had introduced the player to Jovine, himself the nephew of the leader of a Camorra clan and with a record of local drug-dealing. Jovine in turn had introduced Maradona to Cinguerama. Another piece in the chain linking Maradona with the world of prostitutes and drugs was a former underground worker whom Maradona had befriended and made his informal social secretary, or rather the 'friend' who organized his escapes away from domesticity and football and into the wild night. His name was Felice Pizza. The main task of 'Geppino', as Pizza was nicknamed, was to arrange for women to join Maradona in the Hotel Paradiso, and separately to obtain cocaine.

Out of 10,000 hours of taped telephone calls in the course of the investigation, Maradona's name or voice had featured on eleven. Following the intercepts, Maradona and Geppino were questioned by police. Maradona was cleared of any involvement with the Lo Russo ring, but the telephone intercepts prompted local magistrates to instigate separate legal action against him on suspicion of possession and distribution of cocaine. An initial police report had stated, 'The famous footballer Diego Maradona on a number of occasions asked Signora Cinguerama for "gear" in no small quantities. By this we understand cocaine.'

Confirmation of the police investigation into Maradona brought in its wake an avalanche of kiss-and-tell testimonies from a range of statuesque prostitutes and models who claimed to have shared orgies of group sex and drugs with the superstar, in hotels and private apartments. Among the more graphic descriptions was that given by a Brazilian called Susy who worked in Club 21, one of the more sordid bars in the red-light port area. She claimed that after being taken to a hotel, Maradona had paid her between $650 and $800 for a night of athletic sex without condoms. 'He particularly liked to suck my big toe,' Susy stated. Maradona, according to her testimony, also had a weakness for other less conventional sex acts which she said she would allow only if he raised his payment to one million lire. He didn't, so she refused. 'He may be an artist, a great famous world champion, but that doesn't give him privileged status when he's in bed with me,' Susy explained, adding that Maradona had taken cocaine in her presence but that she hadn't.

While a veritable harem lined up to denounce Maradona as a drugged sex maniac, another witness came forward to make potentially the most damaging allegation against the player. On 5 March another element of the twilight zone, one Piero Pugliese, accompanied by his lawyer, a former neo-fascist councillor, presented himself without an appointment at the city's Palace of Justice and demanded to see the prosecutor in charge of Maradona's case. Pugliese personified the close links that existed between football and the Camorra. By day he had worked as a security guard for Napoli. Only later would it emerge that he had also moonlighted as a hired killer for the local Mafia.

Around 1989, Pugliese had temporarily quit both activities after being introduced to Maradona through a friend. He was offered employment as a messenger boy and part-time chauffeur. 'Pugliese formed part of a bad crowd, connected with the Napoli fans, who increasingly surrounded Maradona,' said a close friend of the player. In 1989, Pugliese was among a select group of Neapolitans invited to Maradona's wedding. While in the Argentine capital, he met and befriended a woman, Alessandra Bertero, whom he introduced to Guillermo Coppola. Bertero subsequently agreed to serve as a courier between Buenos Aires and Italy, on behalf of DIARMA, Maradona's marketing company.

According to Pugliese, in 1989 Coppola and Maradona became involved in drugs trafficking and he was asked to play a key role as a fixer. Pugliese got Bertero to collect a package in Buenos Aires and deliver it to him in Rome's international airport. From there Pugliese drove to Naples and delivered it to Coppola. Bertero was told the package contained newspapers and magazines. Pugliese told Italian prosecutors that, unknown to his female friend, the package in fact contained two kilos of cocaine. He alleged that Coppola and Maradona had both known about its true contents because both had supervised its final delivery. Pugliese was paid 20 million lire by Coppola through a Naples bank account registered on behalf of DIARMA and for which Coppola and Maradona had signature rights. Conversations confirming Coppola's involvement in the bank transaction and a personal invitation from Maradona to Pugliese to join him at the player's home, were secretly taped by Pugliese's lawyer.

Pugliese's allegations opened up yet more legal proceedings against Maradona, accompanied, as they usually are in Italy, by carefully placed leaks to the media that provoked a succession of damaging stories about the world of drugs into which Maradona had allowed himself to be drawn. Both Maradona and Coppola subsequently admitted that they had been present when the package had arrived, but denied that it contained cocaine. But they were unable to disassociate themselves from Pugliese. Coppola said that he had given the 20 million lire to Pugliese after being told that the part-time chauffeur wanted to build a football school on the outskirts of Naples. 'I thought it was a good idea and he promised he would return the money in thirty days,' was Coppola's explanation. Maradona said that Pugliese had asked him for another loan while he was training in Rome with the Argentine team for the 1990 World Cup, this time to buy some land. Pugliese had apparently promised he would be able to repay the loan because he was owed some money for winning on the pools.

The women who had kissed and told on Maradona disappeared almost as suddenly as they had appeared. Journalists pursuing further scandal stumbled on bogus witnesses, among them a false Susy who was prepared to give further details in return for money. The real Susy had returned to her native Brazil to pursue a career in modelling. The credibility of Pugliese as a witness proved more difficult to puncture. By confessing to five gangland murders and offering further information on the Camorra, the former hit-man obtained not only police protection, but also a more sympathetic ear from the prosecuting authorities. Testimony from turncoats, or *pentiti* as they were called in Italy, had become a key weapon in the battle against Mafia figures. Thus Pugliese was a witness the authorities felt they could ill afford to mistreat as long as he remained credible.

In subsequent statements Pugliese changed his evidence. He claimed that the original package had been smuggled into Italy on board a plane with the entire Argentine team and its manager Carlos Bilardo, and that Maradona had spent his six years in Naples on the Camorra's monthly payrole. Both allegations were denied by Bilardo and Maradona. Pugliese also claimed that Maradona, acting under orders from the Camorra, had deliberately underminded his team's efforts to win the championship in 1987–88 because the organization did not want to pay out millions of lire to those who bet on the club's victory. Not even those who lost believed that.

But Pugliese's evidence did raise question marks over Coppola's credibility. The manager's position before the Italian legal system was further undermined when within a year he found himself embroiled in a second criminal action, this time linked to a Buenos Aires nightclub killing. Among those who testified against Coppola in Italy was Massimo Crippa, the Parma midfielder and member of the Italian squad. He told prosecutors that he had seen Coppola offer Maradona cocaine during a party on a boat anchored in the Bay of Naples in 1990. The coke was delivered by courier in an outboard and handed personally to Coppola. 'The coke has arrived,' Crippa is alleged to have heard Coppola say. Coppola himself declared soon after returning to his native Argentina towards the end of 1990 that Maradona 'does not and has never taken drugs'. He claimed he had decided to 'separate' temporarily from Maradona because he missed his two daughters and his elderly mother.

For his own defence, Maradona relied on Vincenzo Sinischalsci, one of Naples' most talented lawyers. Sinischalsci had defended members of the terrorist Red Brigade faction. He was politically opposed to the institutional corruption that had built up in Italy in the post-war years. While he retained an in-built suspicion of Coppola, towards Maradona he felt sympathetic. Sinischalsci saw Maradona as a genuine if uneducated poor boy made good whose only real passion in life was football. He thought the twenty-nine-year-old star still had the 'mind of a fifteen-year-old', and that his inherent immaturity made him susceptible to pressure and quite incapable of winning out against the powers that conspired against him.

Sinischalsci never denied that his client had taken drugs, but he considered this a minor offence in the wider context of the institutionalized corruption which he knew existed in Naples. As one of the lawyers in the city who pursued the Camorra as both a symptom and the cause of this corruption, Sinischalsci had never stumbled on any evidence suggesting that Maradona was actively involved with the Camorra, although he recognized that his client may have been inadvertently used by the gangs and their henchmen. Ultimately Sinischalsci believed that the Maradona case had nothing to do with drugs, but everything to do with power.

Thus, in his legal submissions, Sinischalsci was only too happy to have Maradona make thinly veiled references to an alleged plot against him. In one statement, Maradona denounced a 'vendetta on somebody's part, on account of matches I was not supposed to win' and mentioned that 'football interests' may have been responsible. Contrary to what was widely speculated at the time, Maradona was not referring to his non-co-operation with Italy's black-market pools, which were tightly controlled by the Camorra. Maradona insisted that he had never won or lost a match deliberately as part of a 'fix', and there is no evidence to contradict this. On the contrary, the Camorra appear to have accepted from the outset that Maradona's presence on the pitch was so prominent and his performance so idiosyncratic that any fix would have been immediately identifiable.

The matches he was not supposed to win included some of those that he had won out of sheer dogged will power and in the face of considerable opposition. They included Argentina's victory over Italy in the 1990 World Cup. But the real local anger and resentment was generated by the matches Maradona had either lost or failed to play in, and this, in the eyes of the Camorra and the *tifosi*, justified, if not a frame-up, at the very least a concerted attempt to bring the one-time King of Naples to his knees.

In a legal system such as Italy's where simple allegations, not yet proven, are given wide publicity without fear of libel, and where individual cases, without formal charges being laid, often take a long time to get to court, the phone taps, the kiss-and-tells and Pugliese represented a huge collective onslaught on Maradona. By the time Pugliese made his allegations, Maradona had already made up his mind that there was no alternative but to leave Italy, and instructed his new manager Marcos Franchi to do everything possible to break his contract with Napoli. 'My last weeks in Italy were taken up exclusively with seeing how I could help Diego break with Napoli,' Franchi recalled, thus playing a part that one of his predecessors had already played in Barcelona.

For its part, Napoli was no longer prepared to offer Maradona the protection it had afforded in the past. On 17 March 1991 the club doctors abandoned their former lax régime and randomly dope-tested Maradona twice after a home match against Bari. The first test was carried out personally by the team's doctor, Arcangelo Pepe, the second by a couple of outside doctors brought in by the club and approved by the player. Both tests proved positive. Maradona's urine was found to contain cocaine. There were only small traces of it, the remnants of the drugs he had snorted a couple of nights earlier. But they were sufficient to earn him an immediate suspension and the instigation of proceedings against him by the Italian football authorities.

'As a sportsman, I say again that I have never betrayed the principles which inspire a loyal and correct sporting activity, in which I have participated with energy and passion,' Maradona declared soon afterwards. Sinischalsci's defence, somewhat more elaborately developed, proved even less convincing. In essence the lawyer argued that his client deserved to be exonerated as a player because he had taken cocaine simply for his own pleasure and not to enhance his performance. It would take Maradona six years to admit publicly what really was happening in Italy. 'In Naples, drugs were everywhere, they practically brought it to me on a tray,' he said in an interview with *Gente* magazine, while claiming that he had wanted to fail his drugs test in a desperate attempt to get help and treat a long-term addiction.

On the night of 1 April 1990, Maradona broke through the vigil that permanently attended his Naples home for the last time. Accompanied by Franchi, tired and tearful, he boarded a plane and flew back to Argentina. The following day, his team colleagues and the *tifosi* gathered silently in the San Pablo stadium, their emotions poised between anger and sorrow, as if at a funeral. It was a striking contrast to the scenes of unrestrained jubilation that had greeted Maradona's arrival six years earlier. He had, as the Italians say, fallen 'dalle stelle alle stalle' – 'from the stars to the stables'.

For Maradona the nightmare was far from over. Four weeks later, the police raided an apartment he had lent to El Soldadito, the chauffeur and friend he had brought out of the poverty of his father's home town. The police discovered Maradona collapsed on Soldadito's bed after a day of drinking and drug-taking with some women friends. Beside the prostrate star were several grams of cocaine. One of the policemen shook Maradona. As he woke, the player, bleary-eyed and unshaven, struggled to make sense of where he was. 'Where is Claudia?' he was asked. He tried to think of his wife, but could barely make sense of time and place. 'No . . . yes, Claudia is at home . . . this isn't my home,' mumbled Maradona.

Since returning from Italy, Claudia and Franchi had been considering getting Maradona professional help, but were unable to dictate events. He had spiralled out of control, falling deeper and deeper into a drug-induced hole which won him few new friends. By the time journalists were tipped off by police of their imminent raid on El Soldadito's flat, Maradona could not even count on his old ally President Menem to save him. Under siege himself from the media for his ongoing marital problems and the involvement of a close relative in a drugs ring, Menem was only too happy, on this occasion, for justice to take its course against Maradona. The widely held suspicion, never convincingly disproved, was that Menem had fed Maradona to the wolves to save his own skin.

20

COPING WITH COKE

A Sunday night in April, an approaching winter in Buenos Aires. Diego Maradona faces his family as he has never done before. In his Buenos Aires apartment – not the one where the police busted him for drugs just hours earlier, but the one he shares with his wife Claudia and two young daughters since returning from Italy – the core of the Maradona tribe have gathered as if at a wake. Claudia has been joined by Maradona's parents Tota and Chitoro, his sisters and brothers, and his manager Marcos Franchi.

Maradona is dressed casually – a pair of football trousers, a T-shirt. He is barefoot. It should be like any other Sunday, a time for relaxation among close friends and relatives, after the football. Instead Maradona finds himself having to cope with the silence of his family, and the humiliation of being the subject of scientific scrutiny. The atmosphere has been dictated by the presence in the room of the kind of people who do not normally grace the Maradona household: two well-spoken psychologists, part of a medical team which has been assigned by a judge to help Maradona out of the black hole into which he has fallen. Much as he dislikes it, Maradona has little choice but to swallow his pride. Since being arrested on suspicion of cocaine possession and consumption, he is on bail, pending further investigations. Under Argentine law, the alternative to therapy is prison.

Ever since he can remember, Maradona has had a privileged position in his family. The first son, adored by his mother, always encouraged by his father, venerated by his brothers and sisters, had become the family's saviour, pulling them out from poverty and winning them status with his fame and success. But that night, the Maradonas sit not as worshippers but as onlookers to a tragedy with which they cannot fully come to terms. In their eyes there seems to be not so much adulation as pity and disillusionment. As for the psychologists, the intensity of their looks leaves Maradona with little doubt that in that room, at that moment, he is neither star nor hero, but a patient. Instinctively, he tries to shut them out. Medicine men have accompanied him all his professional life, but he has trusted only those outside the mainstream of orthodox practice.

These psychologists come from well-established institutions which do not have the study of football on their curriculum. They do not care a damn whether Maradona is the greatest football player in the world or a fishmonger. He's got a bad drug problem and needs to be cured. In their view there can be no privilege or immunity for those suffering from addictive illness. During their first encounter, the look in Maradona's eyes leaves the chief psychologist, Dr Ruben Navedo, with no doubt about the player's deep-rooted resistance to putting himself in the other's hands. 'It's as if he is telling me there and then, I don't believe in shrinks, I just don't believe in this. So I ask Diego for the first time what he is thinking, what he is feeling, and he says, "I don't believe in this." So I say, "Well, let's talk then," and that is how we begin.'

Maradona's professional life has come to a grinding halt, and those who manage his affairs realize that without medical help the future is bleak. Franchi, the manager, is still kept in the dark about the true history of the player's drug-taking. Maradona tells him he has only been taking cocaine for a few months. But what concerns Franchi and the other Maradonas, particularly Claudia, is the reality of a depressive in their midst, a man who seems to have lost sight of where he is coming from and where he is going, who seems to have lost all sense of motivation. In his football shorts and T-shirt, Maradona still cuts a defiant figure, but he is putting on weight again, his mind is all over the place, as a player he is unhirable. Following his positive dope test in Italy and then arrest in Buenos Aires, he has also become unmarketable. On hearing the news, Japanese companies are the first to start withdrawing from promotional contracts.

So the 'game plan' devised by the shrinks gets going. Some of the aspects of the plan have been applied before, in earlier, less dramatic low points in Maradona's career: the 'detoxification' involving a strict diet based on fresh fruit and vegetables, a lot of water and no alcohol. There is also a routine daily work-out in a nearby gym and jogging in Buenos Aires' Palermo Park. Other measures lock Maradona unwillingly into a less familiar territory of self-denial. Franchi and the psychologists, in consultation with Maradona's parents, 'select' who Maradona can and can't see. Those judged to have a bad influence on him are temporarily cut out of the Maradona circle and denied any access to the player. First among them is Guillermo Coppola. The doctors and Franchi consider him without question the 'baddie in the film' whom Maradona does not need on his road to recovery. They blame Coppola for having dragged Maradona into the wild nightlife of Naples, only to abandon him when the player's relationship with Napoli football club reached a critical stage. Coppola feels he is being unfairly blamed. He tells anyone who wants to hear him that his period in Italy coincided with Maradona's greatest footballing success. He considers himself, like Maradona, a victim of envious power play.

Those who are allowed to get in touch with Maradona are his first manager, Jorge Cyterszpiler, and the two former national coaches Carlos Bilardo and César Menotti. Of these two, Menotti shows particular nobility. Since leaving Barcelona, he and Maradona have not been on the best of terms. They have clashed publicly on the subject of football, and have cut themselves off from each other socially. But Menotti rings Maradona as soon as he hears he's been busted. 'I know things haven't being going too well between us recently, mate,' Menotti tells his former protégé, 'but I'm here for whatever you need.' Maradona would never forget that gesture of generosity.

The reason that Maradona's first manager and his two coaches are allowed as visitors is that all three are judged to have played a positive role in exploiting Maradona's talent as a football player, and giving him 'targets' to which to work, while respecting him as a person.

Maradona himself still finds difficulty, in the cloud of neurosis and paranoia in which he is submerged, in distinguishing between real friends and those simply out to take advantage of him. But among those he asks to see is Adrian Domenech, with whom he formed a friendship long before he became famous. It was with Domenech that Maradona as a young teenager had spent some of the genuinely happy moments of his life. They had shared their inexperience as young footballers with Argentinos Juniors and nights out to the cinema and the local pizza bar with their respective girlfriends, unhassled by the paparazzi and the burden of multi-million-dollar contracts. Later, when Maradona became famous and rich, he offered to pay for the less successful Domenech's wedding party and honeymoon to Barcelona. Domenech refused. He felt his marriage was his responsibility and wanted to go on owing Maradona nothing more than friendship. Ten years later, Domenech woke one morning to see his old friend's picture splashed on the front pages of the newspapers and glaring at him from the TV screens. He had not seen much of Maradona since he had gone to Italy, but the sight of him on the day of his arrest on cocaine charges shocked him deeply.

In the following weeks, Domenech tries to break through the sense of imprisonment which Maradona conveys. 'He is a prisoner in his own house, he can no longer change his clothes and go out to the cinema as we once did. The media are at the entrance to the flat, and even if he wants to the doctors won't let him.' He unreservedly devotes his time to Maradona, eating what he eats, training with him and helping restore in Maradona a sense of self-worth. If there are 'good guys' in Maradona's life, Domenech is one of them.

Another player who is brought in at an early stage to help out in Maradona's rehabilitation is Sergio Batista, the bearded international midfielder. Batista and Valdano are among Maradona's close friends in the national squad. Valdano is the philosopher of the Argentine team, the left-wing intellectual forever glimpsing capitalist plots in the world of football, the man who first encourages Maradona publicly to criticize FIFA in the Mexico World Cup of 1986. When Maradona is arrested by the Argentine police, Valdano announces that the action is all part of a conspiracy to divert attention from the problems of the Argentine government and destroy a footballing genius. Such a statement is hardly conducive to Maradona's recovery. If there is one thing he has never lacked it is paranoia. A more positive role is played by Batista, who volunteers from the outset simply to keep Maradona company, out of the glare of publicity. He shares with his friend memories of better times, when the two managed to enjoy themselves without hindering their performance on the football pitch. Once the two players had amused themselves on the eve of a major international by filming a spoof interview with a video camera, in which sex was the major topic discussed. Batista reminds Maradona that he was a captain once, the inspiration of successive World Cup victories, the pride of a nation, the undisputed international star.

Maradona is by nature introspective. With friends he has never lost sight of his roots, reminding them of the tough times he had as a young child, but the memories are never subject to self-analysis, his views about the world that surrounds him rarely coherent. Now, for the first time in his career, Maradona is having to explore his life in order to help himself and others understand the nature of his 'illness'. He is having to order his ideas, decide whether he really wants to go on playing football or retire, discover whether it is possible to choose his own destiny freely rather than be a prisoner of it.

Drug-taking is the one subject that he has until now discussed only with a very small, intimate group of friends. So secretive has he been on the subject that he has not even attempted to explain it to his parents. Ever since he was a kid he has wanted little more than his parents' approval, and now fears they will disown him. He begins, in his private analytical sessions, to share this side of himself with others who have no interest in the drug itself, other than to see it eradicated from his life.

Images flash before him of those moments when his drug-taking led him to hurt those he loved, and also put his career at risk. It begins with him taking cocaine just for fun – in Barcelona – and develops in Italy to the point where it was both a symptom and a cause of his life falling apart. Claudia had seen him taking cocaine in Barcelona at a party and reprimanded him for it. But only afterwards did the drug, with its ensuing clandestine nights, impossible mornings and unpredictable and often violent mood swings, seriously affect their relationship. Already the partnership that had been formalized in a Hollywood-style wedding was under strain as a result of Maradona's infidelities.

'You feel alive,' Maradona will come to say, 'but the truth is that it doesn't help you, it doesn't make you strong. It makes you weaker, starts killing you gradually.' He pauses. Thinks. Continues. 'At first it's a huge emotional shock. You feel as if you want to destroy the world. Then a terrible loneliness and fear takes you over. And then you begin to doubt, and everything comes tumbling down . . .' He recalls going round the house, locking the doors behind him so that his young daughters would not see him snorting, and the times he forgot to do so and was so coked out of his brains that he was unable to communicate with them.

At no stage does Maradona admit that he has ever taken drugs with the deliberate intention of enhancing his play, nor does he acknowledge the full extent of its negative impact on his professional motivation and competence. Suffering the after-effects of drugs, Maradona has missed training sessions and matches, played badly on occasions, lost his stamina and concentration.

What he does recall is the frustration of a childhood steeped in poverty where parents and children do not have the time or money to share their inner truths. His father, returning day after day from the bone-crushing factory, talks only of work, devoting what little spare time he has to making sure that Diego works at his football.

Like so many addicts before him, Maradona shares his past with a mixture of sadness, regret and relief: feelings of guilt and remorse at letting his family and some of his friends down, relief that he no longer has to hide it from them. And yet Maradona does not allow himself to be defeated by a terrible sense of shame, still less failure. Of the childhood images that return time and time again in his counselling sessions, one seems clearer than any other: the memory of falling into the cesspit at the back of his garden and being rescued by his uncle Cirilo. It is an image that reassures him of his capacity to surmount even the worst crisis of his life, that secures him in his belief that sheer will power to win in football will allow him to succeed in spite of his personal failings, just as he has done before.

And yet as the therapy extends over a period of time, Maradona begins to feel that the psychologists treat him not only as if he were ill, but as if the only way forward were a radical change in lifestyle. His sense of paranoia is revived. He fears that the psychologists are out to anaesthetize his character, turning his rehabilitation into a scientific obsession. One day he has a nightmare. He dreams that he dives into the swimming pool he has in his country house at Moreno on the Argentine pampa and touches the bottom. As he turns and tries to reach the surface he realizes that the water has turned black and he cannot see anything. Nor can he make any progress. When he finally struggles to the surface, he lifts his hand and it is all black. He then starts drowning. At that point, he wakes, covered in sweat.

Maradona is being subjected to two daily counselling sessions. A man with only primary education, whose only real passion has been football, is on the couch being asked about his childhood and his inner fears by two disciples of Freud and Jung. Maradona feels himself running out of things to say. He hates the long silences that greet his inability to remember. He resents the time spent without a ball at his feet, talking to two academics who have probably never watched a football match in their lives. 'So what are your thoughts?' the second psychologist with a Peruvian accent asks him at the start of an afternoon session. 'What the fuck am I meant to think if you were here only two hours ago!' Maradona explodes. They call in Claudia, ask her to calm her husband down. But on this occasion at least, she fully sympathizes with him. 'Look, I've never taken drugs, but I wouldn't know what to tell you either,' she says.

The concept of defeat is not one that Diego Maradona can handle easily. Ever since he entered the public consciousness as a young magician showing off his bag of footballing tricks on TV, he has had it engrained in his mind that he is the best. By the time he gets to Italy, his self-image, fuelled by the media and his fans, pitches him well beyond the normal aspirations of most mortal sporting heroes. He becomes a saint, a messiah, sent by God and acting on his behalf. Football becomes couched in divine terms of intercession. In Mexico, a cheat goal is the Hand of God, followed by an act of brilliance that captures the public imagination by far surpassing the talent and skills of normal footballers. In Italy, Maradona falls, but his self-projection is that of a martyr sacrificed by the very people who elevated him in the first place. He is the victim not of his own weakness but of the betrayal and conspiracy organized by latter-day pharisees. His submission to the Italian and Argentine courts is a plea for mitigation that defies the laws of Caesar. Thus Maradona does not assume personal responsibility for his drug-taking. He blames it on the pressures that others built up around him.

And yet public pressure can bring about Maradona's resurrection as surely as his crucifixion, most surely in Argentina, where a whole national identity, for better or for worse, is tied up with the boy from the shanty town who claimed a title as one of the best footballers of all time. Just a few days after returning to his country from Italy, Maradona is greeted like a hero by thousands of fans when his presence in the crowd is noticed at the start of a game in the Boca Juniors stadium. 'Olé, olé, olé . . . Diego, Diego . . .' they chorus. Another chant also reverberates through the stands. 'In Argentina there is a band, a band of vigilantes, who have ordered the arrest of Maradona. But we know that Menem also snorts.' Similar expressions of street-level solidarity accompany Maradona days later as he emerges from the police station after his arrest. The fans scream abuse at the police, while applauding the player. To much of the outside world, the image of an unshaven, seemingly physically wrecked Maradona busted for drugs looks like the end of the story. But in the eyes of many of his countrymen, even that image carries an inference of divinity: policemen become transformed into centurions, crowds weep openly at the suffering of their saviour, and once again there is the whisper of betrayal and conspiracy. As a nation, Argentina cannot, will not, blame Maradona. In an opinion poll conducted by the country's biggest-selling tabloid, *Clarín*, 71 per cent of those questioned say they believe Maradona to be innocent. A similar percentage say they still see him as their idol.

Maradona and his people interlock. They need each other. When Maradona goes before judge Amelia Berrez de Vidal, after his arrest for drugs, he is asked how many drugs he has dealt in. But this is no ordinary criminal before a court of justice; this is Maradona, who refuses to acknowledge any other kingdom than his own. His statement to the judge has the bland defiance of Christ before Pilate. 'Madam judge, the only thing that I've dealt with in my life is football for my country and I can swear that on the life of my daughters.' Maradona feels he has nothing to answer for.

Soon after returning from Italy, Maradona thinks of quitting for good and devoting himself fully to his wife and daughters. But the echoes of 'Olé, olé, Diego, Diego' that reach him deter him from such self-denial. He owes his existence to football. He feels that the cure for his addiction lies not in lying on the couch, pouring out his life story, but in drawing on that strength of will that has given him the commitment and the determination to succeed in the past. The doctors looking after him, and his own manager Franchi, have their doubts. They do not believe in conspiracies, only in human frailty. In Italy Maradona loses control of his life and needs the help of others to tackle the problems afflicting him. Between them, they argue over what is best for him.

Three months into his rehabilitation course, Maradona says he has had enough of talking about his childhood and secretly quits his counselling sessions. On his own initiative, he begins a tentative return to the only profession he has ever learned. The fifteen-month ban imposed on him as a result of his positive dope test in Italy excludes him from full-time football. But he scores two goals in an indoor amateur tournament played in a local sports club, quickly following this with an appearance at a charity match for which he briefly trains with Boca Juniors.

Among those keeping a close watch on Maradona's 'recovery' is Carlos Bilardo, one of the few soccer coaches who has managed to inspire the player with a careful mixture of indulgence and discipline. It was under Bilardo that Maradona reached what was arguably his professional peak, in Mexico in 1986. Bilardo is no longer national coach, having quit after Italia 1990. But he has been appointed manager of the Spanish club Sevilla and wants Maradona to join him once the fifteen-month ban is lifted. On paper, Sevilla appears to be in a similar predicament to that of Napoli when the Italian club first tempted Maradona in 1984. Sevilla FC is a southern club that has never been able to rival the success or status of central and northern rivals, namely Real Madrid and Barcelona. It is once again struggling to avoid relegation from the Spanish first division. And yet Bilardo makes it clear from the outset to Maradona that all he is aiming for in the following season is to have Sevilla end up somewhere between fifth and eight position in the league. 'We have to accept that the championship is going to be fought out for some while between Real and Barca,' he says.

Within Sevilla, some officials do not like the prospect of having Maradona. They consider him a liability, not only too hot to handle, but also not worth the trouble. But the club's president Luis Cuervas and his vice-president Jose Maria del Nido are on Bilardo's side. During the year, Seville as a city has attracted international interest thanks to the staging there of the Expo Fair. It is no longer Spain's provincial backwater. It has built a new international airport, a network of motorways and a 'bullet train' link with Madrid. To have Maradona is to carry on where Expo ends, bringing in its wake some lucrative broadcasting and sponsorship deals.

Bilardo's offer is also well received by Marcos Franchi and by Ruben Navedo, the one psychologist who has been retained as part of the player's counselling programme. Together with Bilardo, they persuade Maradona that it offers him the challenge of returning to mainstream club football, while minimizing some of the pressures which led him into the black hole in the first place. There is a problem, though. Napoli considers that it still owns Maradona and, despite his chequered history, expects him to honour the remaining year of a contract signed in 1987. It declares him non-transferable and initially rejects an offer of £2.5 million from Sevilla after Cuervas has announced that Maradona is already his. Maradona feels that to go back to Italy would be the equivalent of committing himself to a living death. Quite apart from the pending court cases against him, both those involving drugs and the paternity suit, he has not lost his belief that there is a conspiracy out there waiting to crucify him once and for all. Through his manager Franchi and lawyer Bolotnicof, Maradona puts a set of conditions to Napoli which he knows the club will be unable to meet: he wants a villa in Capri, a guaranteed holiday every six weeks, and a cancellation of a £2 million debt. Napoli has been plunged into a financial crisis since his departure, and is having difficulties in getting bank guarantees for any investments. It cannot afford to let the matter lie. Sevilla for its part has already promised publicly that it will deliver Maradona.

Into this apparent impasse, there enters a power broker in the figure of FIFA's general secretary, Joseph Blatter. At first glance, FIFA seems an unlikely organization to give Maradona a helping hand. Maradona has broken rules and discipline. He has criticized FIFA as an autocratic, uncaring organization. And yet Blatter sees that there is much to be gained on this occasion by coming to Maradona's rescue and getting him back into the game. For better or for worse Maradona remains one of world football's few genuinely charismatic personalities. Blatter and Havelange have their eyes on the US World Cup in 1994 and Maradona can help make it a commercial success. He can also help encourage the start-up of the new American football league. As one FIFA insider puts it, 'Our governors want to be seen to be doing everything they can to help the game, and the Maradona brokerage provided a perfect PR vehicle. In the end it became an emotional decision for Sevilla to get Maradona, and a rational decision for Napoli to get rid of him. But FIFA at the time could gain on the back of both of them.'

Blatter is so convinced of the advantages to be gained that with Havelange's blessing he takes personal charge of negotiations with all three parties. No matter if FIFA's statutes specify that such mediation should be carried out by the organization's Players'

Celebrating on the touchline in South Africa during Argentina's Group B World Cup match against South Korea, 17 June 2010

A disastrous 4-0 defeat by Germany at the Cape Town Stadium sees Argentina head out in the quarter-finals

Surrounded by fans after a GCC Champions League victory for Al-Wasl, 30 May 2012

The hero greets his fans from the balcony of the Vesuvio hotel in Naples, 25 February 201

The patron saints of Argentinian football watch over the team's Group F World Cup match against Nigeria, 25 June 2014

Maradona and Roberto Baggio take part in the Interreligious Match for Peace in Rome, 1 September 2014

Meeting Pope Francis at the Vatican, 4 September 2014

Maradona leads a football workshop with schoolchildren in Barasat, India,
12 December 2017

With Vladimir Putin and Pelé at the State Kremlin Palace for the final draw for the 2018 World Cup

Centre of attention at the World Cup in Russia, 2018

Maradona becomes coach of Dorados de Sinaloay, Mexico, 2018

Maradona flags fly high during a match between Gimnasia y Esgrima La Plata and Estudiantes as part of Superliga Argentina, 2 November 2019

Watching Gimnasia y Esgrima and Patronato from his throne, 8 February 2020

Maradona's casket waits in the funeral chapel at the Casa Rosada in Buenos Aires, 26 November 2020

The funeral is screened in front of the Casa Rosada, with three days of national mourning declared

Status Committee. It is in the nature of the autocratic governorship conducted by the Havelange/Blatter axis that key decisions can sometimes be steamrolled by the top.

Months of protracted negotiations are resolved in a five-hour meeting between Blatter and the two club chiefs in FIFA's headquarters in Zurich. In an interview with the author in March 1996, Blatter recalls that night in late September 1992 as an achievement of which he remains proud. Time, and the criticism the non-accountability of the Havelange régime is increasingly facing, have added their dose of gloss to the event. 'That night I explain that Maradona is like a member of a family. He has failed his family and been punished for it. But he has served his punishment. The same family must now do everything possible to bring him back into the fold,' Blatter tells me.

And yet for all his insistence that his brokerage is done on 'ethical grounds', the agreement that is finally thrashed out has a financial spin to it that reinserts the Maradona name fairly and squarely back in the world of big business. Ironically the £4.5 million transfer deal Napoli's president Ferlaino agrees to includes TV rights ceded to the European TV consortium Telecinco, which is partly owned by his rival Silvio Berlusconi, the president of AC Milan.

It is as if everyone is suddenly prepared to be part of a happy universal footballing family, thanks to Diego Maradona. After the deal is signed, Blatter declares to the world press that FIFA now expects Maradona to 'stop making insulting comments against football leaders whether at club, federation or international level'. Give us another, Joseph.

Seville, the city of Don Juan and Carmen, is, in the words of the Spanish writer Camilo José Cela, 'like the blue of the sky and the green of the olive trees', ever changing, inspiring even the dullest of minds. It has none of the exclusive sophistication of Barcelona or parts of Buenos Aires. Sure, it has its share of saints and crucifixes, but it never takes itself too seriously, nor anybody else for that matter . . . It is a gypsy town where football, like bullfighting, is played and watched in the atmosphere of a fiesta.

They like Mexican waves here. If a game looks like turning dull, the fans liven it up with some rhythmic flamenco hand-clapping, or some cheeky verse reworked to the music of *Guantanamera* or the *Marseillaise*. To get by in Seville all you need is a combination of two things, a sense of humour and a thing the gypsies call *duende*, which really means soul. Ever since anyone can remember, Sevilla's Sánchez Pizjuan stadium has been the favourite venue for internationals, because Basques, Cataláns and Castilians who play for the national squad know that tribal loyalties can be cast aside here in an atmosphere of Andalusian good cheer. What other stadium in the world would have a huge mural covering its outside wall with the emblems of all the country's clubs?

Sevilla gains thousands of new members thanks to him, much to the envy of its town rival Betis, which considers itself more rooted in the working class and yet has never had huge resources. Within four days of Maradona's arrival, Sevilla has grossed an extra £2.2 million in ticket sales. Maradona rents a spacious and comfortable luxury apartment from a bullfighter friend called Espartaco in a quiet residential suburb outside the city. He learns flamenco and dreams of being a bullfighter. In a dream, Maradona comes to Seville dressed as a bullfighter in colours which he particularly admires, green and gold. Out on the field Maradona tries to find his feet again, and recreates some of his old magic in partnership with Simeone in two memorable games, one against Real Madrid, the other against Sporting of Gijón. But these are just two games out of twenty-six he manages to play for Seville.

Today it is hard to find a local fan who can remember his presence in any of the others. Maradona remains overweight and finds it impossible to submit himself to discipline. Bilardo's World Cup formula of indulgence mixed with strictness doesn't work in Seville. There is much too much of the first and far too little of the second. The manager's attempts to ensure that Sevilla gets value for money from Maradona are made no easier by the demands put on the player by the new Argentine international coach, Alfio Basile, a one-time defender with Racing whose philosophy of football is somewhere between Menotti's 'poetry' and Bilardo's pragmatism. Basile recalls Maradona for a series of matches with the national squad. Sevilla officials are angered by Maradona's constant absences, but Maradona goes off anyway. All through his professional life he has resisted any attempt to restrict his freedom of movement, however contractually bound, and he is damned if he is going to make an exception for Sevilla's crusty right-wing president Cuervo after taking on the likes of Nuñez and Ferlaino.

Maradona becomes dogged by scandal again. One night he is stopped for speeding by the police after driving his Porsche at 200 kilometres per hour along one of the city's main avenues; on another he gets embroiled in a drunken brawl in a well-known discotheque. He is prevented from entering by the bouncer because he is wearing trainers. 'Who do you think you're talking to?' Maradona asks him. 'People kill themselves to kiss these shoes.'

His escapades become so notorious that the local press, until then sympathetic towards him, can no longer ignore them. Seville is a small town where gossip travels fast. Local journalists pick up kiss-and-tell stories even at siesta time when neighbours spy and whisper on the comings and goings at the Maradona house. One of Diego's favourite haunts becomes a notorious local brothel called La Casita. Often he takes along his team mates. On one occasion, the debauchery of an entire football team thanks to Diego Maradona becomes the subject of a magazine exposé.

They are not puritans in Spain, but even in Andalusia, among the rich and powerful, there is an inherent streak of social orthodoxy that reacts when it feels itself threatened by anarchy. Maradona stretches the tolerance of the Sevillans to its limits. The club directors are not the most popular in town as it is. They have cynically squandered the club's resources, investing little in the stadium and speculating for their own personal profit on the land surrounding it. They cannot afford to be seen to be taken for a ride by Maradona. The player's debauchery is carefully documented by a team of private investigators hired by Cuervas. Armed with a heavy file, the club president tells Maradona that unless he starts playing football properly he will be considered in breach of contract. Maradona decides he doesn't like the contract anyway and wants to quit.

The crunch comes during a game Sevilla plays against Burgos in June 1993. Thirty minutes before the end, with Sevilla one goal ahead, Bilardo orders Maradona on to the substitutes' bench. The manager has become increasingly aware of the player's lack of match fitness and his failures to turn up at training sessions. He has been watching Maradona gradually lose his momentum and decides he will not be able to hold the game together with Maradona on the pitch. Maradona takes it as a personal insult, betrayed by the one manager he has always instinctively trusted. In a very public act of defiance he walks over to Bilardo and calls him a son of a bitch and jostles him. 'I'm going to have this out with Bilardo, man to man,' Maradona tells journalists. 'If, that is, Bilardo is a man . . .' The violent exchanges continue afterwards in the changing room where Maradona and Bilardo punch each other. It is an incident that Bilardo would like to put behind him and of which he talks only reluctantly. 'During that match, I didn't think Diego looked all that good . . . he then comes up and insults me . . . after the match I went to his house, but I was told he wasn't there, that he'd gone to Madrid. So then I went again and found him and then we started talking. We said what we wanted to say to each other and then we agreed to put it behind us,' Bilardo recalls. 'We beat the shit out of each other,' is how Maradona remembers it.

Bilardo emerges from the incident convinced that Maradona has made his mind up that his days with Sevilla are over and there is no going back. The match with Burgos is Maradona's last appearance in a Sevilla shirt.

'I'm going because they don't love me,' Maradona says. 'But you know what I really love. To be with the gypsies. Here in Seville, the only Virgin that interests me is the Gypsy Virgin.'

Seville should be a turning point in the life of Diego Maradona. A time to think of quitting football, period. For a while he considers doing just that, although the thought of never playing another game, of abandoning what he was brought into the world to do, fills him with horror. He shares his inner doubts with those who have tolerated his moods since Italy – his manager Franchi, his personal trainer Signorini. While still in Seville he is visited by his psychologist. Together they recognize that addictions cannot be cured, they can only be arrested or managed, and that if Maradona is to survive he will have to tread a thin line between the god-like status and the human frailties which have combined to bring about his downfall in the past.

There is something in Maradona that cannot accept defeat. If things have not worked out, he convinces himself, it is not because he has lost his will to play, but because Sevilla has in the end failed to present a sufficient challenge. Only his fellow countrymen are now prepared to offer him that, by demanding that he lead their national team into the next World Cup in the US. And yet there is a patient in Maradona still, a part of him that blames the pressures of fame for his addiction, and that desperately wants to be left alone in the intimacy of those he feels he can love and trust. In the past sheer will power has resolved the contradictions in Diego Maradona. But after Seville he is no longer so sure of himself. He needs the approval of others to begin believing in himself again and his form has not been so good of late.

In fact it's been pretty miserable off and on the pitch. For only the second time in his professional life, Maradona has suffered the ultimate indignity. He has been left out of the national squad for the vital World Cup qualifying round because Basile considers him surplus to requirements. The last time that happened to him was in 1978, when Menotti judged him too inexperienced to represent Argentina. Now age, not youth, is the excuse that Basile uses, judging Maradona no longer able to pull through the psychological and physical setbacks he has suffered. Maradona feels humiliated. 'I won't play for Basile again if he comes begging on his knees,' he says at the time.

Again those who surround him have no option but to take his precarious psychological state into account before signing another contract. In spite of his rehabilitation programme, Maradona continues to veer in and out of drug-induced depression. He knows how easy it is to lose one's way in life, how difficult to regain it. Only later will he recall one night when he thought he'd lost it. As always when he's decided to snort cocaine at home, Maradona makes his way to the bathroom, in the dark so as not to disturb the children or Claudia. It is four o'clock in the morning. He is setting out the cocaine lines, one alongside the other, when he hears a gentle tap on the bathroom door. 'Dad, can I come in?' whispers a little girl's voice. It is his elder daughter Dalma. He is taken so much by surprise that he can hardly utter a word. He throws the cocaine into the toilet. He opens the door and Dalma comes in and sits on the toilet seat. 'What's wrong, Daddy, why are you like this and not asleep?' Dalma asks. Maradona is shaking. 'No, my little mum, I can't sleep.' And Maradona can't hold it together any more and so he starts talking and talking and talking, not knowing what he's talking about. A horrible feeling, a truly horrible feeling, Maradona would later say . . .

After the disgrace of Seville and the bust-up with Basile, Maradona once again avoids a total breakdown by leaning on his parents and escaping to his roots. With his mother and father he returns to their birthplace in Esquina. There, once again, he kicks a ball when he feels like it, avoids the media and goes fishing. He begins to feel at peace with himself again, though a certain restlessness still nags at his soul. Marcos Franchi knows that Maradona has to play club football again, but the problem lies in finding a team that will suit him in the fragile circumstances through which he is living.

Maradona is no longer making as much money as he used to and
there are doubts as to whether he will ever again secure a lucrative
transfer deal. Outside Argentina, the feeling has been growing that
Maradona has finally blown it.

October 1993. Another lifeline is thrown to Maradona when he
is offered a contract with a club seemingly made to measure. This
time it is the turn of Newell's Old Boys, a legacy of the British
presence in Argentina and their contribution to the early days of
football. It was formed in 1903 in the provincial town of Rosario
by former pupils of a local Anglo-Argentine commercial school. It
is not only one of the less successful first-division clubs, it is also
only one of two clubs in Rosario, and it is the other, named after
the town, which is the more famous. Local folklore has it that the
'blue and yellows', as Rosario FC footballers are called, had as their
most committed fan none other than Ernesto 'Che' Guevara. He
was born there. No matter that El Che left Argentina at an early
age and devoted his life to spreading international revolution out
of Cuba. His spirit lives on in the terraces of Rosario, to the extent
that some left-wing Argentine intellectuals like Osvaldo Bayer urge
Maradona not to betray him. So why does Maradona, who has
never had much love lost for the English and who claims to talk
for the people, opt for Newell's?

He justifies the move as part of a new grass-roots philosophy he
claims to have developed while in Esquina and travelling around
the interior of Argentina. 'It might seem a cliché,' he says, 'but
this year I've been lucky enough to travel all over Argentina, to
look at my country and get to know it, and I've begun to realize
whole areas of it have been neglected. I want to decentralize
football. It can't be good to have twenty top teams inside 20
square kilometres.' In reality the explanation is rather simpler.
Walther Cattaneo, Newell's president, works hard on Franchi and
Maradona to convince them that he can generate money from local
businesses and sponsors to buy out the player's remaining contract
with Seville – about $4 million – and pay him a monthly salary of
about $25,000. In the circumstances it is an offer that Maradona's
financial advisers think it foolish to refuse.

Once the deal is signed and sealed, Maradona receives the blessing
of the Virgin of Rosario before making his way to the stadium
for the inaugural ceremony marking the latest resurrection of his
career and the rekindling of the hopes of a nation. As the crowd

erupts, Maradona is handed a commemorative plaque. 'May Our Lady of Rosario protect you as a man and as an idol,' it reads, 'and may today's miracle provide an example of faith, hope and charity. Welcome back to life!'

Maradona plays only a few games for Newell's Old Boys, but his heart doesn't seem in it. Again there is no championship to be won, only a slightly higher position to be gained in the league table. And yet he is followed everywhere, the pressure for him to succeed huge from the outset. In order to lose weight, he has submitted himself once again to a drastic régime of diet and drugs, seemingly oblivious to the pernicious consequences of such a course. The fact that he seems to grind to a halt well before the end of each match after a tremendous spurt of initial energy, that he is breathless in post-match press conferences and that his face is unnaturally drawn, does not worry the TV officials, members of the local media and other vested interests who look to Maradona for the revival of national football as a lucrative business. Those who now urge Maradona to press on include Basile, the national coach. Basile's luck has run out. After a series of unbeaten matches without Maradona, Argentina are trounced 5–0 by Colombia with Freddy Rincón and Faustina Asprilla the men of the match. Argentines hate being beaten by Colombians, whom they regard as racially inferior and lacking in seriousness. The defeat is a national humiliation as interpreted by *Gráfico*. It prints its cover entirely in black.

In the end, though, it is the call from the tribe that returns to haunt Basile, as it has done with other football managers. With the Colombian score mounting in the River Plate stadium, a familiar chant has begun to spread through the terraces: 'Maradooona . . . Maradooona . . . Maradooona . . .'

Soon the only question Basile and others seem to want to ask Maradona is not will he play in the next World Cup, but when will he be fit enough to join the national team again? 'The key is just for him to keep on playing,' says Basile. Among Argentina's senior officials there are those who do not look kindly on Maradona's return. They include Julio Grondona, the long-serving president of the Argentine Football Association. Conservative and austere, with a knack for quiet diplomacy, Grondona has survived various changes of government in Argentina. Presidents, whether members of a junta or democratically elected, trust him to keep his politics to himself. Over the years he has grown to dislike Maradona, his very opposite in background (he is Spanish, Maradona is Italian) and attitudes. Grondona regards Maradona as a showman, an unstable maverick who breaks too many rules. Grondona has had to spend a lot of his time making sure that Argentina's image as a football nation survives Maradona's endless falls, and is tired of it. He fears that Maradona's presence in the high-profile World Cup in the US could be a disaster.

And yet Grondona is not a man to swim too energetically against the current and late in 1993 it is clear that for him to oppose Maradona would probably cost him his job. The combination of TV, marketing and club interests that straddle the Argentine football industry want Maradona back to boost their flagging fortunes. Grondona thus raises no public objections when Basile, also reluctantly, brings back Maradona for the crucial two-leg play-off against Australia. It is an encounter that Argentina has to win in order to qualify for the US competition. And she does, thanks to Maradona. Once again he is reinstated as saviour of the nation.

In the following weeks the relentless pressure of popular expectation begins to build up yet again round Maradona. Yet again they want him to show that he is the best in the world. His performance for Newell's disappoints after the initial euphoria. And those self-doubts about who he is and where he's going make him retreat into old habits.

In February 1994, Maradona surrenders to the irrational act of a troubled mind. It is late summer and he is relaxing in his country home of Moreno with a group of friends, some team mates from Newell's, his father Chitoro and his favourite uncle, Cirilo. Outside the gates of his driveway, a group of journalists are on guard duty, hoping to get a comment from the player about his virtually broken contract with Newell's and his plans for the future. Maradona asks them to leave him alone, to leave his children alone. The journalists say they will once he has given them one coherent statement. Maradona starts to insult them. One of his friends takes the garden hose and sprays them with water. Another mocks the journalists by pretending to masturbate. Maradona himself picks up an air rifle and, leaning on the roof of one of his cars, takes careful aim and then shoots at the gate, injuring four journalists.

Those injured sue Maradona. Two cede to pressure from the

Maradona camp and settle out of court, while the others consider it a point of principle to see that justice applies as much to the famous as to the ordinary hack. The investigating magistrate, a local man determined to assert his independence from political interference emanating from Buenos Aires, is determined to make an example of Maradona. But he subsequently discovers the huge vested interests that Maradona can move in the country. He receives discreet pressures from President Menem to be lenient, and the opposite message from Grondona, which suggests that the football chief's personal vindictiveness towards Maradona has not abated. Grondona believes that Maradona should be prosecuted like any other citizen and if found guilty of assault should face a jail sentence. He is angry that yet again Maradona has turned the sport he loves and cares for into a platform for public scandal.

Unaware of the political intrigue behind the scenes, public reaction veers towards collective sympathy for Maradona. Those who argue that he deserves to be treated like a common criminal, regardless of his status, are in a minority – at least in the local media. Instead the incident seems to confirm still more clearly Maradona's place in the litany of national sporting heroes whose eccentricities – however outrageous – are blindly accepted for the greater good of the nation. They include Carlos Monzón, the Argentine boxing champion who was popularly forgiven in spite of first throttling his wife and then throwing her to her death, and 'Ringo' Bonavena, who remains a national hero in spite of dying in a shoot-out in a Las Vegas brothel.

Menem, several players from Boca Juniors and Marcos Franchi are among those who publicly suggest that what Maradona needs is not further legal action against him but a period of being left alone. Many of Maradona's fans simply see the incident in Moreno as confirming him as king. In the language of the terraces he has had the balls to tell those wankers in the press where to get off.

In the end it is left up to Maradona to demonstrate just how powerful his hold is on the Argentine people. With the legal action against him still pending, and the journalists he had shot at still recovering from their wounds, Maradona confirms that he is willing and able to captain his side in the US World Cup. The announcement is greeted with the popular euphoria one would expect from a football-crazy nation that has only one high priest.

21

TESTING POSITIVE

In the late afternoon of 30 June 1994, the president of the Argentine Football Association, Julio Grondona, had a mobile phone nearly pushed down his throat as he walked away from Dallas Cotton Bowl stadium. He had been watching his national team train before their World Cup tie against Bulgaria. Seconds earlier a pack of mainly Argentine journalists had laid siege to FIFA's press officer, Andreas Herren. They wanted him to provide some credible explanation for the feverish comings and goings of some of FIFA's senior officials and doctors over the previous twenty-four hours. In the bureaucratic language of FIFA, a curt no comment or similar obfuscation speaks volumes. It is confirmation that something is indeed afoot. And on this occasion the press officer's inability to clarify anything was the signal the journalists needed to home in on a more exploitable quarry.

Over a direct phone link with a radio station in Buenos Aires, Grondona confirmed what two Argentine journalists had been tipped off about hours earlier but could not bring themselves to report: Diego Maradona, their hero, the man of magic, football genius and international star, was the player whose drugs test had proved positive.

The news had been broken to Maradona twenty-four hours earlier by his personal trainer, Fernando Signorini, as he lay half asleep in his room at the Babson College residence in Boston, the city where Argentina had played its opening World Cup ties. Gently but persistently to shake Maradona out of his profound slumber and to prepare him for a training session or match had become one of the regular aspects of Signorini's job since Maradona had first taken him on in Barcelona in 1983. Faced with Maradona's immobility, Signorini began as he had done on countless previous occasions: 'Diego, come on . . . let's go . . . get up . . .' he said as he shook the player over and over again. Only when Signorini uttered the words 'It's all over' did Maradona show the first signs of reaction. Still half asleep, he recalled who he was and where he was.

Over the last week, he had been in a great mood, as if the personal nightmare of the previous World Cup in Italy belonged to another planet. Journalists, Argentine and non-Argentine alike, warmed to the image of the slimmed-down, seemingly fit Maradona who spent his practice sessions hanging about the touchline, in idle banter with some of the more eccentric of the fans that year – three old men dressed in togas who followed the Argentine team wherever they went. Maradona led Argentina to a convincing 4–0 win over Greece, and a hard-earned 2–1 victory over Nigeria. After this second match, he was accompanied off the field by a Green Cross nurse and told that he was one of two Argentine players picked for a dope test. 'Don't worry, I'll show them that I'm worth more than they think,' Maradona had told friends, confident that he had nothing to worry about from a competition that was going his way. This had been billed as Maradona's return to greatness, and certainly the early stages of USA '94 had come alive thanks to him. He was one of the few players of whom the majority of Americans had heard. There were no whistles or jeers in Boston.

These images flashed across Maradona's mind only to disintegrate when his eyes cleared sufficiently to see the expression on Signorini's face. 'What's wrong, Fernando?' he asked. 'They've killed us,' Signorini replied. 'The test was positive and they've decided to suspend you.' Maradona felt he had fallen into a black hole. In silence, he staggered out from his bed and made for the bathroom. 'I killed myself training, I killed myself training, and now they do this to me!' he screamed before breaking out in sobs. Signorini was rarely surprised by anything that Maradona did, but the scene he witnessed that day – an international star reduced in an instant to a human wreck – was not one he would easily forget. He later recalled, 'It seemed as if Diego's whole world had come apart. He was crying from the deepest depth of his soul, completely out of control.'

Not since the assassination of John F. Kennedy had a single news item out of Dallas provoked such an international reaction as that which followed the announcement that Maradona had tested positive for drugs. The bulk of British journalists, who had found themselves shedding their dislike of the player in the early stages of the competition, reverted to their previous opinion, condemning him as a confirmed cheat and a disgrace to the game. Some, like Ian Ridley of the *Independent on Sunday*, were more sympathetic. Arguing that Maradona had been brought down by an act of mere folly, Ridley wrote, 'Those with a passion for watching the game that matches Maradona's passion for playing it, however, will long remember where they were, and those being barbecued in the 100-degree heat of the Texan city will recall the coldness that gripped them when they heard the news. Say it ain't so, Diego.'

Similar voices were raised in other parts of the world where Maradona had long since been metamorphosed into a god. In Dhaka, over 20,000 Bangladeshis staged a spontaneous demonstration chanting, 'Dhaka will burn unless Maradona is allowed to play.' Not surprisingly the greatest sense of collective shock was felt in Argentina. Renewed popular enthusiasm for Maradona among his fellow countrymen had persuaded him to come out of semi-retirement to give it his last shot, playing for his national team in the US. 'My only ambition is to represent the national colours once more and then quit,' he had said. Thousands of Argentine fans had flown to Boston, while millions more had stayed glued to their radio and TV sets for the opening games. Not since Maradona had led his team out against England in the 1986 World Cup had there been such a clear-cut national enterprise as winning in the United States, the country which represented everything an Argentine loved and hated most.

When Maradona scored Argentina's third goal against Greece after setting up an extraordinary combination of passes between three of his colleagues, the country's most popular radio journalist had screamed, 'Gardel is alive, Gardel is alive!' – a reference to the legendary Argentine tango singer who died in Paris in the 1930s.

And yet when the news of the dope test filtered through, it was not Gardel's magical tango that was recalled, but the day of his death in June 1935, which, like that of Perón, left much of the nation desolate and seemingly orphaned. Argentines fell into a stunned state of shock or wept openly. Only gradually, just as had occurred following Argentina's defeat in the Falklands War, did the grieving express itself in anger against the alleged culprits. Argentines prepared publicly to question Maradona's personal responsibility were in a minority and were promptly vilified as traitors. They included Bernardo Neudstadt, a TV commentator who made a habit of pushing his ratings up by adopting the opposite view to his competitors. In an uncompromising attack on Maradona, Neudstadt painted the player as an irresponsible dope head and a national disgrace. But public sympathy in Argentina remained overwhelmingly on the side of Maradona. It was not just that society remained emotionally identified with him, but also that without him people stood to lose money, position and influence. It was not easy to disentangle a football industry that for better or for worse depended on Maradona's resurrection from the dead. A genuine collective catharsis might have happened had Maradona himself made a public apology. But instead the image that he chose to give to the world was that of a genius unfairly treated, who had once again fallen victim to a conspiracy.

'They've cut my legs off,' Maradona said in his first press conference following the announcement, before insinuating that FIFA, represented by the president, João Havelange, and the general secretary, Joseph Blatter, had chosen to punish him in revenge for his past insubordination. 'This is a real dirty business. I'd like to believe in Havelange and in Blatter, but after this, well . . . I don't want to say anything . . .' It was an accusation that FIFA, sensitive to the popularity Maradona enjoyed in many of its member countries, would go out of its way to deny. In an interview in March 1996, granted during the final stages of this book's preparation, Joseph Blatter emphasized what he claimed were his continuous efforts to reintegrate Maradona into the 'world football family': 'I've always thought of Diego Maradona as a wonderful football player. One of the darkest days of my life was that day in the US when I realized it was Maradona that failed the test. After all the effort, it was a huge disappointment.'

And yet in 1994, once Maradona had set the ball rolling, there was no stopping Argentina's conspiracy merchants from spinning the tale for all its worth. One of the more imaginative efforts was provided by Fernando Niembro, the Argentine journalist who had persuaded President Menem to made Maradona 'ambassador for sport' during the World Cup in Italy. With Maradona's approval, and with the co-operation of another writer, Niembro produced a novel called *Innocent*, in which fact and fiction are mixed in an attempt to convince a gullible reader that everything is not only possible, but probable. Into Niembro's own-eye witness account of the 1994 World Cup is woven an extraordinary tale in which Maradona falls victim to a CIA plot to ensure the order and stability of the competition. At one point an agent for the CIA dresses up as a priest and administers Maradona a host spiked with drugs.

The man who in fact administered Maradona's 'cocktail of drugs' prior to the match against Nigeria was no CIA agent but one Daniel Cerrini, a member of the player's 'inner circle' of trusted friends and advisers that was periodically subject to change or modification. Cerrini had been introduced to Maradona in the summer of 1993, soon after the player had returned to Argentina following his brief post-Naples period of playing with Sevilla. Maradona was overweight, unfit and depressed after an unsuccessful season. By contrast, Cerrini had all the attributes of an Adonis: a relaxed, reassuring manner and a handsome, permanently tanned face atop a body which bulged with carefully sculptured muscle tissue. Cerrini ran the New Age Gym in Buenos Aires. He was also a body-builder whose main claim to fame had been to win the Mr South American Youth Body competition eight years earlier. His other 'credentials' were off-the-shelf diplomas as a physical trainer and a dietitian, neither of which were recognized as formal professions in Argentina.

From the moment of his first meeting with Cerrini, Maradona seems to have regarded him as his physical ideal, and was easily seduced by what was claimed to be a rapid and fail-safe course to recovery and well-being. The Cerrini method involved a combination of intense training, drastic diet and supplements of vitamins and minerals, and additional weight reduction and energy-giving drugs over a limited period. Maradona willingly succumbed to it in an effort to lose weight and regain his fitness in time for the start of the football season playing with the Argentine team Newell's Old Boys. Superficially Cerrini brought about a dramatic turn-around in Maradona's body shape, making it lose all its excess fat and defining his muscles. The plump face Maradona had displayed in his last weeks in Sevilla became taut and stretched to the bone, almost emaciated.

Maradona played only seven games with Newell's before resigning after an argument over his contract. But he emerged from the experience convinced that he both could and should once again set his sights on playing in the World Cup. Maradona insisted that Cerrini should be part of his personal team, working alongside his long-time trainer Fernando Signorini. A few weeks before Argentina's pre-World Cup international tour, the three men took off to a remote farm in the middle of the Argentine pampa. The idea was typically Signorini's and sprang from his close observation of Maradona's personal and professional life over the previous decade.

'I chose the place because it was Spartan. It had a TV that hardly worked, and no hot water. Our only luxury was a small radio on which we listened to music and followed some football matches,' recalled Signorini. 'I remember talking to Diego soon after we arrived. I said, "Look, Diego, if we you want to get to the top again, you've got to start from the bottom. Go back to what it was like in Villa Fiorito. Feel hungry." He was soon shaving himself in the sun just as he remembered his dad doing when he was a kid.'

What worried Signorini was the presence of Cerrini. The more he found out about him, the less he trusted him. Among those who had investigated Cerrini's background on Signorini's behalf was Dr Nestor Lentini, the head of the Argentine National Sports Clinic. Lentini confirmed not only Cerrini's lack of convincing medical credentials, but worse, his association with a positive drugs test that had resulted in the expulsion of his girlfriend from a female body competition in 1989 for the alleged use of anabolic steroids. Despite this discovery, neither Signorini nor Lentini attempted to persuade Maradona to rid himself of Cerrini. It had long been an unwritten rule in Maradona's inner circle that no one would denounce an individual until he had lost the personal trust of the player. Such tribal complicity persisted as long as the chief was happy, and Cerrini had so far ensured that Maradona was just that.

The tensions in Maradona's medical team simmered beneath the surface in the weeks leading up to the World Cup. In former years the Argentine squad had enjoyed a lax régime of medical controls during that period, knowing that random dope tests would only be carried out once the tournament had got underway. Prior to the US World Cup, however, FIFA updated its regulations to include the right to carry out random tests during the qualifying rounds. So distrustful was Lentini of Cerrini and the influence he was having on Maradona that he conducted regular analyses of the player's urine samples to ensure that the dietitian had not introduced illegal substances into Maradona's régime. The controls met with the approval of the Argentine team's official doctor, Ernesto Ubalde, who resented the fact that he was unable to win Maradona's confidence to the same degree as Cerrini.

Between Cerrini and Signorini there developed continuous arguments over what Maradona's ideal weight should be. Signorini suspected that Cerrini's diet was designed not for a footballer with a medium- to long-term set of sports commitments in front of him but for an athlete requiring a quick fix for a short-run competition. Body-builders who had trained under Cerrini had found how dramatically they could lose energy and regain weight once they had reached their 'peak'. Signorini felt that the Cerrini method was full of potential risks in a competition like the World Cup, and was determined to make it less extreme. 'I felt that Cerrini had always judged his success by how good he and his patients looked in photographs. That didn't seem to be a guarantee that Diego would play good football,' Signorini told me.

Maradona had returned from Sevilla weighing 92 kilos. In the just over one-month period that he took to prepare for Newell's Old Boys, his weight came down to just over 70 kilos. That was the weight that Cerrini wanted Maradona to be for the World Cup. Signorini insisted on 77 kilos. The two men were at odds over what would ensure speed, agility and strength, while preventing dehydration. The days of Mexico's World Cup, when Maradona had been allowed to eat when and how he wanted, were long past. Unknown to the outside world, the Argentine camp in the run-up to the US World Cup had an almost surrealistic atmosphere about it, with Maradona caught in the middle of a major argument over his weight.

For Argentina's opening game against Greece, he weighed in at 76.8 kilos. He told Signorini and Cerrini he had never felt better. The word spread out from the Argentine camp that Maradona was in crack form and was really looking forward to playing in the competition. But someone who had followed the player's career from the outset was worried by the Maradona he saw in a pre-match training session in Boston. Horacio Pagani, the veteran football journalist for the Buenos Aires newspaper *Clarín*, recalled, 'When I got to the States, everyone came up to me and said what a fantastic physical state Diego was in, but when I saw him training I couldn't believe it. After ten minutes he seemed out of breath. Later when I interviewed him just after he'd given his urine sample for the dope test, he went on again about how happy he was. He said he was living some of the happiest moments of his life. He either was truly not conscious of what he'd taken, or else he was a total impostor.'

Two days before the Nigeria game, another of the few journalists with whom Maradona felt at ease, José Manuel García of the Spanish sports daily *MARCA*, visited him at his Dallas hotel. García had not had time alone with Maradona since the player's brief season with Sevilla in 1992–93. He was impressed by how well he looked and by his positive frame of mind. Maradona's only problem was that he appeared to have caught a cold as a result of the contrast between the stifling Texas heat and the excessive air-conditioning in the hotel. He talked with difficulty, through a blocked nose. García drew the conversation to a close with typical Andalusian jocularity, 'Diego, you've got a hell of a flu coming on there. I'd better go before you tell me to bugger off.'

Smiling, Maradona rose from the sofa he had been sitting on and said, 'Don't worry, I'm going to see the Prof. He'll give me something for the nose so I can sleep better.'

The Prof was Signorini's nickname. Prior to the game with Nigeria, the decongestant was just one of several products that Maradona was encouraged to take by his medical team. These included a weight-reducing supplement which Cerrini had included as part of the player's crash diet programme. On arriving in the US, Cerrini had purchased the supplement as a replacement for a product he had brought with him from Argentina. It was available over the counter in the US and was widely used in amateur sports, but it contained a substance which featured on FIFA's proscribed list of performance-enhancing drugs. Cerrini later claimed that he had overlooked rather than ignored this fact, and therefore saw no reason to communicate it to Maradona prior to the match. Maradona for his part denied that he had defied FIFA regulations by knowingly taking a banned substance to aid his activity on the field.

On 1 July 1994, FIFA's World Cup organizing committee circulated a memorandum on the results of two separate laboratory tests carried out on the urine which had been collected from Maradona five days earlier. Under the reference heading, 'Sample Number FIFA 220, collected June 25, 1994 in Boston, match Number 23, Player D.A. Maradona, Argentina UCLA CWAO4 Identification Number', the memo listed the substances which Maradona had taken: 'The samples A and B contained the following substances listed as prohibited substances, stated in Doping Control Regulations, Chapter 3.5.A (Stimulants) of the FIFA prepared by the FIFA

Sports Medical Committee for the World Cup 1994: Ephedrine, Metephredine, Phenylpropanolamine=Norephredine (Listed substances); Pseudoephedrine, Norpseudoephedrine (substances are not listed, but from the chemical content and the biological effect similar to the Ephedrin and Norephedrin, could possibly be metabolites).'

The memorandum was the outcome of a system for doping control which FIFA had been refining in the run-up to the US competition. In Maradona's case, the system had initially involved the official doctor of the Argentine team, Dr Ubalde, filling in all the medicaments and the respective doses taken by each of his players on an official form (0-1), as well as detailing any treatment undergone in the seventy-two hours preceding the match. The completed form handed in to the FIFA doping test made no reference to any banned substances, but according to Ubalde was consistent with the information made available to him by the rest of the medical team prior to the match. At half-time in the Argentina–Nigeria match, Maradona's number 10, printed on a small plastic disc, was one of two per team drawn by lot from two small fabric pouches by a member of the FIFA Sports Medical Committee and witnessed by a FIFA commissioner and an official representative of each team.

Following the match Maradona was required to provide a urine sample, again in the presence of officials, which was then separated into two bottles, sealed and sent to FIFA's laboratory in Los Angeles. After an initial test proved positive, FIFA, again according to regulations, allowed the Argentine delegation to exercise its right to a second test, on the second bottle. Among the Argentines who unanimously confirmed the earlier findings, and raised no objections to the fairness in which the test was carried out, was Maradona's own lawyer, Daniel Bolotnicof.

In all, nearly five days elapsed between the moment Maradona was led off the field at Foxboro and the formal announcement by FIFA at a press conference in the Four Seasons Hotel in Dallas that the player was being withdrawn from the competition after failing a regulatory dope test. In that interlude, the growing realization that Maradona was in the frame had led to an extraordinary series of behind-the-scenes discussions within FIFA. In the history of one of the world's most powerful sporting bodies, few players had exercised the minds of FIFA officials as much as Maradona. His lack of discipline on and off the pitch, and his constant outbursts against authority, provided a destabilizing factor in a sport that was expected to govern itself by a universal set of rules and regulations. Equally, however, Maradona had over the years personified the lengths to which football could become transformed into a money-spinning enterprise. He had proved himself a natural crowd-puller, a TV entertainer and, while no diplomat, the best-known and, in large sectors of the Third World at least, the best-loved footballer in the world.

In Maradona FIFA had a player who had proved time and time again his potential to generate millions. He had arrived in the US prepared to buckle down and get on with the job of playing football. He and other players found themselves having to play during some of the hottest hours of the day in a scorching summer, as required by FIFA's television contracts. But Maradona did not, as he had done in Mexico in 1986, make a big public fuss about it. Some alarm bells did ring internally within FIFA when, after his first goal against Greece, Maradona rushed over to a TV camera and screamed into it. He may simply have wanted to tell the world that he was back, but the image of his crazed expression broadcast to billions of TV viewers around the world struck a discordant note in a competition that was supposed to entertain, not act as a vehicle for revenge. Arguably, if they had not subjected themselves strictly to the regulations, FIFA officials could have justified drug testing Maradona on the basis of that one TV shot and the exhilaration that he had shown since arriving in the US. There is no evidence to support Maradona's suggestion that when the test finally came it was part of a wider plot against him.

Only afterwards, when the test had been confirmed, did all FIFA's old prejudices towards Maradona surface – and with a vengeance. Maradona was now regarded as a liability, the bad boy of the football world who had stepped out of line once again. With FIFA desperate to convince the Americans that football was a sport worth having, there could be no room for rebels, let alone an unreformed dope head. Within the organization no senior official was now prepared to protect him.

Julio Grondona, the long-serving head of the Argentine Football Association, led the collective charge. Some of his colleagues had expected him to press for a cover-up. Far from it. No sooner had Maradona tested positive than Grondona privately told his colleagues within FIFA that they could count on his 'full co-operation' in imposing whatever penalty they deemed fit.

The most hardline reaction was led by Lennart Johansson, the UEFA president, and seconded by Antonio Matarrese, president of the Italian Football Federation. Both men had closely followed Maradona's tumultuous life while playing in Europe, and felt that his influence on the game as a whole was a bad one. Looking at the full spectrum of European clubs, they saw many footballers who could claim much of Maradona's talent without having to drum up so much controversy. Matarrese, in particular, appears to have found it hard to forgive Maradona for the way he had tried to divide the Italians in the 1990 World Cup.

In the end, though, it was left up to Joseph Blatter and João Havelange to consider how to punish Maradona in a way that would preserve FIFA's claim to fairness and integrity. It was Havelange's success in keeping previous World Cups as undisturbed as possible by issues of religion, politics and ethics that had endeared him to companies like Adidas and Coca-Cola, always with an eye on the global market. These multinationals were FIFA's financial lifeline in sponsorship terms.

Havelange was sensitive to Maradona's popularity in the Third World. He also attached great importance to the presence of Latin American and African teams in the competition. There was a strong element of political self-interest in all this, since Havelange owed his long-running presidency to tactical alliances with Third World officials. Backed by Blatter, he therefore resisted calls from some of his international committee to have the whole Argentine team thrown out of the competition. Maradona was automatically suspended from further World Cup games, but in an attempt to defuse the controversy over his case in what remained of the tournament, further sanctions were held off until after the outcome of three separate investigations. One was by Julio Grondona, and the other two by members of the FIFA Sports Medical Committee, the Chilean Dr Antonio Losada and the Swiss Professor Jiri Dvorak. Maradona took advantage of the breathing space to accept a lucrative contract with Argentine TV to commentate on Argentina's final game.

The FIFA World Cup organizing committee that met in Zurich on 24 August 1994 – exactly two months after the Nigeria match – to decide finally on the Maradona dope case concluded that he was not guilty of consciously drugging himself in order to enhance his performance and that he had not been aware of the exact components of the drugs that formed part of his diet. It nevertheless ruled him guilty of a breach of the FIFA Doping Control Regulations. It also held Cerrini responsible for administering these substances to him. Both Maradona and Cerrini were banned from any footballing activity for fifteen months and each was fined 20,000 Swiss francs. In not punishing Cerrini alone, FIFA had taken a tougher stance than it had in 1986. During the World Cup in Mexico a Spanish player tested positive but was exonerated after the Spanish football authorities had skilfully shifted the blame to his doctor. In reaching a judgement on Maradona's own complicity, FIFA officials took into account his previous record of drug-taking. In so doing there was a parallel between the Maradona case and that of Willie Johnston, the Scottish winger, who was expelled from the 1978 World Cup in Argentina and also had a previous record of drug abuse. Johnston's FIFA ban was three months shorter than Maradona's, but the Scot was banned from ever playing for his national team again. No official in Argentina dared propose that for Maradona on his return from the US.

On the contrary, within days of FIFA's decision, Havelange received an unprecedented appeal on Maradona's behalf. In a five-page letter, President Menem claimed to speak for the fans not just of his own country but of the whole world, and appealed for clemency. It was an extraordinary letter, which said as much about Menem's own political self-interest as about the nature of Maradona as a national symbol. Menem suggested in effect that Maradona should be treated as a special privileged case, and that for all his flagrant undermining of the rules, not just once, but time and time again, he should be allowed to get on with playing football.

'I was very worried when I heard Maradona declare publicly [after his test] that it was "as if they'd killed me",' wrote Menem. 'I therefore think that special consideration should be given to the psychological impact that a period of inactivity could have on a player with a personality like Maradona's ... As President of the Argentine people I am not mistaken in asserting that I represent everyone by interceding on Maradona's behalf so that he can end up his sporting days not as a player sanctioned by FIFA, but giving joy to fans all over the world with the magic of his game.'

Menem was aware that Havelange had for most of his presidency run FIFA much as he had run Argentina, like a medieval war-lord, suppressing debate and extending patronage. Menem believed he had the measure of Havelange by appealing directly to him. Havelange was sympathetic, conscious of the popularity that Maradona still enjoyed. But he was bound by FIFA's regulations, which made it impossible for him to overturn a decision taken by the committee – even to attempt it would risk a major outcry. Just how seriously FIFA regarded the Maradona case is evident from the minutes of an internal meeting soon after the ban was imposed. At it Joseph Blatter, with Havelange at his side, described the Maradona case to members of the Sports Medical Committee as 'the most serious' during the World Cup and confirmed his official endorsement of the ban. Thanking Professor Dvorak for his 'scientific support in this matter', Blatter concluded, 'The decision taken has proved to be the right one.' Next spoke the Belgian chairman of the Sports Medical Committee, Michel D'Hooghe, who made it clear that he wanted lessons to be drawn from the case and regulations tightened up. D'Hooge declared, 'The Maradona case has cast a shadow over the whole tournament,' adding that it was of the utmost importance that in the future information regarding medication, including self-medication, be improved to prevent abuse, and overall doping controls made stricter. The meeting submitted for further consideration by the Executive Committee a recommendation that in future every player should be subject to the direct authority of his national association and treated exclusively by his team's physician.

The call for reform accepted as given the honesty and pro-fessionalism of national associations and team doctors. It also accepted the fallacy that testing during the competition and qualifying matches was all that FIFA itself had to do to comply with its own cardinal principles: the preservation of the ethics of sport and the protection of the physical and mental integrity of the player. The key post-US meeting of senior FIFA officials rejected once again the introduction of FIFA-supervised random doping tests during training sessions at club level, even though FIFA's own doctors had confided privately that this was the only credible deterrent against drug-takers, who could often count on the complicity of their medical advisers and even club officials. Blatter's meeting concluded that from 'a practical point of view, it is quite impossible to carry out doping tests during training sessions at club level'.

Both in its sentencing and in its recommendations for reform,

FIFA misled the public about the Maradona case. The evidence shows that responsibility for what occurred should be shared far more widely than they admitted, and that there is a need for much tougher regulations than those which for political and commercial reasons are deemed acceptable by FIFA. Interviews with many of those most closely involved point to the chaotic administrative structure inside the Argentine camp, including the total lack of management controls on Maradona himself. The monitoring system which some members of the Argentine medical team had imposed in the weeks leading up to the World Cup proved ineffectual and had anyway completely broken down by the time Maradona reached the US. Relations between Maradona's dietitian Cerrini and Dr Ernesto Ubalde, the team doctor, were so bad, the degree of mutual mistrust so great, that neither man bothered to communicate what the other was doing. At the same time Cerrini appears to have exercised an increasing influence over Maradona, to the detriment of Ubalde and the player's personal trainer Signorini, who found their control over the actions of the team's captain growing less and less the closer the first match approached.

The Maradona who ceded to Cerrini was not the Maradona whom journalists and millions of viewers had observed preparing for the World Cup. Beneath his public air of self-confidence, Maradona was suffering from an acute crisis of insecurity and paranoia. He was feeling his age and the heavy toll of years of self-abuse, while at the same being fully aware of just how dependent the rest of his team were on him, and the responsibility that rested on his shoulders. Maradona's long-running mistrust of conventional medicine had deepened to the point of an obsession. Cerrini may have struck other doctors as a quack, but to Maradona he was the latest in a long line of medicine men on whom he could rely to help him produce magic.

One member of Maradona's inner circle, closely involved in events of US '94, told me, 'By the time he got to the US, Diego was demonstrating once again his total lack of confidence in conventional medicine. He felt, both psychologically and mentally, that he was different to all other players, and that therefore he deserved special treatment, in keeping with his special status. He desperately wanted to succeed in the World Cup and had convinced himself that only Cerrini could get him there. It was of course a completely mistaken view, but one that could only have sprung from a neurotic.'

Under the normal practice followed by a team's medical team in a World Cup competition, the last-minute changes to Maradona's régime of pharmaceuticals introduced by Cerrini should have been conveyed to Ubalde, as the official doctor. Ubalde subsequently claimed that he, Signorini and the team's cardiologist Dr Roberto Peydro were given no such information. And yet to blame only Cerrini for professional negligence as Julio Grondona did in his report to FIFA should fool no one. As Maradona himself came close to stating publicly after his suspension, Cerrini was picked as a convenient scapegoat by Argentine officials, doctors and FIFA, as a cover-up for their own complicity in the affair.

This somewhat eccentric dietitian of whom few people in the outside world had ever heard fitted the bill of villain easily. The reality, however, is that Cerrini managed to do what he did because no Argentine official was willing to stop him. As long as Maradona declared his allegiance to him, they felt that they had no alternative but to allow Cerrini the rope he wanted. What mattered was that Maradona played in the World Cup. How he got there was of secondary importance. It was a view shared by the FIFA hierarchy.

By banning Maradona and refusing to assume wider collective responsibility, FIFA was acting with an eye to its own commercial interests. By shaming the player rather than accepting that the system was at fault, FIFA could assure the public that apart from that one unfortunate incident – clearly sensationalized by the press – it had been a dope-free World Cup. It was a message that sponsors liked to hear.

But how great was Maradona's personal responsibility? It was certainly not in his nature to ask too many questions of Cerrini, still less to submit himself to official controls even if these had been offered. As a senior FIFA official involved in the investigation told me in his organization's defence, 'Maradona didn't ask what he was eating or drinking. If someone had his trust, and Cerrini clearly did, he trusted him completely. Even if there might have been some doubt raised by the change to the drugs he was taking, he didn't really want to know. He just wanted to play, with whatever means.'

The position ultimately taken by FIFA was, if anything, lenient in effectively giving Maradona, a player with a previous record of cheating, the benefit of the doubt. It did not accuse him of deliberately drugging himself to enhance his performance as the International Olympic Committee did Ben Johnson. FIFA also took the view that a claim of ignorance on behalf of a player clearly prone to manipulation could never be accepted as a defence. The negligence and lack of professionalism with which Maradona was indulged and allowed himself to be indulged came close to wrecking the spirit of the '94 World Cup. And yet what happened in the United States was not a sporting aberration but formed part of a pattern that had been developing since Maradona's early days as a star.

22

CHASING DIEGO

After the dope test on Maradona proves positive in the US World Cup of 1994, someone flies a private plane over the Boston stadium, trailing a banner. 'Maradona Prima-Donna,' it says, as if destined for a tombstone. In a helter-skelter of a career, Maradona seems to many to have taken the final fall. For days, commentators have been debating his ability to pull through the tunnel of public disgrace and out the other end. He has trained with humour and good grace, and then played his first games with energy and skill, 'marshalling the residue of old gifts', as one British journalist, Ken Jones of the *Independent*, puts it. Now the same commentators have taken to writing obituaries, reflective pieces on a disastrously flawed genius who has finally come to grief on football's last frontier.

Back in Argentina, Maradona does not, cannot, give up. While still banned from playing football, he tries his hand at management, first with the small provincial club Deportivo Mandiyu, then with the more ambitious premier club Racing. It's only a year since he declared in an interview that he can't see himself as a manager. 'I can't teach players things which only I can do,' he tells the Argentine author Alicia Ortiz, while still in Seville. But a year is a very long time in the life of Diego Maradona. As it turns out, his short spell as manager proves disastrous not just because the players cannot replicate his natural gifts, but because their own talents are not fully exploited. Maradona proves a distraction rather than an inspiration. Mandiyu are relegated after a game in which Maradona is filmed screaming at the referee that he is a 'thief and a liar' and a 'gutless coward without balls'. His subsequent management of Racing also proves to be both short-lived and controversial. During it, Maradona runs away from his home and disappears for several days on an apparent binge of drink and drugs. He is found after Claudia has appealed to the presidency for help in her search.

That this does not turn out to be Maradona's final breakdown is due in large part to the re-emergence in his life of Guillermo Coppola. Slowly but surely, Coppola re-establishes his friendship with Maradona, interrupted when he resigned as the player's manager in 1991. Coppola is not Argentina's most popular man. Some of Maradona's friends blame him for the player's nose-dive into the drugs scene in Naples. The Argentine police have investigated him in connection with the murder of a Buenos Aires nightclub owner. And yet Coppola himself is sure of his ground with Maradona. He feels that the best way to deal with him is with a mixture of indulgence and sharp business advice.

Most important, Coppola has a talent for networking and securing deals. In Naples he was called upon by Maradona to put his finances in order. Now eight years later Maradona once again turns to Coppola to pull him out of the mess he's got himself into. Coppola does this by repackaging Maradona and selling him to the growing commercial interests dominating Argentine TV. Under a complex deal Coppola gets America 2, a TV station, effectively to finance Maradona's return with Boca Juniors in exchange for exclusive rights on a series of matches. It is a remarkable coup given that in the aftermath of the World Cup Maradona's marketable value appeared to have sunk to an all-time low. Next Coppola pulls off several publicity stunts aimed at re-establishing Maradona's international profile without him even having to kick a ball.

In September 1995 in a personal fax from Maradona the world press is invited to Paris for the launch of a new international players' union. The 'solidarity' event is beautifully timed to coincide with a controversial judgement by the advocate general of the European Court of Justice, Carl Otto Lenz, giving players much greater control over their own transfers.

Maradona arrives at Paris's five-star Hôtel Le Méridien Etoile wearing a black sweatshirt and an ear-ring made up of his daughters' milk teeth. He is looking tired after an overnight flight from Buenos Aires and less thin than he should be after a month working out in Uruguay with Daniel Cerrini, the same dietitian he took with him to the US. Maradona does not blame Cerrini for anything, having convinced himself that he was an innocent victim of a much wider game plan against him by FIFA.

He continues to use Cerrini's services in open defiance of the post-US FIFA stipulation that players should entrust themselves only to doctors officially endorsed by their teams.

Journalists have gathered in the hotel lobby, but Maradona is whisked past the majority of them to a private reception screened by security guards. I am among a privileged few allowed to play fly on the wall. As a porter struggles with Maradona's suitcase, one of his entourage shouts, 'Look after that bag, it's got the medicines!' *Plus ça change*, I reflect silently. While Maradona receives a massage in his room, Didier Roustan, a journalist with the French TV Station 2, a friend of Eric Cantona, huddles in a corner with two of Maradona's lawyers, Bolotnicof from Buenos Aires and Sinischalsci from Naples. They seem to be playing parts in a French cop movie. They are in fact talking serious money. Having helped organize the event, Roustan, less a journalist than a dealer, is worried about cash flow. The debate, never fully resolved, is whether the founding stars, some of them millionaires, should each put up $7,000 as a sign of good faith in the brotherhood of soccer. While Roustan seems to take the idea of the union seriously, Bolotnicof and Sinischalsci see it as a simple marketing exercise for their client. It explains their reluctance to be too tied down on figures.

By the time Maradona reappears, looking refreshed but still older than his thirty-four years, a full team of eleven star players have gathered. They are led by those who, like Maradona, have had problems with the authorities: Gianlucca Vialli, who is refusing to play for Italy; George Weah, who has just transferred from Paris Saint-Germain to AC Milan in a cloud of accusations of bad faith; and last but by no means least, Eric Cantona, who is, like Maradona, serving a worldwide ban from soccer, for practising a Kung-Fu kick on an irate fan.

Privately Maradona is hugely relieved with the turn-out. Before leaving Buenos Aires he panicked, thinking that perhaps he had after all lost all credibility among his colleagues around the world, and that Paris would turn into a public humiliation, worse even than Boston. And yet once he sees that some stars have made an effort, his thoughts turn against some of those who haven't. His anger is particularly vented at Pele, Platini and Franz Beckenbauer, all of whom he feels have become FIFA apparatchiks. He is also disappointed that no fellow Argentines or Spaniards have bothered to turn up, even though several of his former colleagues, including Valdano and Redondo, are just south of the border.

And yet this event is intended to put disappointments and setbacks in the past, and to signal that Maradona is back in business. More people have turned up than expected, Maradona tells journalists. He mentions Ruud Gullit and Khristo Stoichkov as among those who have telephoned messages of support, and Gascoigne and Platt among the Englishmen who would have got there if they had not been otherwise engaged. Later, in a crowded press conference, Maradona and Cantona hug in the spirit of the Argentine independence hero General San Martín, whose statue adorns the nearby Métro station Argentine. In the capital of countless radical uprisings – and the city where FIFA was founded with noble ambitions in 1904 – the two rich mavericks claim to want to set the seal on a new charter for footballers' rights. Cantona explains that football is a sport that brings joy to millions and that therefore footballers deserve to be treated with respect. Maradona extends the meaning of respect to cover sympathy for those players 'unfairly' subjected to drug tests whose consequences are out of all proportion to the act itself.

The only drawback is the large egos of the two protagonists. Maradona and Cantona seem uneasy in each other's presence, cramped by each other, like two supermodels hogging a narrow catwalk. At one point, Maradona loses patience with Cantona's philosophical ramblings, interrupting questions and answers with, 'Is Eric going to take all afternoon?'

For all the tension, however, Maradona remains one of Cantona's biggest heroes. 'In the course of time, it will be said that Maradona was to football what Rimbaud was to poetry and Mozart to music,' Cantona said in an interview in 1995. It was in January of that year that the two players met in Paris to discuss the formation of the union. Cantona agreed to it on condition that Maradona would be its president. The Frenchman felt that Maradona's skills as a footballer and his popularity, particularly in the Third World, were what mattered, not his personal life. Cantona believed that geniuses not only could but should be excused their human failings.

Maradona was in the French capital collecting the annual best player prize from the magazine *France Futbal*. Coppola was there too, making sure that Maradona enjoyed himself in a hectic series of escapades to local nightclubs including Queen's, a favourite venue for well-heeled Parisian gays.

After the players' union is announced, Cantona and the other players evaporate from the scene, leaving Maradona to run his own show with a series of impromptu dialogues which demonstrate that he has retained some of his old skills for seducing the media. Asked to comment on British football, Maradona delivers a personal tribute to the management skills of Glenn Hoddle and Kevin Keegan. 'English football used to be so static,' he says, 'players seemed to be waiting for the ball to come to them as if it was being transported by a plane that drops bombs. Now everyone moves around. Hoddle and Keegan have transformed the game. And now I enjoy watching English football from Buenos Aires. Congratulations.'

Later, surrounded by mainly Argentine journalists, euphoric at the prospect of the renewed copy flow that will emanate from the occasion, Maradona conveys a sense of being genuinely enthused with his project. He declares his hope that his 'union' will act as the channel for the frustrations and grievances of rich and not-so-rich footballers worldwide who feel that club owners and FIFA officials need to have their power checked. Only when a journalist with a Swiss accent asks him a provocative question about whether his real intention is to strip FIFA of its prime assets does Maradona cut the dialogue, suspecting that he is being deliberately provoked or, worse, spied upon under orders from Messieurs Havelange and Blatter. The announcement of the union has in fact thrown the world of football's governing body into a slight panic. The men of Zurich do not like revolutions. Only when word comes back to them from Paris do they relax, satisfied that there is more mouth than muscle in Maradona's revolutionary army.

In Paris Maradona shows himself to be a man of many moods: arrogant, manipulative and paranoiac. Only in private, in a small trusted circle, does he show that there is a different side to his character. When the media pack has disappeared, he slouches in an armchair in one of the hotel's empty drawing rooms. His main concerns are twofold: firstly, how and where to buy some dolls for his two daughters; secondly, how to get hold of a decent cheese sandwich. Operation Dolls, as Maradona calls it, takes top priority as Coppola first tries to contact a toy shop with my mobile, and then enlists the help of a female colleague to carry out the purchase, brandishing a wad of dollars. Only when this is done does Maradona rub his stomach: 'Now, for the sandwich, I'm dying of hunger. Let's go look for it.' We all laugh together.

As my colleague who claims to know Maradona more intimately than I do puts it, 'When Diego is in a good mood, it is easy to fall into the trap of thinking he is just a regular guy.'

Only later does one discover than while the world media were gathering to listen to Maradona's revolutionary pronouncements, Coppola was out arranging the evening's entertainment at Queen's (he is a connoisseur of Parisian nightlife) and seeing to the other items on his client's shopping list: shirts and ties from the Versace store in the Faubourg St-Honoré. As for Operation Cheese Sandwich, that turns out to be as easy as walking on water. Leaving the hotel, Maradona is instantly recognized by a couple of photographers who have hung around just in case. They are soon joined by a growing crowd of onlookers, increasingly desperate for an autograph, a touch or just a glimpse of the star. Maradona dons a pair of gold-rimmed dark glasses and, seemingly basking in the popular recognition, begins to strut down the Boulevard St-Cyr. At one point, a young urchin pushes his way through and tries to get himself photographed with his arm around the star. Maradona grimaces and pushes him violently to one side. He tries to relax again, but seems overwhelmed by the pressure building up around him. He remains the unpredictable, pampered individualist with more than a few hang-ups.

Suddenly Coppola breaks from the entourage and on to the road, weaving his way in and out of the traffic until he intercepts a Rolls-Royce convertible. It is chauffeur driven and its owner, a silver-haired businessman, seems genuinely surprised by the sight of Coppola's tanned, Versace-framed features. 'Stop, stop,' Coppola cries. 'It's Maradona. Can you give him a lift?' There is no gun in his hand but the tone of the voice says it all. It is the statement of a man who is convinced that the world of Maradona is beyond good or evil. Without waiting for an answer, Coppola takes a running jump into the back seat, followed closely by Maradona and a friend. All three are laughing hysterically. Seconds later, the silver-haired man, ashen-faced, and struck dumb by the shock of it all, gesticulates to his chauffeur to drive on. I imagine they are driving into the setting sun, somewhere in Hollywood. Then I remember that this is Paris, and that that is Maradona.

The next morning, I wring the stardust from my eyes and catch an early train back to London. An intrepid female colleague who has been chasing an interview with Maradona for months decides to go back to the hotel. Maradona is supposed to have caught an early plane to Istanbul, where he is due to make a token appearance at a charity match for the children of Bosnia. But after the night out arranged for him by Coppola, the star is on his bed, dead to the world. Coppola and Maradona's lawyer Bolotnicof have hangovers too, and know that it is more than their lives are worth even to attempt to wake their client.

My colleague is no green girl. But even she is taken aback by the scene that confronts her when she is ushered into Coppola's room. The man who likes to claim for himself the title of best friend and adviser of the 'number one player in the world' is lying completely naked, scratching his balls and laughing. The butt of his humour is one Bayarm Tutumlu, a Turk of dubious distinction who has organized the charity match in Istanbul at considerable personal cost, and who is now running up and down the corridors of the Hôtel Le Méridien Etoile, tearing his hair out. Maradona emerges at three that afternoon. They get to Istanbul for the charity match.

From there Maradona catches a plane for Seoul, arriving a day late to join Boca Juniors. The visit has been the subject of intense behind-the-scenes debate. Those who have strong reservations about it include key advisers to the South Korean government committee bidding to host the 2002 World Cup. As one would later reveal to the author, 'We were of the opinion that Maradona was unpredictable. He had a history of drug abuse and had a reputation of cheating. In our view it wasn't the kind of image that we wanted to be associated with. The risk was that a Maradona visit might backfire on us and wreck our bid.'

And yet South Korea also experiences intense lobbying from the Argentine government, led by President Menem. He is convinced by Coppola (a friend of his son's and of at least one key official in the government) and other representatives of the Argentine football industry that Maradona will ensure the diplomatic and commercial success of Menem's official visit to Seoul. In the end the South Korean government is also convinced that Maradona and Boca Juniors will help raise the profile of South Korean football, as well as put Argentina behind Seoul's bid for the World Cup. (In fact Julio Grondona, the Argentine representative on FIFA's executive committee, backed Japan's bid until the football authority swung behind a joint hosting option at its meeting in Zurich in May 1996.)

The Maradona visit becomes a political issue. 'It was handled directly government to government,' a South Korean official later recalls. The source lives to regret it. Maradona has never and will never be a good diplomat. He is too impetuous, too individualistic. He causes a rumpus with the staff at the hotel he is staying in, and fails to appear at an officially arranged photo opportunity at which he is meant to give a short football lesson to some South Korean children.

None of this really matters in Argentine terms. The negative details of the trip are carefully excluded from the reports sent back to Buenos Aires. Instead the image is of Diego as a resurrected genius. Gathered in Seoul are an impressive extension of the Maradona tribe and all its offshoots: a collection of genuine friends and hangers-on, relatives, past and present managers, football officials, middle-men, TV moguls, journalists, all excited by the prospect of Diego's return to football. Once again, a conglomeration of vested interests rests on Maradona's shoulders. Thus does the god make his way back into the world.

October 1995. On a return visit to Argentina to research part of this book, I attract more attention from the local media in five weeks of Maradona studies than I ever did in the five and a half years I worked as a correspondent out of Buenos Aires, covering wars, government overthrows and debt crises. Fellow journalists pursue me from La Bombonera to the old riverside encampment in Corrientes where Maradona's father was born, requesting interviews. It is a reminder, as if I needed it, of just how central Maradona is to the Argentine collective psyche.

Back in Buenos Aires I am invited to appear for the first time on Argentina's most popular chat show, *Hola Susanna*, for a special programme dedicated to Maradona. The show's host, Susanna Giménez, belongs to Argentina, old and new. As a young actress she burst into the gossip columns as the lover of the boxing champion Carlos Monzón. She was lucky to escape from the affair alive. Monzón found it difficult to distinguish between his women and his sparring partners, a flaw that ended tragically when he pushed Giménez's replacement over his balcony after a fight.

Monzón later died in a car crash after being paroled from prison while Susanna pursued her career. I meet her when she is officially turned fifty and firmly established as Argentina's best-loved personality, sex symbol and chat-show hostess. Bottle-blonde and brash, she looks like a younger version of Zsa Zsa Gabor. By her own

admission she is living proof of surgical wizardry, describing herself
as a 'pioneer grandmother – with plastic boobs and jeans'. She is also
a happy component, like so many of Maradona's entourage, of the
New Argentina of President Menem, where a visit to the surgeon
for a lift of one kind or another, like a shirt from Versace, is a
status symbol. But Susanna is no bimbo, just as Maradona is no
fool. She has developed her career on TV, just as Maradona has
done on the playing fields of Argentina, thanks to an instinctive
feel for what the majority of Argentines love and cherish.

The entrance to her studio is a swimming pool filled with letters
– just a week's fan mail. This is but one of several programmes
she has dedicated to Maradona: in part because she admires him,
much as she did Monzón, as a man who has done and said what
he feels, but also because he ensures high ratings. I have watched
a clip of one of her earlier Maradona specials. In it she dresses up
as a majorette and leads a company of Granaderos, the President
of Argentina's ceremonial guard, in a march past Maradona, his
wife and daughters. My programme is an altogether more sober
occasion, carefully managed to avoid any major controversy. 'I'm
never going to say anything critical about Diego,' confides Giménez
flirtatiously, 'because I want him back on my programme!' The
following week is Maradona's birthday, and she wants to make
a show of the party.

Her other guests are Coppola, the Argentine journalist Fernando
Niembro, the former coach of the Argentine national squad Carlos
Bilardo, the Argentine TV commentator Mariano Grondona and an
Argentine post-graduate Oxford student called Esteban Hubner. It
is Hubner who is asked to kick off the show, for he is the reason
why the programme is taking place. He has invited Maradona to
give a lecture in Oxford, and the event is being billed by Giménez,
inaccurately, as the 'greatest academic honour ever to be bestowed
on an international sportsman'. Hubner tells of how he once worked
as a buttons in a Buenos Aires hotel Maradona had stayed in, taking
an instant liking to the player and developing an admiration that
would intensify as he grew older. Once in Oxford, he became
obsessed with the idea of bringing his icon to the UK.

Picking up the theme, Grondona notes that Maradona is the only
Argentine foreigners ever ask about, so he deserves to be brought
to the citadel of academic learning. Grondona is regarded by his
fellow countrymen as one of Argentina's most profound thinkers,
an ex-university professor who believes in 'intellectual' TV. His

final contribution to the Giménez show is to remind the audience of Maradona's mystical qualities. 'He was born in a stable,' Grondona muses. (Actually Maradona was born in a hospital named after Eva Perón.)

Niembro is there as the author of an earlier book on Maradona, the fictionalized account of his downfall in the US World Cup which has the player being deliberately doped by the CIA. Niembro defends his underlying thesis, that Maradona was the innocent victim of a plot to get rid of him by FIFA. By his own admission, Niembro has no evidence for this whatsoever, but he knows that it is a theory that touches many Argentine hearts, and sells books. That he still feels confident enough to spout on about it before a live TV audience and millions of viewers, more than a year after the World Cup, demonstrates the extent to which Argentines are prepared to delude themselves when it comes to Maradona.

The rest of the chat show has Bilardo reminiscing about Maradona's skills as a footballer, and Coppola declaring how good his client feels with his return to full-time football at Boca. As for myself, I warn that Maradona might encounter some hostility when he gets to the UK. 'They'll ask him about drugs, and the Hand of God, although no one has forgotten that second goal against England . . .'

And so they do, on an evening in the Oxford Union debating chamber which sums up Maradona in a way that few of those present really grasp at the time. The image which Coppola tries to project to the outside world is that of Maradona finally earning universal respect after years of unjust treatment at the hands of the media and officialdom. No matter that Maradona's doctorate is a sham – the orthodox Jewish society that organized the event has no authority to give him a scholar's cap and gown. What matters is a scroll that commemorates Maradona as the Master Inspirer of Oxford Dreams. And a sense of those dreams is conveyed when Maradona agrees to kick a golf ball from one foot to the other, and balance a football on his head. The request comes from a student who has watched him doing it while training for the US World Cup.

Questions about the Hand of God and drugs are brushed aside with a mixture of evasion and humour. 'It was not the drugs that stopped me playing, but I made a mistake and accept that,' he says. 'There are a lot of powerful men in football. They've tried to kill me, to destroy me, but they cannot. They want to destroy me as I'm one of the few players who says things that these people do not like.' And the Hand of God, any apologies, any regrets, Diego? Clutching a plastic arm donated to him by the students, Maradona smiles with the smile of an angel. 'At the time it cured everything,' he says. It's as simple as that.

Maradona delivers his 'lecture' in a faltering monotone as if reading from a prepared script he has not read over enough times. In fact it has been penned by Coppola and Bolotnicof, and presents the audience with a kind of philosophical coherence that Maradona alone is incapable of conveying. As a portrait of a life, it is surgically selective if not downright dishonest. 'As a boy, football gave me a rush of joy,' he says, 'but I did not see how people who brought such joy could ever be considered shallow or empty. It was my destiny to bring this kind of happiness to the people . . . I was interested only in playing and in feeling the clamour of the stands, this unpredictable chemistry which defies definition. Big business did not interest me at all. But since it was part of football, I had to keep it in mind.'

The lecture winds up with a veiled criticism of FIFA and the way that football has lost its purity to the ruthless men of money. The speaker then offers his credo to the audience, the four noble truths of Diego Armando Maradona: 'Family, friendship, solidarity, justice'. What more can one expect from God?

23

MARADONA REDIVIVUS

B uenos Aires in January 2010, the start of a World Cup year. Superficially, Maradona is a man transformed; his latest act of irresponsible behaviour – a foul-mouthed rant against some journalists – led to a dip in his poll ratings but is turning into a mere blip on his road to redemption as coach of the national team. His past infidelities have been forgiven and he lives openly with his latest girlfriend while his ex-wife manages his financial affairs. He is reconciled with his daughters – doting grandfather to the child of one of them, a footballer's wife; supportive dad to the other, a successful young actress. He cuts a trim figure, and there has not been a health scare for a while, his former addiction to cocaine apparently behind him.

Such is the public persona. And yet dig beneath the surface and Maradona remains the same unpredictable, erratic genius I discovered while first researching this book fifteen years ago. His occasional descent into violence – of word or deed – is the product as much of his environment as of his inner demons: his upbringing in the lawless lands of the shanty town, his long-term drug abuse, the hangers-on and opportunists who have made their own habit of making use of him.

Argentina is Latin America's failed state, forever falling short of its huge economic potential. It is noted for the corruption prevalent among its politicians and businessmen, and the wheeler-dealers who pervade the football industry from top to bottom. It is a world Maradona moves in and out of with ease, the vested interests ensuring that despite his human failings and wasted brilliance he is allowed to give more of himself. For all his public raging against the establishment, Maradona has spent most of his adult life being nourished as much by the powerful as by the hardcore fans who venerate him from Buenos Aires to Baghdad. His arrogance and natural vindictiveness have dented his popularity around the world. But among his loyal fans, the collective memory hangs on the moments of sheer magic he produced as a player, a natural talent that learnt to control a ball in the dust before becoming rich.

The southern neighbourhood of La Boca is where the myth of Maradona as the people's idol has endured the longest. Boca Juniors is the club he has always claimed as closest to his soul. Boca likes to see itself as the home of the marginalized, drawing to its bosom the dark-skinned Maradona lookalikes. Murals and sculptures have immortalized him in and around La Bombonera, the stadium that has received him as player and fanatical fan. Although the museum is dedicated to a litany of eccentric legends from Rattin 'the Rat' to Gatti 'the madman', Maradona retains pride of place as the undisputed greatest of them all.

Late one evening in September 1996, Diego Maradona sat facing me across a table in an Italian restaurant in London, looking at the first edition of this book which I had just handed to him. After months of chasing him around the world, I hoped this would be a defining moment by which I could measure his willingness to come to terms with himself. And yet this was not destined to be a night of revelations. Maradona was flanked by his then agent Guillermo Coppola and Gianluca Vialli. They collectively conveyed an image of threatened conspiracy, although I could only guess at the nature of the conversation I had interrupted. I imagined it might have something to do with the rumour that Maradona wanted to play for Chelsea. Whatever it was, he wasn't going to talk more about it there, and soon I watched him depart into the night, in the direction of one of the capital's hottest nightspots.

Maradona saved his reaction to my book for a few days later, while he was visiting the southern Spanish resort of Alicante for a 'health cure'. Pouring out his latest confession about his drug addiction, he slammed all those who had helped me, accusing them of betrayal. 'Burns has pissed all over me,' he declared on Spanish radio.

In Alicante, Maradona went on a bender. In the early hours, he returned to his hotel in a state of mind one eyewitness described as 'very strange and disturbed'. He then got stuck in the lift when the electrics failed, and kicked its doors until his foot bled. After the fire brigade rescued him, he went on kicking at tables and chairs, screaming until daybreak when the hotel management presented him with a bill for the damage. Approaching the age of thirty-seven, past his sell-by date as a player, and staring into the abyss, it seemed that this might be the start of the final chapter of Maradona's turbulent life. But he had fallen from the stars to the gutter before, only to get up again. This turned out to be far from the last twist in his helter-skelter life.

A few weeks earlier, after missing five penalties in a crucial phase of the local league championship, Maradona had announced he was quitting Boca Juniors. The man who had invoked a benign deity in justifying his dishonest goal against the English in Mexico '86 now blamed 'witches' for casting a negative spell on him. Maradona was continuing to struggle with a drug problem for which he was seeking help from an array of doctors – senior officials at Boca Juniors privately warned that they feared Maradona might fatally collapse in the middle of a match, his heart simply giving up under the strain of his drug abuse. In one of his characteristically spontaneous outbursts on national TV, he declared: 'Maradona the football player is dead.' He went on playing for Boca until October 1997, but even then news reports that he had finally hung up his boots and beat a dignified retreat from the headlines of world football proved premature.

In January 2000, Maradona stared death in the face. Grossly overweight and suffering from a heart condition that he had inherited from his father, he collapsed while on vacation in the Uruguayan resort of Punta del Este. He was admitted to hospital suffering from hypertension and an irregular heartbeat. Coppola was on hand to tell the media that it had nothing to do with drugs, while Maradona's friend, the Argentine president Carlos Menem, put it all down to a 'stress attack'. Later, the Uruguayan police revealed that analysis of Maradona's blood and urine showed 'excessive consumption of cocaine'.

The exclusive bedside TV images which Coppola negotiated on his client's behalf showed Maradona recovering. But he had put on twelve kilos since he had last quit playing some three years earlier. He was bloated and puffy-eyed, and was hanging on. If he had been almost anybody else, Maradona would have died that day. But then his resilience or mere good fortune has always baffled his doctors. The phone call informing me that Maradona would go on living in the new millennium caught me in conversation with some of his fans on the worldwide net. Micky from Liverpool said that Maradona was wanted by more clubs than Michael Owen would ever be. Charly from San Jose, California, said that Maradona was greater than Pele. Someone in Kathmandu insisted that Maradona was the king of football, while an Argentine doctor recalled being held at gunpoint by Afghan tribesmen and being freed after shouting Maradona's name. He was still adored by the fans all over the world for the player he once was.

It was about that time that Jon Smith, the international football agent who had represented Maradona between 1987 and 1993, concluded that the footballer had ceased to be the internationally marketable product he once was. Smith told me that towards the end of the 1990s he had approached three English Premiership clubs with the offer of Maradona as coach, and was promptly told to get lost.

But nothing is ever predictable with Maradona, and within days of his collapse in Uruguay he was recovering in Havana, Cuba, courtesy of his friend Fidel Castro, with his financial support system in overdrive as his agent touted more exclusive interviews and photographs to a hungry world media. Maradona even spoke of himself in the third person, mocking the self-delusion of those who had predicted his imminent demise. 'Diego Maradona will only ascend to heaven when all four Beatles are waiting to meet him,' he declared. From Havana, British journalist David Jones suggested that the man a worldwide FIFA poll of fans had voted the greatest footballer of the twentieth century, 'isn't merely suffering delusions of grandeur, but is also stark raving bonkers.'

Maradona's latest spell at the La Pradera health spa-cum-holiday complex verged on farce. He rose late each morning, then brunched on fruit and juice brought to him by two white-hatted chefs on a silver service trolley. Occasionally he made his way into a small gym where four sets of ten press-ups, four sets of ten leg-raises and a few half-hearted rolls of the shoulders left him 'panting like an asthmatic walrus'. Maradona, with a shock of dyed orange hair, a tattoo of Che Guevara on his flabby arm and a heart monitor around his ample girth, looked like a clown, an inflated Harpo Marx. None of this seemed to worry Castro, who found ways of making political capital out of Maradona's presence on the island. The local media portrayed him as the good leader of the people, in contrast to the Goliath of the North (the United States) who had refused to give Maradona a visa since the 1994 World Cup doping scandal. 'With meetings like the one I have just had with Fidel, my heart will hold out, and this Diego will be around for a while,' Maradona declared after meeting with the Cuban leader, with whom he shared an air of apparent immortality.

Within a year, in 2001, Maradona was shedding public tears, and not for the first time in his life. He was crying with the emotion of knowing there were still enough Argentines around who respected him so much that they couldn't accept anybody else taking his Number 10 shirt, even at this point in his life when he was really saying goodbye, again. The shirt, signed by Argentina's class of 2001 – the likes of Javier Saviola, Gabriel Batistusta, Javier Zanetti, Hernán Crespo, Juan Román Riquelme, Andrés D'Alessandro, Marcelo Gallardo, Pablo Aimar and Juan Sebastián Verón – was handed to him at a testimonial match between an Argentine XI led by himself and a Rest of the World XI, part of which seemed like a rogue's gallery of bad boys, gifted players and legends of the past – men like Carlos Valderrama, Hristo Stoichkov, Eric Cantona and René Higuita.

It was November in Buenos Aires, warm, sunny and sweetly smelling of faded jacaranda. Prior to the match, Maradona, wearing a turban, had paid a visit to his friend (now ex-president) Menem, who was under house arrest for alleged corruption. It was later reported that in the Buenos Aires Hilton, where he and his entourage had set up camp, Maradona had stalked the corridors wearing an Osama bin Laden mask he had purchased after 9/11 and worn at fancy dress parties in Havana.

On the day of the testimonial Maradona wore his Number 10 shirt, and waited until a local rock group called The Paranoid Rats finished their dedicatory verse: 'I want Diego to play for ever'. He then walked out into La Bombonera, his beloved coliseum, just as he had done on countless occasions before, to the roar of 60,000 fanatical fans, gladiator of the people, with his two young daughters at his side. The stadium was draped with the blue and yellow of Boca, and blue and white, Argentine colours. The barras bravas packed the terraces. They bounced with joy, chanting 'Maradoo, Maradoo' and unfurling a giant banner bearing the words 'Thank You, Diego'. It was a sign of their indebtedness to the eternal memory of his genius. That the event had been sold as Maradona's definitive farewell appearance in the midst of the worst political and economic crisis afflicting Argentina in years was an achievement akin to Don King's staging of the Ali-Foreman fight in Mobutu's Zaire. This was Maradona's version of a global people's sporting event, his very own rumble in the jungle.

And yet there was no championship at stake this time in La Bombonera. Maradona's enduring self-belief was focused on his uncontested crown as the greatest player who ever graced the turf. The reality check showed that the man trotting across the pitch looked a trifle overweight for his forty years, at eighty-four kilos.

There remained in Maradona a desperate, unfulfilled need to find meaning in his life, to recover a sense of purpose, to harness his talent and genius for the game. Back in 1997, just before another descent into drugs, overeating and overdrinking, Diego had promised not only to help Boca become great again but also to help Argentina qualify for the 1998 World Cup in France, with him playing in the national team. It didn't turn out quite that way. The fulfilment of the dream was postponed for another day although the urge for self-justification persisted.

In *Yo Diego*, his autobiography published in 2000, Maradona talked about his natural talent: his ability to rotate his ankles was one factor that enabled him to do things with his left foot that most mortals struggle to do with their right hand. The extreme rotation of the ankle was accompanied by his panoramic field of vision on the pitch, with an ability to see the outcome of a move as it developed. Jorge Valdano famously liked to tell the story that after *that* second goal against England in 1986, Maradona said to him, 'I could see you running along, but I didn't pass because I thought I could do it." Valdano said, 'Son of a bitch, on top of everything he was doing he could see me!'

But only Maradona himself could really describe the second goal as the kind that you dream of as child, dribbling down the right of the field, beating Beardsley, Reid and Butcher, seeing Valdano unmarked to the left but deciding to go it alone, shaking off Fenwick by feinting inside and going outside, pulling Shilton out of position, then scoring, leaving Butcher to pick up the pieces as a late arrival. Maradona recalled: 'Every time I see it again, it seems almost a lie that I achieved it. It's almost a dream . . . but I scored the best goal in my life.'

For Maradona, his performance and Argentina's victory that summer of 1986 was a slap in the face for all those who had criticized the team coached by Carlos Bilardo in the final weeks leading to the tournament. 'Once we had the cup in our hands, we went back into the changing room and started singing the rudest chants from the terraces,' he remembered. 'We were directing them at everybody . . . We were all standing on the benches, screaming like mad men: "And this one is for all you motherfuckers out there!" '

While admitting to his own drug addiction, Maradona put at least two dope tests down to part of an unspecified conspiracy, and denied he had ever taken drugs to enhance his performance. As for that game with England in the Aztec stadium, he admitted using his hand in the first goal against the English, only to feel no regret or need to apologize. The goal, he said, was sweet revenge after all the Argentine *chicos* who were killed like 'little birds' in the Falklands War. It made him feel like an Argentine version of the Artful Dodger stealing an Englishman's wallet.

Maradona hit out at referees, FIFA, money-grabbing players and corrupt politicians, and placed himself, predictably, on the side of the genuine fan. 'I am the voice of those who have no voice, the voice of many people who feel represented by me because I always have a microphone in front of me, while they'll never get the chance to have one in their godforsaken lives.' He felt no need to justify the fact that he had remained remarkably silent during the latter days of the military regime that cost the lives of between 9,000 and 30,000 people between 1976 and 1983. After playing not far from the killing fields (Maradona's flat at that time was one street away from one of the junta's notorious detention camps), he was happy to have his picture taken with leading members of the Camorra in Naples, not because he was in their pay, but because he felt entertained. He ended his autobiography by insisting that, having reached the age of forty, he could with all honesty claim that he had harmed no one but himself and owed nothing to anyone but his family.

In 2001, when he returned to La Bombonera for his testimonial, he did so after another tortured struggle to get fit again, submitting himself knee to surgery at a clinic in Colombia. The irony of getting into shape in the land of white powder seemed lost on Maradona's most fanatical fans. Only when the game got under way did he realize the extent to which he had been sacrificed on the altar of collective self-delusion. From the outset it was clear that he was not fit enough to play much more than a small part of the full ninety minutes at a competitive pace. So the game was choreographed to accommodate him as he was then. The other players slowed their pace, took the sting out of their tackles, and made sure that Maradona got the ball as often as possible. He seemed so slow in mind and body that he barely tackled and let passes go awry.

There was something deeply sad about the best player the world had ever known being shown charity. But to say that the pathos was resolved in pantomime was to belittle the emotion that swelled up around Maradona to protect his dignity, and the complicity of the players to ensure that it was so.

Given his poor condition, everyone knew that Maradona was incapable of scoring a goal on his own merit. So with the Argentina XI ahead on goals, scored by others, a penalty was created so that Maradona could take it. He strode forward, chest puffed out and legs moving like tree trunks, and kicked the ball into the back of the net, with a little help from Higuita the goalkeeper who barely made any attempt to save it. Later, when presented with another opportunity in front of the goal, Maradona tried to chip Higuita from thirty meters. This time Higuita turned the failing missile into a moment of brilliant riposte, gesturing to Maradona with a scorpion kick similar to the one the Colombian employed against England at Wembley. By then the match was well into its second half and Maradona could hardly walk, let alone trot. He was limping badly and drenched in sweat. It was hard not to feel for the man, reduced to a fractured prop in the game that he loved so much, acted out in his honour but not played as he knew it should be. But Maradona had been there before, struggling to reconcile his love of football with the personal wreck he had become, and yet always surviving. Looking dangerously out of breath, he took a bottle of water and emptied it over his head – a ritual baptism – just when the match seemed to be deflating like a punctured balloon. Temporarily refreshed, Maradona played to the home crowd, ripping off his Argentine shirt and revealing the Boca Juniors one below. It was as if his whole life was being played out in slow motion – tears welled up in his eyes again and he gave two fingers to the celebrities, politicians and football executives who had paid for comfortable VIP seats and gestured in solidarity to the stands where the dark-skinned and the unemployed, the thugs and the thieves were sitting.

It was at this precise point that Maradona's most loyal fans, the wild, lawless, shirtless ones of the standing-room only terrace known as *la doce* ('the Twelve' – so-called because the passion is equivalent to having a twelfth player), already pogoing their tribal dance and vibrating La Bombonera, let off a stream of firecrackers like an artillery barrage, filling the whole stadium with the smell and reverberation of gunpowder. The cacophony of chanting gained such frenzy and energy that it broke through the stadium, across the country, and across the globe, leaving TV commentators worldwide speechless and repeating inanities such as, 'This is incredible.' Maradona was carried on his team-mates' shoulders, eyes to the heavens, arms outstretched in supplication, crying as he'd never done before for his failures and his victories, for times past and passing, and the sheer mesmerizing seduction of immortality.

Beyond the stadium, Argentina as a nation sunk into its deepest crisis in living memory under the presidency of Fernando de la Rúa. A crisis of confidence in the government's ability to tackle a soaring public sector deficit plus high unemployment led to a run on bank deposits which in turn led to the highly unpopular *corralito*, an official ban on withdrawals of savings. Riots ensued in Buenos Aires and other parts of the country. In the capital, shops and banks were looted and the congress building was set on fire. Clashes between protestors and riot police left twenty-seven civilians dead and hundreds injured in the worst outbreak of political violence since the end of the Falklands War, almost twenty years earlier.

The Argentine national football team was preparing itself for the 2002 World Cup finals in Japan and South Korea, hoping that a win would raise the nation's morale, as it had done in 1978. In a climate of political disintegration, there was talk of Maradona standing for the Argentine vice-presidency on a joint ticket with his friend, the former Peronist president Carlos Menem, who had recently escaped a jail sentence.

After de la Rúa was forced to resign, Argentina entered a period of political limbo as a series of interim presidents struggled to maintain control. Protestors and sectors of the media publicly blamed the political class, using the slogan '*que se vayan todos*' ('away with them all'). In January 2002, a new interim president, Eduardo Duhalde, the former Peronist governor of Buenos Aires, abolished a fixed exchange rate, allowing the Argentine peso to devalue by more than two-thirds of its value and throwing over half the population into poverty. The following year, fresh elections were brought forward and Néstor Kirchner, another Peronist, was sworn in as president on 25 May. Argentina, a country that had once surpassed Europe in terms of prosperity and was supposed to be self-sufficient in food and oil, found itself with a depleted middle class and growing signs of malnutrition among significant swathes of the population.

In a political language that echoed the populism of General Juan Peron and Evita, Kirchner promised to tackle his country's social problems, embarking on a radical renegotiation of the country's massive debt and announcing a realignment of foreign policy away from the United States and towards other emerging nationalist Latin American leaders like Hugo Chávez in Venezuela and Eva Morales in Bolivia. Despite moving quickly to pursue outstanding cases of human rights violations by the military and curbing the judiciary of allegedly corrupt judges, Kirchner's style of politics reflected that of his past as a governor of the oil-rich province of Santa Cruz. He began to rule Argentina as a personal fiefdom, handing out favours, including lucrative business contracts, to friends and building power blocks beyond congress among local authorities, the trade union movement and a disenfranchised social underclass.

Maradona began to warm to the new political environment, finding that it suited his own personal interests. In 2004, he and his childhood fiancée and long-suffering wife Claudia Villafane divorced following the admission that he had fathered an Italian boy called Diego Sinagra while playing in Naples. Maradona eventually moved to a new house in the luxury residential neighbourhood of Ezeiza, close to acres of land owned by the Argentine National Football Association where the national squad had its impressive training quarters. In 2004, the area was a strong Peronist fiefdom, allied with the government. It was rumoured that Maradona's house purchase had been facilitated by local mayor Alejandro Granados, whose son owned a local football club – flush with funds – and other similarly shadowy business interests. Only later would it emerge how Maradona had followed up his move into high-value real estate by allying with Granados, his friends, the ruling Kirchners and the Peronist party that had dominated Argentine politics since General Peron's coming to power in 1945. In April 2008, Granados announced that Maradona had become a member of the Peronist party and registered with the legendary Number 10. In August 2009, he enthusiastically backed the government in its efforts to win back state control over the financially lucrative TV football coverage.

Four years before officially signing up as a Peronist, on 18 April

2004, Maradona was admitted to the intensive care unit of a Buenos Aires hospital suffering a suspected heart attack following a cocaine overdose, the latest in a series of near-death health scares. And yet reports of his death once again proved exaggerated. Within a year, looking obese and unfit, he agreed to gastric bypass surgery in order to deflate his stomach and reduce his appetite. Following the operation he was put on a strict diet of lightly mashed, easily digestible foods and no alcohol. One of the stories circulated in the past suggested that one of Maradona's blowouts had involved the consumption of seven pizzas, several cakes and lashings of champagne. Within weeks of having his stomach stapled by a Colombian doctor, Maradona was looking notably thinner as he embarked on a brief yet financially lucrative career as a TV presenter.

During a thirty-episode chat show called *La Noche del Diez* ('The Night of the Number 10'), Maradona enticed a range of international stars – from Pele to Mike Tyson, Robbie Williams to Julio Iglesias, and his favourite politician Fidel Castro – to play or say a few words. In the opening show, Maradona and Pele exchanged personally autographed national shirts, headed a ball to each other for nearly a minute and played a tango song – with Pele on guitar and Maradona singing. Pele praised Maradona as an example of how to beat addiction, calling him an inspiration for his own son, who had been jailed on a drugs-related charge. Maradona shed tears as he publicly thanked his family and friends for helping him to rebuild his life after a series of relapses. Although the performance pushed the TV show to the top of the ratings, not everyone was convinced. A spoof episode posted days later on YouTube had a puppet Maradona making a series of indecent proposals to some real-life girls in an English pub before ending his show in a state of debauched abandon, snorting large quantities of cocaine from a sugar bowl.

When Robbie Williams was interviewed by Maradona, the audience was treated to another mutual admiration session, with both men agreeing that Argentine women were the world's sexiest, and that George W. Bush was an 'idiot and a murderer'. The political theme persisted when Maradona interviewed Castro for his programme. Maradona told his audience that interviewing the Cuban leader had been his dream, although in fact the two men had met on several previous occasions. Maradona's alliance with the Cuban leader sprang from an instinctive rebellious streak he had carried within him since his childhood days of survival in the shanty town of Villa Fiorito. 'For me he is a god,' Maradona said of the veteran communist leader prior to arriving in Havana with his TV crew. The pre-recorded five-hour interview (heavily cut for the final programme of the series) showed Castro praising Maradona for his solidarity with the latest Latin American campaign against US imperialism. 'We have struggled for various years against the United States,' said the Cuban leader, seemingly happy to show the world that, contrary to rumour, neither he nor Maradona were at death's door.

Ratings for the final *La Noche del Diez* were lower than the series' start, suggesting that Maradona's popularity remained, as it always had been, based more on football than politics. Viewers were getting tired of a programme that was such a blatant exercise in self-promotion and seemed to get Maradona no nearer to another comeback on the pitch. And yet the following days saw Maradona stepping into a new arena, protesting against the presence of George W. Bush at the 2005 Summit of the Americas in Argentina. TV images from the time show him drawing the attention of the rest of the world to an otherwise lacklustre and politically sterile conference of talking heads from north and south of the Rio Grande. They show Maradona leading a colourful trainload of protestors to Mar del Plata to join thousands who had converged on the coastal town in a 'Say No to Bush' demonstration. The train was temporarily named the Alba Express as a tribute to the 'Bolivarian Alternative for the Americas' (Alba was the regional trade pact being promoted by Castro and the Venezuelan president Chávez). When Chávez took the podium before an anti-globalization and anti-Bush demonstration at a nearby stadium packed with over 40,000 people, Maradona was at his side. Not everyone was pleased. Mexican president Vicente Fox, a close ally of Washington, described Maradona as being ideologically confused. 'He has a good foot for kicking, but he does not have a good brain for talking,' Mr Fox told journalists. Maradona was once again in the limelight.

While still working on his TV show, Maradona returned to his old club Boca Juniors as a vice-president. His decision to hire Alfio Basile as the new coach while also keeping a close relationship with the players resulted in a marked improvement in the first team's performance after a disappointing season. Boca went on to win the Argentine league championship and the Copa and Recopa

Sudamericana, a success story that prompted the first stage in a long, drawn-out campaign by Maradona to realize his ambition of coaching the national team.

But before this started, the global publicity wheels of Maradona Inc received a fresh spin when BBC TV made a successful bid to have the player agree to an interview with Gary Lineker. Unless you were prepared to pay huge sums, getting an interview with Maradona had become an increasingly difficult assignment for most journalists since his retirement from full-time football. Lineker himself had the frustrating experience of travelling all the way to Argentina for a TV documentary in 1997 only for the Argentine star to fail to turn up. This time the BBC calculated that they were dealing with a more predictable subject, given his reported success in tackling his weight and drug problems, and the new incentive to his life he had found both as a TV star and with his return to Boca. The project was timed to coincide with the run-up to the World Cup, an event that ever since 1986 had been personified by Maradona, whose outstanding performance showed football at its best.

An advance production team led by BBC sports director Jason Bernard and a 'fixer' arrived in Buenos Aires on 6 March at the tail end of a sweltering summer and had an early meeting with Claudia Villafane, Maradona's ex-wife who was now his manager. Her biggest initial concern was whether the BBC had brought along a handbag catalogue for her from London, as promised. Lineker flew in two days after Bernard had established a rapport with Maradona over dinner.

Over the next five days the BBC team struck lucky, filming Maradona with his family and friends, playing football, being a TV star, celebrating goals from his box in La Bombonera and talking to Gary as if they were long-lost friends. The two met while Maradona was changing for the Masters game, an event attended by a large contingent of *barras bravas* who all had free tickets. As Bernard reported later, it was the first time Maradona and Lineker had met since a centenary game at Wembley in 1987; unsurprisingly, Gary was apprehensive. But what followed could almost have been scripted. The two hugged and Maradona said, 'Nice to meet you, old friend.' When they shook hands, Gary joked, 'Was that the hand?' referring to the infamous 'Hand of God'. Maradona replied, 'No – it was the left.'

Lineker, in the words of the sports writer Jim White, looked a 'paradigm of good health: slim, elegant, prosperously attired in pink shirt and black suit', in contrast to his interview subject, who had spent the past decade 'pursued by devils to whom he must have pledged his soul in exchange for World Cup triumph'. The last time White had looked at Maradona for any length of time on a TV screen, he seemed 'plagued by drink, drugs and fast food', as if attempting 'some mad David Blaine-style stunt, seeing how long he could live while attached to a mechanical tyre: the former genius of the game had been transformed into an almost spherical blimp.' But White was pleasantly surprised by Maradona's seemingly healthy appearance. And what in other times might have been a cruel exercise in public humiliation turned into a riveting piece of TV sports journalism, with a polite, Spanish-speaking Lineker engaging with a seemingly relaxed, gracious and good-humoured Maradona, supported by his family despite his divorce, and reserving the full gambit of his emotions for the Boca goals and, irony of ironies, the moment when a referee failed to spot an opposition hand ball.

For British viewers, there were other treats in store – not least an entertaining if provocative account by the man himself of his two legendary goals in the Aztec Stadium in 1986. 'The other guys seemed reluctant to join in the celebrations,' Maradona commented over the archive footage of him running alone into the corner of the Aztec stadium after the hand of God, 'I was saying, "Come on guys, let's do it properly, let's go the whole hog." '

Months later, Argentinian hopes of repeating their World Cup successes of 1976 and 1986 were dashed when they were beaten 4-2 by Germany in a tense quarter-final shoot-out in Berlin. The match brought back memories of the 1990 final in Rome, when the defending champions lost their crown to Germany 0-1 after a controversial penalty award, with players and officials from both sides trading punches on the pitch. Argentina's national honour was restored when its football team clinched the Olympic title in Beijing in 2008. The campaign to victory was notable for two things: confirmation of the extraordinary talent of the Barcelona youngster Lionel Messi, and the looming presence of Maradona.

When the first football was kicked in those Olympics, a large majority of the fans watching the event locally supported China. But, as one commentator put it, 'Things settled down when pictures of a relaxed-looking Diego Maradona filled the big screens.' The sight of Maradona, up in the commentary box or in the stands, hinted at celebrity, and the chants for China soon morphed into support for Argentina. It was hard to gauge the precise reason. Was it the memory of Maradona as a star player or his support for Castro and other revolutions? But the popularity of the Argentine team personified by Maradona was not lost on sponsors, PR firms and TV rights people, for whom the beautiful game was synonymous with big money.

It was during these Olympics that Maradona took a further step towards realizing his dream of managing the national squad. When Argentina won gold, he rushed down into the changing rooms and joined in a high-profile celebration with the players as if he was their coach, even though the hero of the hour was actually Sergio Batista, the manager of the Olympic squad. And yet in Batista, a veteran of the 1986 World Cup who had recently taken over responsibility for the youth divisions of the Argentine Football Association, Maradona had not so much a potential rival as a useful ally and scout. In the aftermath of the Olympics, while Batista faded into the background, Maradona kept in touch with several of the gold-medal-winning players, thanks to his friendship with Gabriel Heinze and his personal ties with Sergio 'Kun' Aguero, his youngest daughter Giannina's partner and father to her child. The opportunity to make a fresh move came later that summer, as Argentina's struggling attempt to qualify for the World Cup put increasing pressure on manager Alfio Basile, less than a year after his appointment as national coach. Basile was forced out in October 2008 after securing only four wins in nine matches, the crunch point coming when Argentina was defeated 1-0 by Chile, the first time it had lost to its Andean neighbour in thirty-five years.

After the match, a complex network of vested interests contributed to intense lobbying in support of Maradona's appointment as national coach, despite fears that his personality was ill-suited to the demands of the job. The campaign is thought to have included personal phone calls to the President of the Argentine Football Association, Julio Grondona, by three Latin American presidents – Chávez of Venezuela, Morales of Bolivia and Argentina's own head of state, Néstor Kirchner, all of whom had been seen to ally themselves politically with Maradona during his latest anti-US phase. Grondona and other AFA officials were also made aware of the extent to which the commercial value of the Argentine national squad would be boosted with Maradona at the helm. For example the Renova Group, owned by Russian billionaire Viktor Vekselberg, which had brought the rights to twenty-four Argentine team exhibition matches for $18m in 2006, forecast a doubling of profits as interest soared as a consequence of Maradona's latest return. Within the footballing world, Heinze and Aguero had already led the equivalent of a dressing-room revolt against Basile, persuading other players in the Argentine squad to vote with their feet in favour of Maradona, in what one AFA insider described as the equivalent of a 'palace coup'.

While many of the manoeuvrings took place behind the scenes, they were only too evident to Riquelme, a key player in Basile's squad and the only member of the team to take a public stand against Maradona. In truth, ego was mixed with principle. This was in part because Riquelme feared losing his influence in the team under Maradona's tutelage, but also he genuinely objected to the underhand way in which Basile's removal had been orchestrated. Riquelme quit the national squad, saying of Maradona: 'We don't think the same way. We don't share the same codes of ethics. While he is the coach of the national team, we can't work together.'

Riquelme was admired for his elegant, unhurried style and his ability to prise open defences with incisive passes and well-placed free kicks. Since returning from a long stint in Europe to play for Boca, he had become something of a local hero. But critics, some of whom were close to Maradona, argued that Riquelme's strong personality on the pitch was more often a curse than a blessing, dragging the whole team down when he underperformed and making it difficult to change systems. The Boca Juniors playmaker, who made more than fifty appearances for Argentina and scored seventeen goals, officially missed Maradona's first two games in charge because of club commitments. However, his decision to quit followed Maradona's publicly veiled suggestion that the national squad could work better without him. Maradona said in an interview that he got up at four o'clock every morning to think about team selection and that much of his deliberating had been over how to introduce Riquelme without disrupting the team.

Without Riquelme, and with Maradona as coach, the previously lacklustre Argentina began playing well, beating Scotland and France as well as Venezuela in a World Cup qualifying match. But the controversy which had never been far from Maradona's life resurfaced as Argentina stumbled in subsequent games, beginning with a humiliating 6-1 defeat away to Bolivia something Bolivian fans would celebrate on YouTube as just revenge for the racial discrimination shown to their families and friends living in Argentina as immigrants. A succession of four defeats in five games left Argentina lying in the play-off position in the South American qualifying zone. Argentina and Maradona's reputations were thrown a lifeline when a dramatic ninety-third-minute goal from the Boca Juniors veteran Martin Palermo secured a 2-1 victory over Peru. Maradona, in raptures, aquaplaned across the rain-drenched turf in celebration. The winning goal was, Maradona insisted, another miracle from San Palermo.

Days later, Argentina faced Uruguay in a match they needed to win to be guaranteed a place in the World Cup. Argentina's rollercoaster progress through the qualifying round until then had been widely seen as a product of Maradona's eccentricity as a coach. Maradona's campaign to control and direct the national squad involved him in a much-publicized brawl with manager Carlos Bilardo and a dispute with the Argentine Football Association over the appointment of other assistants. In his first year at the helm, Maradona capped over seventy players and experimented with back fours, midfield sixes and four-pronged attacks, preceded by a training regime that accommodated Maradona's enduring habit of waking late. The regime – if one could call it that – confused stars like Lionel Messi, Gonzalo Higuain and Carlos Tevez who had been moulded by the discipline of the European teams they played for. Only weeks before Maradona had taken over as national coach, Messi – his proclaimed successor – had been warned by Barcelona's incoming manager Pep Guardiola, after being discovered on too many nights out with Ronaldinho, that he faced being sacked if he continued to arrive tired for training.

'What is your dream?' asked Guardiola of Messi in a crisis meeting.

'Well,' answered the young player, 'I would like to be the greatest in the world one day, like Diego.'

'Well then, you have two options: you go on partying, and you will be out of here within days. Or you start going go to bed early, be up on time for training and then you might become one of the best in the world.'

Days later, Ronaldinho was on his way out of Barcelona and Messi had buckled down to Guardiola's regime, which in many ways was poles apart from Maradona's. In the following months, Messi, like Tevez, would suffer sustained criticism from Argentine fans who accused him of not playing his best. But the players struggled to come to terms with Maradona's style of management, forever switching teams and strategies. Maradona called up seventy-eight players, leaving even the most experienced football commentators struggling to see a method in the madness. Martin Samuel of the *Mail on Sunday* noted that Maradona had approached the job of coaching Argentina 'like a kid given the new FIFA 2010 game on Playstation and a bucket of blue smarties.'

In the critical qualifier, Argentina beat Uruguay 1-0. The victory was overshadowed by Maradona's sexually explicit, foul-mouthed rant at his growing army of media critics. 'There were those who did not believe in this team and who treated me as less than nothing,' a wild eyed Maradona declared, clutching his crotch. 'Today we are in the World Cup finals with help from nobody but honour. To all of you who did not believe in us, and I apologize to all the women here, you can suck my dick and keep sucking it. I am black or white, I'll never be grey in my life. You can take it up your ass.'

Victim, knight, defiant rebel, foul-mouthed aggressor – only Diego Maradona could claim to be all four in one statement, and get away with it. Two months later, Maradona emerged from a FIFA ban and flew to Pretoria to check out the Argentine squad's facilities, having lined up a series of lucrative appearances in the run-up to the World Cup. Despite their poor qualifying campaign, Argentina approached the tournament hoping that the hand of God would come to the rescue and secure success. The Argentine squad was certainly not short of star players – Messi, Higuain, Teves, Sergio Aguero, Nicolas Burdisso, Javier Mascherano and Diego Milito among them. The question of whether Maradona would manage to mould them into a cohesive unit with a clear personality, capable of beating the opposition, and also have luck on his side remained. A huge responsibility – and no small part of the marketing behind the Argentine team – fell on the shoulders of Messi, FIFA's footballer of the year and one of the great performers in world club football. At FC Barcelona, Messi's natural talent is supported by a very motivated and interconnected team which had allows him to flourish as a player. By contrast, Messi's ineffectual performances in several of Argentina's World Cup qualifying matches appeared at least in part to be caused by a system that seemed to rely excessively on him as a playmaker and director. Nevertheless, Maradona later appeared to have high hopes of building on Argentina's performance against Uruguay in which Messi linked up well with Veron. Certainly with Maradona as coach, and South Africa as host, the 2010 World Cup will not be a dull event. Everything is possible, divine intervention and tears included.

24

A DEATH FORETOLD

I owe to my pursuit of Cristiano Ronaldo an unexpected reunion with the enduring spirit of Diego Maradona. In March 2019, I encountered the legendary Number 10 Napoli shirt on a visit to a recommended pizzeria in Turin, after visiting the Juventus headquarters and talking to fans and executives about Ronaldo's first season in Italy.

The sky-blue shirt was hanging, defiantly, like a totem near a poster of another hero of the south of Italy, the popular comedian Totò. While Diego was not there physically, he had also not yet, like Totò, passed to another world. Maradona's presence on this planet as well as his legacy was a subject of continuing fascination that generated passionate loyalties, transcending borders, races and cultures.

By March 2019, I had for years been trying to leave Maradona behind me and was exploring the rivalry between Ronaldo and Leo Messi, two modern icons of the game, but fans worldwide continued to have Maradona as a point of reference and comparison when deciding on the meaning of football greatness. And while I ate my pizza that night, I reflected that it was Messi's Italian immigrant grandmother, Celia Cuccittini, whose memory he would invoke by dedicating his best goals to her in heaven (she died in 1998). It was Celia who encouraged him as a young boy not to worry about his small stature but to dream of becoming the best footballer in the world one day – as good as Maradona.

The first Argentine star with a claim to inherit Maradona's crown as his country's, if not the world's, best ever player, Messi was born a year before the legendary World Cup in Mexico. It would prove a tough legacy, following in Maradona's footsteps, overshadowed as much by his larger-than-life personality, always destined to provoke controversy and hyperbole, as by his undisputed genius as a player.

The first record I have of the two talking to each other, however briefly, was in 2005, during Messi's first season with FC Barcelona's first team, when he brought the Nou Camp to its feet, scoring his first La Liga goal against Albacete. Messi was having lunch at home the next day when he received a phone call from Argentina. Maradona congratulated Messi for playing well in a string of games and encouraged him to look to the future and keep on scoring.

Later that summer, Maradona invited Messi onto his wacky *La Noche del 10*, the Argentine TV show named after the shirt number he made globally famous. Maradona at the time had temporarily drawn back from his cocaine lines and was in the recovery zone after a couple of near-death health scares related to his drug misuse and binge eating and drinking.

The programme always featured Maradona playing football-tennis with his sports guests. On this occasion it was Maradona and the similarly aged Enzo Francescoli, the Uruguayan-born River Plate star, against Messi and Carlos Tevez, the emerging young Argentine thoroughbreds. Maradona's team ended up losing 10-6 and everyone took it in good part. Messi was not one to gloat, even if he might have been tempted to. As for Maradona, his resilient sense of self-belief had survived worse setbacks in his life. Moreover, by then an idea seemed to have formed in his head, that of seeing his professional future somehow tied up with Messi's, not competing for the title of best player in history – for there was something in Diego Maradona that believed he was beyond such comparison – but as his coach.

'I've seen the player who will inherit my place in Argentine football and his name is Messi,' Maradona would say a few months later, in February 2006. 'He is beautiful to watch – my kind of player in our blue and white jersey. He is a leader and is offering classes in beautiful football. He has something different to any other player in the world.' And yet Maradona and Messi belonged to different life forces.

As Fernando Signorini, the physical trainer of the Argentine national squad who worked with both of them, told me when I caught up with him in Buenos Aires in 2017:

> Physically and technically there is much in common but there is a gulf between the two when it comes to personality. Messi was not born, like Diego was, in a shanty town, nor did he have to fight for survival from an early stage. As a young teenager Diego was playing for the youth team of Argentinos Juniors, getting up at four in the morning to go and play in an away game across the country, on pitches that had no decent changing rooms, let alone hot water or lighting, and where you had to face growing violence from the fans. Messi, at the age of twelve, was taken to Barcelona and put in a glass house and protected.

As I was to discover, the relationship between the two Argentine football stars was not so much a tension between egos, since Messi for much of the time both on and off the pitch didn't seem to display his ego, nor did he seem much interested in football history, but rather a scarcely veiled Freudian rivalry between a forceful father (Maradona) and an understated son (Messi), competing not for the love of a wife or a mother but for the admiration of a nation.

As the World Cup in South Africa loomed, any doubts that Maradona may have had about Messi's character not being captain material had been replaced by an open courtship, as the Argentine coach struggled to put together a coherent team and system that would ensure qualification. Messi was viewed by coach Maradona as his most important player, but without the captain's armband, which was worn by Javier Mascherano. Messi nonetheless came to be seen by many of his countrymen as a cause as well as a victim of the team's dysfunctionality. Only as the tournament progressed was Argentina's underachievement also blamed on Maradona's failings as a coach.

Maradona listened to Messi's suggestion that he should replace the 4-4-2 system – two wingers, two centre-midfielders and two forwards – with a 4-3-1-2, or a 3-4-1-2 system, with play focused on the attacking front three, but still with enough players to defend.

The revised system worked well enough for Argentina at the start of the 2010 World Cup against opponents Nigeria, who offered plenty of space. A frenzied crowd of Argentine fans at the Ellis Park stadium bounced up and down and chanted their support as an overweight and slightly self-conscious Maradona gesticulated from the touchline. Among the players, Messi was the outstanding performer although it was a goal by his team colleague Heinze that secured victory.

Maradona had further cause for celebration when in the next match, again thanks to Messi, Argentina won 4-1 against South Korea, then 2-0 against Greece. Exactly twenty-four years after the infamous 'Hand of God' goal against England at the quarter-finals of the 1986 World Cup in Mexico, the player-turned-coach leapt for joy in the technical area.

After the match against Greece, Maradona hit back at the media for questioning his team and its management and said he was happy with Messi's performance. 'People should relax,' he insisted, with typical bravado. 'This team is going to show everything it has.' And yet the Argentine team evidently had nowhere near the quality of the best years of FC Barcelona under Guardiola, where Messi thrived in a collective masterclass of creative, attacking football.

As things turned out, what the team had – including Maradona and Messi – was not nearly enough to win the 2010 World Cup. Despite beating Mexico, Argentina were knocked out in the quarter-finals by Germany. Their 4-0 loss was the national team's worst margin of defeat since 1974.

Back in Argentina, Messi received harsher criticism than Maradona. After all, Diego, as a player, had led a similarly average team to win the title in 1986 thanks to his genius. Messi playing with Maradona as coach in South Africa 2010 came nowhere near Mexico 1986. In South Africa, not for the first or last time, a less successful World Cup campaign left Argentine football with a sense of humiliation as well as loss. It showed Messi was yet to earn his mythological status as the nation's new hero; and it also led to a belated realisation that Maradona was human after all, with his shortcomings as a national coach cruelly exposed.

And yet Fernando Signorini, the Argentine team's physical trainer who had known Maradona from his days in Barcelona, has positive memories of the World Cup in South Africa. As Signorini told me, he felt privileged to be part of the unique circumstances that brought Maradona and Messi together during the campaign. 'It was a marvellous experience while it lasted: Diego, whenever he was out of the media spotlight, showed real tenderness and respect for the much younger Messi when they talked with each other. All that idea that there was somehow a rivalry between them was an invention of some sectors of the media,' Signorini told me.

Several years after first interviewing him in the early 1990s for the first edition of this book, I had caught up with Signorini again on a return visit to Buenos Aires where I had lived and worked as a journalist during the 1980s. He told me this story about a training session he had witnessed with Maradona as coach and Messi as a player in preparation for the 2010 World Cup.

We had been training for about forty minutes when Diego shouted out, 'That's it, let's all go back to the dressing room.' And as everybody heads off, I notice that Leo picks up the ball and puts it in front of the open goal on the left-hand side of the penalty. He hits the ball and it flies to the left, three metres above the bar. Messi makes a gesture of resignation and then starts walking despondently towards the dressing room, shoulders crunched, head bowed. So, I catch up with him, put my arm round his shoulder and tell him, 'You are on your way to becoming the best player in the world and you are walking to the dressing room having hit that shit ball...'

At that point I heard Diego say, 'Hang on, lad, come here...' Then Diego puts the ball in exactly the same spot, steps two metres back and, putting his hand on Messi's shoulder, tells him: 'Look, when you go and hit the ball, don't take your foot away so quickly. Because without it the ball doesn't know what to do...'

And at that moment Diego steps up, and kicks the ball straight into the net. There and then I felt the history of Argentine football summarised, in these two guys. It contradicted what some people claimed – that Diego was jealous of Leo. No way was that true, because someone who is jealous of another has nothing to teach him.

Certainly, Maradona's role as coach in the 2010 World Cup gave the competition an aura that the 2014 World Cup, in which Diego was no longer a central character, lacked. As Maradona's English translator, Argentine journalist Marcela Mora y Araujo, told me: 'There was a concerted effort by the likes of Juan Sebastián Verón to publicly defend Messi from the hard time he was being given by some of the media. This, in conjunction with an obvious bonding with the supreme ego that was manager Diego Maradona, helped turn around the press's attitude. Some way into the tournament, the love conquered all, and although Argentina didn't win the trophy, snippets of the fun Messi and Maradona had with their talent delighted us all.'

Maradona was removed as national coach after the World Cup 2010. As had happened before when meeting adversity and humiliation in his career, Maradona suggested that he had been the victim of an injustice by higher authorities, blaming the long-term president of the Argentine Football Association, Julio Grondona (who was later exposed during the FIFA-gate scandal) and also criticising the director of the national team, Carlos Bilardo, who was never given much credit for his role as coach of Argentina's victorious 1986 World Cup team. Bilardo also worked with Maradona during a less-than-successful time in Seville.

In 2011 Maradona took up a new managing job with the United Arab Emirates side Al-Wasl, after reportedly agreeing an annual salary of 3.5 million euros (£3 million). The club's home ground, Zabeel Stadium, sat on the fringes of Dubai's old town. Since the discovery of oil in the 1960s, Dubai had been transformed, with luxury hotels and ten-lane motorways, and its expatriate-heavy population had risen from 50,000 to over three million. And yet it had never been a major draw for the world's fading star players, with the 18,000-seater home stadium only occasionally more than half full.

As recalled by Patrick O'Brien, an Irish journalist there at the time, Maradona arrived that August at the Jumeirah Zabeel Saray Hotel on Dubai's palm island 'exactly as you'd expect him to – almost an hour late and flanked by an entourage longer than Sheikh Zayed Road. The UAE Pro League is where great careers go to rest so there was giddy curiosity in the air of the venue, moved from Zabeel Stadium to accommodate the hundreds of journalists in attendance.'

Apart from doing his health no harm, it was a great marketing exercise, strengthening his popularity in the Arab world. As O'Brien suggested: 'Dubai's ultra-strict illegal substance policy may have been good for Maradona. Drying out is easier in the desert. And he was good for Dubai, too. Maradona is what Dubai does. The biggest names, the best cars, the tallest buildings; Dubai's self-conscious image exists by showing off. Having the Burj Khalifa of footballers made sense, regardless of results.'

What soon became evident, as surely as the dust storms that frequently engulf the skyscrapers in this region, was that Maradona had not lost his ability to startle, provoke and outrage, as unpredictable off the pitch as he was on it in his prime.

Al-Wasl had a record of being seven-time UAE champions, but only winning one league crown in the previous fourteen years. Despite expectations that Al-Wasl would challenge for the title, bad results began to roll in. By the following January the club had slipped to seventh position in the league, closer to the bottom than the top, winning only one out of a series of six games. At his weekly press conference, Maradona showed his characteristic defiance, insisting that his gesticulations from the touchline demonstrated not that he was feeling the pressure, but that he was passionate about the game. 'Football is a sport that is full of excitement and joy,' Maradona told the gathered media.

The romantic rebel was still haunted by devils, even though he sometimes showed signs of trying to restrain them. He refused to shake hands with the Al Ain boss, Romanian Cosmin Olăroiu, who declared: 'Maradona doesn't always have a clear mind because of his [way of] life. I don't take drugs. My life is clear. I don't do anything ... Who is Maradona as a coach? He should respect his work and never come to matches wearing short pants.'

Maradona kicked an Al-Wasl fan with his famous left foot during a photoshoot in the stadium, and after a 2-0 defeat at Al Shabab, he climbed into the VIP area of the stands and remonstrated with fans, later claiming they had abused his latest girlfriend, Veronica Ojeda.

It was while Maradona was in Dubai that his beloved mother Tota died. His sense of loss was profound, made worse by the fact that he was unable to get back to Buenos Aires in time to be with her in her final moments. While other less respected women were destined to come and go in Maradona's life, passing each other like ships in the night, Tota endured like an anchor thrown into the dark waters of her son's existence. Whenever it seemed he couldn't sink further, she supported him through his tortuous rehabilitations, and when she could, she held up a protective shield against the other demons, the pressure of media and fans, the predatory nature of those others who got close to Maradona simply to feed off him.

Al-Wasl finished eighth in a twelve-team league, the club's joint worst performance. The board members who hired Maradona resigned, and with the new board came a new coach. Maradona was sacked in July 2012, after fourteen months in charge and following a trophy-less season.

The personality and talent that had allowed Maradona to excel as a player seemed no longer to deliver results on the pitch, and yet he continued to court controversy and attract media attention off it. His most fanatical fans around the world never lost their belief that he remained the best player in the history of football, even if, after the glory days of the World Cup in Mexico, his performance as a player had declined. In the new millennium he became almost a caricature of his former self in his physical appearance and outspokenness.

In February 2014, it was announced, as if a miraculous deal had been struck, that Maradona had again pulled back from the brink and was now not only taking up a manager's role but also expressing his wish to play again, at the age of fifty-three, with Deportivo Riestra, a minnow of a club that played in Primera D in Argentina, the fifth tier of the country's football league system.

The club was based in the Flores neighbourhood of Buenos Aires, and was reported to be planning to ditch its 3,000-seater stadium and move to the nearby Estadio Pedro Bidegain, a ground with a near-44,000 capacity and home to the Primera División champions San Lorenzo.

The deal was conjured up with the encouragement of Victor Stinfale, who media reports described as a close friend and legal representative of Maradona. But the deal also appeared to represent one of those curious coincidences that seemed destined by a higher order, and which punctuated Maradona's life. For Flores was the neighbourhood in which Jorge Bergoglio, the recently elected Pope Francis, had been born and where he had found his vocation as a priest, and San Lorenzo was the team that the Jesuit-trained football-fan pontiff had supported all his life.

In autumn that year, Maradona met Pope Francis in Rome in support of a charity match. Maradona emerged from a private conversation with the spiritual leader and the two men warmly embraced, the player showing genuine love and joy, as if transformed by the moment. 'It's given me a real kick to see an Argentine in such an important place as the Vatican, after we've had so many popes that only cared about politics but not about the kids who go hungry,' declared Maradona. He handed Pope Francis a shirt with the Argentine colours and the Number 10 of his magical playing days. 'He has helped restore the Catholic faith I had when I was a kid.'

Maradona had never adhered to strict Church doctrine in his personal life, nor was a conversion to a life of piety and abstinence thought likely. However, there was no doubting that the 'people's champion', born in a Buenos Aires slum, found himself more engaged with Pope Francis than with any of his predecessors.

It was all very different from the lack of human chemistry in Maradona's encounter in 2000 with Pope John Paul II, a football fan too but doctrinally inflexible and a virulently anti-communist Pole to boot. Maradona, who by then had absorbed a crude form of liberation theology as part of periodic anti-imperialistic, anti-capitalist rhetorical outbursts, looked up at the Vatican gold ceilings and said: 'With all this gold, why does the Pope not sell it to the poor?'

By contrast, Pope Francis and Maradona shared common ground in their Argentine social experience and political affinities. They both came from families that were devoted followers in the 1950s of the populist President Juan Perón and his legendary wife Evita, whose radical redistribution of wealth would for ever be held up by the Argentine working classes as a golden age of socio-economic justice.

And Maradona had been born to a father of Guarani descent and a poor Italian immigrant mother in a shanty town where the inhabitants found solace in their religious icons and communal prayers, and the example of worker priests living the Gospel message of humility, compassion and solidarity. It was in neighbourhoods like the Villa Fiorito of Maradona's childhood that Pope Francis had found his calling as priest and bishop among the outcast and marginalised population, reaching out to the periphery of humanity as a hallmark of his papacy. Thus did the Pope of Good Promise, as I called him in a biography, touch the soul of the Hand of God, otherwise known as '*pibe de oro*', the anti-establishment artful dodger from Villa Fiorito.

On 25 June 2015, Maradona's remaining parental prop, Diego senior, popularly known as 'Chitoro', died, aged eighty-seven. This time the son got there in time for the final days of his father, who had for years suffered from respiratory and cardiovascular problems and had contracted pneumonia. His health had deteriorated after the death of his wife, Tota.

Maradona's childhood memories of his father were of stoical sacrifice – getting up each day to work in a local factory while finding time to encourage his young son's talent and his early start in a professional football career. Chitoro was by nature a quiet, reserved man, if prone to drink, who seemed happiest when hosting *asados*, or barbecues, with his son's family and friends, a practice that he most famously shared with the victorious Argentine squad during the 1986 World Cup.

Maradona deeply mourned both his parents. They had not just been there when he most needed salvaging, but were his enduring point of reference, a reminder of his roots without which his life made no sense.

Well into his fifties, Maradona dreamed of coaching Napoli and even returning to the Argentina squad. But he was chasing windmills. The game that was his heart and soul had been leaving him behind. He seemed outpaced and lost in a highly competitive world of elite high-performance players, slick, well-preserved and thoughtful managers, obsessed with tactics and image, and huge wealthy major football clubs insisting on strict training regimes, guaranteed returns on investment and minimum reputational risk.

He nonetheless took what was on offer. Maradona signed his next coaching job in May 2017 with Al-Fujairah, a small club playing in the second tier of the United Arab Emirates Division. He was tasked with guiding it into the UAE Arabian Gulf League, but he left the following April after failing to deliver their promotion.

During the World Cup in Russia in the summer of 2018, Leo Messi, the record-breaking winner, along with his iconic rival of the modern game, Cristiano Ronaldo of the Ballon D'Or, once again failed to recover the tournament crown for Argentina. Despite the team's defeat, the players looked much healthier and fitter than Maradona, whose bloated face and puffy eyes flashed across the world's TV screens.

Maradona could barely hide his unhappiness and disappointment with his team's performance. He cut a somewhat grotesque image as he watched Argentina from a stadium balcony seat, giving TV viewers an overdose of his theatrical range, from rolling eyes to abusive two fingers, seemingly out of his head on something, less a noble Caesar than a decadent Caligula believing he could still preside over football's equivalent of the Roman theatre.

And yet there were no other commentators arguing that Messi had been let down by his fellow countrymen over the years because of the dysfunctional teams of badly coached players and an Argentine Football Association better known for its political in-fighting than its professionalism, or that Messi's greatness had been more than demonstrated while playing for FC Barcelona. In the ongoing debate among Argentines as to who was the greatest player, Diego or Leo, people remembered Maradona's commitment to the national cause and his winning goals, his genius, not his flawed personality, and in Napoli, of course, he remained venerated among many of the poor and dispossessed. The Napoli stadium, which, as vividly depicted in Asif Kapadia's 2019 immersive documentary, rapturously greeted Maradona's arrival in 1984 as pre-ordained and miraculous, was even destined to change its name from the great apostle St Paul (San Paolo Stadium) to Diego Armando Maradona Stadium, in honour of the legendary player who won the local football club's first ever *scudetto* (the championship shield). Such is football.

It was Maradona who, in the pantheon of football gods, lay nestled between the prolific present-day achievements of Ronaldo and Messi, and a more distant golden past of Pele and Di Stefano. And yet of all his career moves, not since his transfer from FC Barcelona to Napoli in 1984 did one seem so obviously high-risk and controversial as his signing as head coach in September 2018 with the Mexican second division Los Dorados.

The club was based in Culiacán, the capital of the western state of Sinaloa, best known for its links with illegal drug trafficking as made notorious by the jailed cartel kingpin Joaquín 'El Chapo' Guzmán. The clan behind the club, the Hank family, had faced allegations of links to Mexico's violent crime industry. Its patriarch, Jorge Hank Rhon, had a reputation for philanthropy, supporting the poor as well as being the owner of an empire of casinos, hotels, a dog-racing track and a first-division football club, Xolos, in Tijuana, across the US border from San Diego.

The irony of Maradona, a confessed drug addict, signing such a deal, in such a region of the world, produced a flurry of worldwide comment on social media, with one radio reporter drawing the suggestive analogy of a diabetic going into a sweet shop. But the deal was not to find the kind of relief that people imagined.

Sinaloa's notoriety was destined to grow long after Pep Guardiola had left Dorados in 2006, after spending the last months of his career as a player there, prior to moving into top club coaching in Europe. But in sport, the city of Culiacán was much better known for its baseball, Chaco Guzmán's favourite sport, than for football. The local team popularly known as Los Tomateros played in a stadium whose size and capacity eclipsed the one owned by Dorados.

In July 2018, Maradona emerged from his wild appearance at the World Cup in Russia to be presented at a colourful press conference as the new chairman of the Belarusian team Dynamo Brest. But the prospect of spending the winter in eastern Europe, where hardly anyone spoke Spanish, in a country and with people he did not feel instinctively drawn to, left him open to alternatives.

The coaching deal was negotiated with Los Dorados by Argentine football agent Christian Bragarnik, who had Maradona as one of his clients. Maradona was thus persuaded to escape from the pressure of life in Argentina, a nation that seemed to have invested its hopes, dreams and failures in him, and go to the relatively benign climate of Dorados, where people spoke Spanish and where the club had a history of signing Argentine players, among other Latin Americans.

Although his erratic performance from the VIP box during the World Cup in Russia suggested he was heading for another crash landing, Maradona's two seasons at Dorados were not quite a resurrection, nor, as the local PR hype suggested, a transformation and a recovery, but rather an encounter with a romanticised past.

Maradona's rewound good Mexican story was immortalised in a fly-on-the-wall seven-part Netflix documentary series directed and produced by Angus Macqueen, the award-winning documentary maker. Macqueen had a reputation for making hard-hitting investigative films tackling controversial subjects, and knew Culiacán well, having made an early documentary on Chapo Guzmán. He was given complete editorial control, even if he had to accept a certain element of manipulation and careful lawyering of the final cut in exchange for unprecedented access to film Maradona over many months.

Macqueen was surprised by the extent to which various facets of Maradona's life came into renewed focus, like a reincarnation, as he witnessed his passion and his excess, while wondering whether he would keel over mid-dance.

The early sequences show Maradona bow-legged and overweight, barely managing to walk, and at one point hobbling painfully on a crutch towards a small group of ecstatic fans in an empty stadium. Then the camera switches to the changing room where Maradona, with a huge smile, sways his hips freely to his beloved *cumbia* music, joining in a shared dance with his players.

Macqueen spent nine months filming Maradona turning up every day for training and attending match days, celebrating victories and taking defeats badly, and yet for much of the time evidently enjoying himself and finding a real connection with his young players, particularly those who came from the same poor background as himself and who felt motivated by his mystique and the force of his instinctive, primitive enthusiasm for the game.

Maradona seemed to see in some of the players an image of himself in his early playing years, battling against the odds on and off the field, while reliving, although on a much-diminished scale, some of the passion and idolatry he had experienced at Napoli and during his glorious World Cup in Mexico in 1986.

The old demons still lingered. Family traumas, and the hurt he caused, had a habit of interrupting the idyll. Some of this was off camera, as Maradona was visited at different points by a sister, two ex-girlfriends and one of his more recent children, a six-year-old boy, who was paraded before the cameras but did not make it to the final cut.

But the most striking image was that of Maradona physically deteriorated to the point that it was evident that time was running out on him. Maradona told Macqueen that he had not taken cocaine for eight years and there was no suggestion that he ever indulged in illegal drugs while in Culiacán. The film did show Maradona at times slurring his words during a period when he is thought to have continued to take painkillers, anti-depressants and alcohol. It also showed him throwing one or two of his trademark volcanic tantrums, one when he physically lashed out at male and female fans who had taunted him, chanting 'Diego sucks cock', while he blocked them from taking a selfie with their phones in the stadium tunnel. Such was the price of fame when it came to Maradona, because the club he was coaching had just lost a final it needed to win to gain promotion to Mexico's top league.

Maradona was instinctive and aware of the camera, but not always conscious of the damage and chaos it could reveal. He showed himself at his most self-indulgent and narcissistic, taking centre stage in the dressing room after the defeat in a speech filled with despair and self-pity, as if all the players had been temporarily removed from the scene.

And yet to answer the question: what exactly was Maradona doing in a city surrounded by a landscape of heroin poppies and marijuana plantations, and football fans making jokes about sniffing lines of coke with the notes they handled for their match tickets? It was that Maradona simply loved the sport, and no league, team or player was beneath him.

And, at Dorados, the positive energy that players felt they got from Maradona's legend and having him around was enough for them, along with the technical support they got from his assistants, who took care of scouting and game preparation. During his year in charge, Maradona guided the team to two championship finals and within a couple games of promotion to Liga MX.

Then it was all over, or nearly. Maradona, suffering from the ravages of his life, the first body-building injections as a child, the wear and tear on his body inflicted by a mix of brutal tackles from his early years as a player, the dubious medical interventions and quack advice, the cocktails of prescriptions and his own addictions, wasn't mobile enough to play much football himself any more.

In January 2019, the latest health scare had Maradona back in hospital in Buenos Aires being operated on to stem some internal stomach bleeding. But he recovered and returned for a second and final season at Dorados. The team lost in the Clausura finals to Atlético San Luis in extra time. Maradona left the club, citing his health and the pain he was suffering due to shoulder and knee issues in what turned out to be the beginning of the final stage of a life less ordinary.

For months Maradona's health had been declining. Even by the standards of former falls, his final coaching days at Gimnasia y Esgrima La Plata really did look like the end game. In January 2020 he became a pantomime act, watching home games from the sidelines from a mock throne decked in the club colours of blue and white. Promising to sign replica high-backed chairs to raise money for the club, the bloated Maradona seemed less a

king than a parody of himself at his most indulgent. But even
that was deceptive.

He had been suffering for some time from chronic osteoarthritis
in both knees, which caused a lot of inflammation, and had
struggled with his excessive weight due to poor diet. He also
suffered from respiratory and heart problems.

With Argentine football games suspended due to the Covid-19
pandemic, Maradona spent months in lockdown secluded in a
large private house south of the city of Buenos Aires, attended
by his dietitian, physio, holistic therapist, doctor, and the
youngest of his three known daughters, Jana, who shared the
produce of her organic vegetable garden with her father as a
contribution to his detox programme.

Jana was born in 1996 as result of an extra-marital
relationship Maradona had with Valeria Sabalain, who he first
met when she was working as barmaid in a Buenos Aires disco.
Throughout Jana's childhood and adolescence, Maradona
refused to recognise her as his daughter, but reconciled with
her when they met for the first time in 2015. A year later,
Maradona belatedly recognised Diego Junior, born in 1986, as
his son; he had had an affair with Cristiana Sinagra, Diego's
mother, during his time playing for Napoli.

The surfacing of paternity claims both before and after his
divorce in 2003 from Claudia Villafane – the mother of his
first two daughters, Giannina and Dalma – came to epitomise
Maradona's dysfunctional and often egocentric and destructive
personal life, with disputed claims pursued after his death as
family and old girlfriends argued over his inheritance. While he
recognised a second son, Diego Fernando, from his relationship
with Veronica Ojeda, as soon as he was born in 2003, it was
only in 2019 that he admitted paternity of three children born
in Cuba after he moved there in 2000 for drug-addiction
treatment.

On 30 October 2020, a Friday, Maradona turned sixty. He
was mentally and physically wasted, and was still haunted by
the demons he had struggled with throughout the later years
of his adult life: physical disability, alcoholism and depression.

The following day, persuaded that he should try to celebrate his birthday where his heart had always been, on the football pitch, Maradona barely lasted half an hour watching a game between Gimnasia y Esgrima and Patronato in the Juan Carmelo Stadium.

It was the first match day of the Argentine football season after an eight-month suspension because of the Covid pandemic that had killed over 30,000 of Maradona's fellow countrymen. With no fans allowed into the stadium and just a small number of journalists, club officials and players present, along with Claudio Tapia, the President of the Argentine Football Federation, not even the blue and white flags, the players' shirts emblazoned with DM60 and a short firework display in his honour could lift the occasion from its terrible sense of foreboding.

Maradona, who days earlier had been quarantined, having had contact with someone suspected of having contracted the virus, was despondent as he left the stadium after sitting on his 'throne'. The thanks he expressed on his Facebook site for the birthday greetings that reached him from football stars, past and present, turned out to be his final farewell.

Turning sixty, Maradona looked like his father Chitoro when he was twenty years older, only in worse health. Maradona could barely walk as he was assisted from the Gimnasia ground and hospitalised for the last time in his life. He was reported to be suffering from anaemia and dehydration. Then news came that he had undergone brain surgery, after being diagnosed with a subdural haematoma – an accumulation of blood between a membrane and his brain.

Contrary to medical advice, which had recommended days of observation in hospital to aid recovery, Maradona checked himself out and moved back into private accommodation.

He died after suffering a heart attack in his sleep, from acute lung oedema and chronic heart failure, according to the post-mortem, his body finally giving up.

Three part-time employees in a Buenos Aires morgue took pictures of themselves with Maradona's body in an open casket. For a while the pictures went viral on social media. Unlike a photograph of one of the three mortuary assistants subsequently lying 'dead' beside Maradona, this was not fake news. Maradona really was dead.

As well as an unhealthy interest in the dead Maradona's body, there was adulation, ritual and mass hysteria. Thousands of fans gathered in the stadiums where he was venerated. Candles were lit, strips with the legendary Number 10 and adulatory placards were held up. Fanatical followers then converged on the Plaza de Mayo, the square in Buenos Aires by the presidential palace, the Casa Rosada, where his coffin was transferred so that the public could pay their final respects.

The more radical fans, sweating and drunk in the local summer heat, jostled and pushed and chorused popular Maradona chants, and pogoed their traditional insult to the historic enemy of popular folklore on and off the pitch: '*El que no baile es un ingles!* He who doesn't jump is an Englishman!' they chanted. Everyone seemed desperate to hold on to Maradona's presence like a ritual seance.

At dawn on the Thursday following his death, Maradona's ex-wife, the actress turned events organiser Claudia Villafane, and their two daughters, Dalma and Giannina, were the first mourners to be allowed into the presidential palace where Maradona's coffin had been temporarily laid the night before, draped in the Argentine national flag and the Number 10 shirts of Boca Juniors and the Argentine national team that he had turned into enduring totems of his glory days, his nation's reincarnation and himself as sacrificial lamb.

They were followed shortly afterwards by Veronica Ojeda, Maradona's ex-girlfriend and the mother of one of his children. A third former girlfriend tried to visit the coffin before the palace was opened to the public but was stopped by security guards. Then his ex-wife asked that the public visits should be curtailed at 4 p.m. that afternoon, several hours before the scheduled end to the lying-in-state. The entrance was blocked off later that evening.

After the visits were stopped, a group of mourners broke through the barriers and ran into the palace, where they traded blows with security staff before being pushed back into a cloud of tear gas. Riot police by now had also opened fire with water cannon and rubber bullets to disperse the crowd, which extended for over a mile along the surrounding avenues.

With the palace gates once again firmly closed and security around the body stepped up, the coffin was temporarily moved to a private room where a small group of family and friends, including veterans of the 1986 World Cup, prayed and played some *cumbia* music.

That, and what followed, was Argentina's very own national opera of family, friends, passion, loss, delusion, politics, brutality and chaos. It was a stage show produced by a failed state, but which could only belong to Diego Maradona, a grotesque farce as well as a tragedy that nonetheless had all the makings of the only possible end to his life, a show made for and by him and the country he was born in.

When I first began writing about Maradona's life in the mid-1990s, I wrote that the only certainty about it was that when he died his funeral would be as big as Evita Perón's, whose 'shirtless followers', *los descamisados*, considered her a saint as well as a political icon.

And so it came to be with the god Maradona, who fifteen years earlier had said how he wished to be remembered. Appearing on his popular TV programme *La Noche del 10* in 2005, Maradona, interviewing himself, responded thus to the question of what people might say on the day of his burial. 'Thanks for playing football. It was the sport that gave me most happiness and most freedom, like having heaven in one's hands. As for the tombstone – it should just say: Thank you for the Ball.'

On 26 November 2020, the adoring crowds filled the Plaza de Mayo and the surrounding avenues, and lined the motorway to catch a glimpse of the hearse carrying Maradona's coffin, no longer covered in football shirts but now draped only in the Argentine flag, as if part of a state funeral: a politicised act. After the adulation and collective hysteria that had accompanied him most of his adult life, Maradona was accorded a rare moment of intimacy in a private family burial ceremony in the Bella Vista garden cemetery.

Unlike the more famous Buenos Aires Recoleta cemetery, Bella Vista does not boast the mausoleums of the rich and famous, but buries its dead in a simple patchwork field of headstones interspersed with turf and lined with trees.

Maradona's burial was witnessed by just a few family members and close friends, the best known among them being Guillermo Coppola, his manager during the 1980s and 1990s, his best footballing years as well as the years of some of his worst excesses off the pitch. Maradona was laid to rest alongside his beloved parents Chitoro and Tota, anchors to their son, in death as in life, who had chosen this haven of peace.

When all is said and done, I still look back at the 1986 World Cup in Mexico as Maradona's most sublime moment, when he carved out a special niche in football history and the collective memory, even if those in Buenos Aires's Boca Juniors and Naples worship him for what he achieved for the clubs there. Maradona's talent as a player was huge and unique, producing moves of great artistry, during an era of football when attacking players, unseen by multiple TV cameras and unprotected by referees, were subjected to incessant and destructive fouling by defenders. And yet the way Maradona squandered his talent, by letting his roller-coaster life off the pitch reduce the lifespan of his best playing years, made him the last of the football rock stars. It is impossible to imagine him coping with the pace and tactics, let alone dietary and training requirements, required by the elite footballers of the modern game.

The statistics show that over a stop-start, twenty-one-year professional career as a player, Maradona's trophy haul is minimal compared to Ronaldo's and Messi's. Inevitably his monstrous ego and the destructive elements of his personality were part of a darker story.

And yet there was something more romantic, but also more elementally human, about Maradona compared with the remorseless athleticism and slick self-promotion of some of the modern stars. As for politics, Diego was defiant and rebellious, although the activism of some of the younger players in the time of Covid on issues like poverty and racial equality speaks to new generations with arguably more genuine moral purpose.

As a final reflection by this biographer (however unauthorised), it seems to me that much of the mythology and self-delusion surrounding Diego Maradona is inseparable from the Argentine psyche, for ever seeking – and failing to find – a redeemer to lift it from its political and economic failure.

Maradona's ambivalent life and death resonated in the time of Covid, a time of unpredictability, of suffering, of dislocation, and when people searched for healing and hope. The bereaved fans who gathered in the Plaza de Mayo seemed to augur a mass spread of the virus – or its conquest. They clung with nostalgia to the memory of a genius of the game whose time and personality could never be repeated. He was mourned by many around the world. On hearing the news of his death, I tweeted: 'With your genius and your demons you held up a mirror to our humanity, its potential and its fragility. Your poetry in motion will endure. *Que en Paz Descanses*. Rest in peace.'

INDEX

ALSO AVAILABLE BY JIMMY BURNS
BARÇA: A PEOPLE'S PASSION

'Burns' examination of the club's fates and fortunes always goes well
beyond the game itself ... Burns is a brilliant journalist ... Unmissable'
TOTAL FOOTBALL

Founded in 1898, FC Barcelona or Barça has more than 500 local fan clubs
spread across the world, while its championship matches attract a global TV
audience. Former players include such legendary figures as Kubala, Maradona,
Cruyff, Ronaldo, Rivaldo and Lineker, and Barça has been managed by
greats such as Helenio Herrera, Cesar Menotti and Bobby Robson. The
club's honorary members have included Pope John Paul II and opera star
José Carreras. To unravel the background to the Barça phenomenon, Jimmy
Burns has unearthed police files and long-forgotten newspaper reports. He has
travelled with supporters and has talked to people intimately linked to the club,
from managers and players to groundsmen and doctors, whilst also gaining
access to those who have conspired to gain political and financial control.
In *Barça*, he tells the gripping story of the world's best-loved football club.

*

'Excellent ... A densely detailed account of the history of F. C. Barcelona'
DAILY TELEGRAPH

*

ISBN 9781408878200 · PAPERBACK · £9.99

PAPA SPY

A TRUE STORY OF LOVE, WARTIME ESPIONAGE IN MADRID, AND THE TREACHERY OF THE CAMBRIDGE SPIES

'A great story, with drama, betrayal and historical significance'
INDEPENDENT

In 1940 British publisher Tom Burns was sent to Madrid as press attaché to the British Embassy. There he used his considerable ingenuity and his deep love of Spain in the propaganda war against the Nazis. The aim was simple, to keep Franco out of the war and so protect Gibraltar and the western Mediterranean. What Burns didn't know was that his most dangerous enemies were not in Spain but at home, chief amongst them, Kim Philby, head of the MI6's Iberian section. How he overcame these odds is the story told in his son's extraordinary tale of personal courage, wartime espionage and betrayal.

✳

'[In] Jimmy Burns's lively biography ... the murky world of intelligence, counter-intelligence, deception and double agents, provide a series of real James Bonds'
SPECTATOR BOOKS OF THE YEAR

'Jimmy Burns brilliantly evokes the shadowy world of dingy cafes, luxury hotels, propaganda, bribery and betrayal ... Lovers of Spain, lovers of true spy stories and lovers of love itself will adore this enchanting book'
SUNDAY TELEGRAPH

✳

ISBN 9781408803097 · PAPERBACK · £14.99